Proslavery Britain

Proslavery Britain

Fighting for Slavery in an Era of Abolition

Paula E. Dumas

palgrave
macmillan

PROSLAVERY BRITAIN

First published 2016 by
PALGRAVE MACMILLAN

Palgrave Macmillan in the UK is an imprint of Macmillan Publishers Limited, registered in England, company number 785998, of Houndmills, Basingstoke, Hampshire, RG21 6XS.

Palgrave Macmillan in the US is a division of Nature America, Inc., One New York Plaza, Suite 4500, New York, NY 10004-1562.

Palgrave Macmillan is the global academic imprint of the above companies and has companies and representatives throughout the world.

Hardback ISBN: 978–1–137–57820–4
E-PUB ISBN: 978–1–137–55857–2
E-PDF ISBN: 978–1–137–55858–9
DOI: 10.1057/9781137558589

Distribution in the UK, Europe and the rest of the world is by Palgrave Macmillan®, a division of Macmillan Publishers Limited, registered in England, company number 785998, of Houndmills, Basingstoke, Hampshire RG21 6XS.

Library of Congress Cataloging-in-Publication Data

Names: Dumas, Paula E., author.
Title: Proslavery Britain : fighting for slavery in an era of abolition / Paula E. Dumas.
Description: New York, NY : Palgrave Macmillan, [2016] | Includes bibliographical references and index.
Identifiers: LCCN 2015027478 | ISBN 9781137578204 (hardback : alkaline paper)
Subjects: LCSH: Slavery—Great Britain—Justification. | Slavery—Great Britain—History—19th century. | Abolitionists—Great Britain—History—19th century. | Antislavery movements—Great Britain—History—19th century.
Classification: LCC HT1163 .D86 2016 | DDC 306.3/62094109034—dc23
LC record available at http://lccn.loc.gov/2015027478

A catalogue record for the book is available from the British Library.

Contents

Figures

Acknowledgments

My road to uncovering the existence of a proslavery Britain began with a single question that I asked in a graduate seminar at Western University in London, Ontario. In that small seminar, "Slavery and Abolition," I asked who the British abolitionists were fighting against that forced them to take decades to achieve their goals of abolishing slavery and the international trade in slaves. I will be forever thankful to Margaret Kellow, who immediately challenged me to answer that question and who helped me to verify that there was next to no current scholarship on the opposition to British abolition. This led to a master's cognate paper, a PhD thesis, and now this book.

During my doctoral studies at the University of Edinburgh, H. T. Dickinson and Gordon Pentland encouraged me to gain a firm understanding of the place of the slavery debates within the wider scope of British political history, but to also look into how proslavery ideas manifested themselves in the arts and culture of the era and how these ideas could have reached the wider British public. Upon my first meeting with them, they looked at me and confidently told me that my research project would become a book. I am thankful for their unending support and encouragement. Advice from the University of Edinburgh's faculty, including (but certainly not limited to) Frank Cogliano, Andrew Wells, Adam Budd, and Karina Williamson, helped guide my research. John Oldfield's feedback and encouragement to highlight the existence of a culture of proslavery in Britain has had a significant impact on the final shape of this project. Lindsey Flewelling, Megan Ledford, David Løvbræk, and Martha Rybiak provided timely, thoughtful feedback on the penultimate draft of this book. Any errors, of course, are entirely my own.

In order to undertake this research I received helpful financial support. The offer of a Western Graduate Research Scholarship guided me to Western for my master's degree. A College Studentship from the University of Edinburgh enabled me to study in Edinburgh, utilizing the National Library of Scotland's holdings and the wealth of information contained within the University of Edinburgh's print and online collections. I received a small project grant from the University of Edinburgh Development Trust that allowed a colleague and me to organize and run an interdisciplinary conference, Villains, Rogues, and Deviants: Writing the Histories of People We'd Rather Forget, where we presented papers at an early stage in our research. I also presented drafts of my research at the British and Irish History Workshop at the University of Edinburgh, Historical Perspectives Conference at the University of Strathclyde, Enslavement: Colonial Appropriations, Apparitions, Remembrances, 1750–present day at the University of Portsmouth, and the Mid-Atlantic Conference of British Studies at The John Hopkins University.

It would be impossible to name every person who has leant his or her assistance, input, and encouragement to this project over the past nine years. In addition to the individuals mentioned above, I would like to express my gratitude to Hisashi Kuboyama, Tanya Cosentino, J. Neville Thompson, Kevin James, Matthew Dziennik, Sarah Dziennik, Rusty Roberson, Angela Nolte, Louise Settle, Daniel Clinkman, Erin Dee-Richard, and Polly Golding. I would also like to thank the staff at the University of Edinburgh's Main Library, particularly in the Centre for Research Collections, the Annexe, and New College Library Special Collections, the National Library of Scotland, the Mitchell Library, Glasgow University Library, the British Library, the Dana Porter Library, the D. B. Weldon Library, Wilfrid Laurier University Library, Huron University College Library, the Beryl Ivey Library, the British Museum, the Brynmor Jones Library, the Hull History Centre, and the Wilberforce House Museum. The John Carter Brown Library and the Library of Congress kindly provided the images contained within this book and I thank them for this. Palgrave Macmillan, and in particular Kristin Purdy and Michelle Smith, have provided endless support and much-needed advice throughout the publishing process.

Finally, I would like to thank my family for their unending support, including my parents who encouraged me to take on this project, Grandma Betty, who always believed in me, my husband Derek, who has been there for every stage of this process, and our amazing little girls. I could not have asked for better cheerleaders. This book would not have been nearly as enjoyable an undertaking without them all, and so I dedicate it to them.

Paula Dumas
June 2015

Introduction

On June 17, 1783, an MP in Britain's House of Commons brought forth a petition asking for the total abolition of Britain's participation in the slave trade. The timing and content of the petition had been inspired by a recent debate over the right of the members of the African Company to participate in the trade. After the petition was read aloud, former Prime Minister Lord North stated that, while he appreciated the sound, humanitarian sentiments of the petitioners, it would be impossible to abolish the slave trade. He continued, noting:

> it was a trade which had, in some measure, become necessary to almost every nation in Europe; and as it would be next to an impossibility to induce them all to give it up, and renounce it for ever, so he was apprehensive that the wishes of the humane petitioners could not be accomplished.[1]

Again he stressed the impossibility of the goal, regardless of its well-meaning proponents. The petition was allowed to lie on the table and the West Indians in the House could again feel secure in their wealth and their professions. It would take another two generations for slave trading, colonial slavery, and the apprenticeship system that was later established to finally be abolished in the British Empire.

Why did abolition and emancipation take so long if everyone knew that slavery was wrong? In the example above, Lord North clearly acknowledged the legitimacy of the Quakers' concerns. British abolitionists, it turns out, did not proceed unopposed, nor was abolition a universal goal among all Britons. Proslavery sentiments could be found just about anywhere: travel narratives were advertised across the country and reviewed in the biggest periodicals of the period; pamphlets were created and distributed by individuals and organized groups of West Indians in Britain; novels were available to purchase from booksellers and borrow from circulation libraries; plays were performed on stages in London; catchy songs were included in song books; and artwork was created and published by some of the biggest names in political prints and caricatures. These works were read, viewed, and experienced by urban, educated, wealthier Britons with an interest in politics, arts, science, and religion and the leisure time to learn about and experience more of the world than their predecessors. They also point to the existence of a culture of proslavery within a distinct subsection of Britain at this time.[2] The arguments and rhetoric contained within this outpouring of work challenged the louder abolitionist claims about life in the colonies and the nature of the slaves. Members of the West Indian interest formed committees with the expressed purpose of producing their own propaganda and petitions. They even attacked the foundational logic of abolition and sentimental nature of abolitionist rhetoric. Far from being passive, doomed onlookers on the sidelines of the road to abolition, politicians, writers, members of the West Indian interest, and their supporters actively fought to maintain colonial slavery and the prosperity of the colonies and Britain.[3]

Just what is meant here by the term "proslavery?" Definitions of the word vary in their usage and meaning. In his foundational study of American proslavery, Larry E. Tise defined proslavery as "favoring the continuance of the institution of Negro slavery, or opposed to interference with it."[4] In this book, the term "proslavery" refers to arguments and individuals who promoted the institution of slavery as beneficial for them, the colonies, and Britain's national interest in a public manner. This means that some individuals may be classed as supporters of colonial slavery or the slave trade because of what they did or said rather than their personal opinions and beliefs. They may not have held such views in private. *Proslavery Britain* is concerned about the public's potential exposure to the slavery debates and the impact of the popular debate on British politics and abolition.

Throughout this study the term "abolitionist" has been applied to the politicians, writers, and many others who publically expressed any abolitionist sentiments. Here it refers to an individual or ideology that expressed support for abolishing the slave trade and/or slavery (because one could be in favor of ending Britain's participation in the slave trade without necessarily calling for an end to colonial slavery) regardless of the possible motivations behind the sharing of such beliefs. Proslavery is also contrasted with "anti-abolition" and "anti-abolitionist," both of which are used in the context of the pre-1808 debates to refer to people and arguments that were against a proposed abolition of the slave trade. Anti-abolition arguments in this period focused on defects in the abolitionist platform, emphasizing the illegal, illogical, inhumane, or pro-French nature of their aims.

Proslavery arguments, on the other hand, positively promoted slavery and the slave trade. This promotion of the institution of slavery receded quickly from the slavery debates in Parliament following the abolition of the slave trade as politicians became increasingly reluctant to appear supportive of a demonized institution.[5]

The term "anti-abolitionism" requires further clarification because the meaning of the word changes over time and depending on the context of its use, both in the contemporaneous debate and in this study. Whereas prior to the abolition of the slave trade the terms "anti-abolition" and "anti-abolitionist" can be generally defined as above in the context of the parliamentary debates, the words become more changeable in 1807 as Parliament resolved to abolish Britain's participation in the slave trade.[6] They can be used to describe an attack on an abolitionist and his position on slavery in Parliament, but they can also be used to describe a member or supporter of the West Indian interest who opposed immediate abolition. Some abolitionists, however, also opposed immediate abolition. This means that in some cases both "anti-abolitionists" and abolitionists opposed immediate abolition and advocated gradual abolition and amelioration in the 1820s. It was their motivations, chosen arguments, and rhetoric that differed. This study will therefore employ the terms "anti-abolition" and "anti-abolitionist" in the post-1807 period to refer to members of the West Indian interest and their supporters who, throughout the slavery debates, repeatedly opposed the proposals of abolitionists, openly refuted abolitionists' arguments and facts, defended themselves and the colonists from charges of inhumanity, cruelty, and backwardness, and opposed the immediate abolition of slavery.

The term "West Indian interest" here refers to the individuals and organizations that had personal or business connections in Britain's West Indian colonies. The West Indian interest in Britain possessed complex connections to the West Indies through the personal possession of property or slave ownership, family investments, birthplace, or relationships. It also included British and West Indian merchants, traders, ship owners and builders, dock owners, and mortgagees. British West Indians were not necessarily either attached to formal West Indian organizations or politically active. They might have been settled in the colonies, in London, in the major ports of Liverpool, Bristol, and Glasgow, or on a country estate. The West Indian interest in Britain was thus a large heterogeneous group whose members formed a formidable lobbying force in the eighteenth century and possessed much political and financial power at the beginning of the nineteenth century.

Much of this book is devoted to examining and understanding the rhetoric of the West Indian interest as it reflects British proslavery thought and culture. In the late eighteenth and early nineteenth centuries the West Indian interest had to develop new ways to depict, define, and defend itself in Parliament and to the British public because of the growing popularity of abolitionism. Its members possessed close ties to Britain, great wealth, transatlantic connections through practices such as absenteeism and intermarriage, and vital roles in ensuring Britain's economic prosperity and security during war and peace. These allowed the interest to maintain a significant hold on parliamentary decision-making in the face of popular abolitionism. This power became more concentrated in urban areas and more clearly defined as its members organized to fight abolition in the wake of the American Revolution. They also moved beyond straightforward proslavery arguments by beginning to employ pro-colonial rhetoric and familiar depictions of life in the colonies to remind the wider British public of their British roots, their unending support of Britain's investment in the colonies, and their need and worthiness of Britain's protection and compassion.

The term "amelioration" also requires some explanation. According to J. R. Ward, amelioration refers to concerns regarding raising the standards of practice of colonial slave ownership that began in the second half of the eighteenth century and became a more defined method of plantation management from the 1790s onward.[7] Ward notes that by 1823 "amelioration" meant different things to different people. Whereas the West Indian colonists viewed amelioration as a method to reinforce slavery and make the institution more efficient, humanitarians believed that amelioration could lead to a better social state with less racial hierarchy and subordination in the colonies.[8] In this study the term "amelioration" is used to describe an effective method employed by the West Indian interest to delay and defeat calls for abolition as well as to demonstrate progress and the material benefits of slavery for the slaves in the colonies. It most frequently refers to the period after 1823 when Parliament formally asked the colonies to institute reforms on the plantations to benefit the slaves. The term "slave" is used here to denote enslaved men, women, and children.

Finally, it is vital to define the term "culture." In his study of English anti-slavery, David Turley defined culture as "the range of ways of responding to and judging the world within contained limits common to a group."[9] In this study, culture is used in much the same way. Proslavery culture involved a set of shared goals, principles, viewpoints, and practices possessed by members of the West

Indian interest. It centered on the beliefs that slavery was necessary for the survival of the colonies and that the slave trade was necessary to develop, maintain, and increase production on colonial plantations. These viewpoints compelled absentee planters in Britain to promote slave trading and colonial slavery while opposing abolition in print and in Parliament. Writers, artists, politicians, satirists, members of the West Indian interest, and their supporters expressed these beliefs in a number of accessible formats that were distributed throughout urban Great Britain for an intended audience of elite, politically active Britons. These will be discussed widely in Chapters 2 and 3.

How does this study differ from the countless studies of British slavery and abolition? By concentrating solely on the proslavery position in this period, this study is able to expose and explore abolition's opposition. The West Indian interest and their supporters advanced powerful, influential arguments to challenge abolition and defend slave trading and owning; they affected the timing and nature of abolition and emancipation and their history deserves to be told. Perhaps historians have been cautious about investigating the proslavery case or embarrassed by the existence of Britain's proslavery past, or maybe they continue to be influenced by the first generation of historians of British abolition who focused on the work of abolitionists and moralized the debate. Douglas Hamilton has argued for the need to recognize Britain's role in creating the institution of the transatlantic slave trade in order to fully understand and be proud of her role in suppressing the trade.[10] This study seeks to tell the story of proslavery in Britain and to do so in a non-judgmental, analytical manner so that it might first formally recognize the value of proslavery works; second, acknowledge the existence of a proslavery culture within a narrow segment of the British public; and third, better inform our understanding of the great victory of abolition.

Generations of British historians have attempted to understand why Britain ended its participation in the slave trade and why abolition and emancipation occurred when they did. Until the mid-twentieth century the conventional history of abolition depicted abolition as the successful outcome of the work of saintly abolitionists.[11] This interpretation required anti-abolitionists to be treated as either a stagnant, inhumane force standing in the way of human progress or as insignificant in (or even absent from) the story of abolition. Historians have since begun to consider economics, slave resistance, the historical and international context of the anti-slavery movement, and the work (and motives) of abolitionists to provide a more balanced, intellectual history of abolition.[12] This broadening of the scope of research has led to two opposing theories about the origins of popular abolitionism and the movement's ability to gain political backing. As such, historians of British slavery and abolition tend to take sides as to whether it was mainly economics or humanitarian efforts that shaped the processes of abolition and emancipation.[13]

Studies of proslavery sentiment do exist. The study of American proslavery thought, for example, has benefited from generations of historical research.[14] In contrast, there has been limited scholarly interest in British proslavery arguments and rhetoric. As Christer Petley recently noted, historians such as Gordon K. Lewis, David Brion Davis, and Roger Anstey repeatedly oversimplified the lives of the proslavery advocates, their campaigns, and their ideology in their histories of British slavery and abolition.[15] Proslavery arguments and rhetoric taken from specific slavery debates in Parliament and in major publications have also been examined.[16] These studies tended to characterize proslavery arguments as defensive, but, as discussed below, there was a variety and strategy to these arguments for which the West Indian interest has never fully received credit. Their size, strength, composition, and motivations have also been the focus of historical study. Researchers studying Britain's West Indian colonies have attempted to assess the origins and extent of the decline of their power and influence that contributed to their inability to effectively fight abolition.[17] David Beck Ryden completed a detailed chronology of the formation and activities of West Indian societies in Britain and examined how they responded to the abolitionist threat. His research led him to conclude that the planters were facing decline in the period due to three major factors: first, that mercantilist policy was working against their interests; second, that it was no longer easy or inexpensive to control their slaves; and third, the overproduction of sugar caused economic decline.[18] These factors, he maintained, combined to explain the timing of abolition.[19] Ryden and Srividhya Swaminathan have noted that a detailed study of proslavery is missing from the historiography of British abolition.[20] *Proslavery Britain* helps to fill this gap.

Chapter 1, The Proslavery Position, is an examination of the proslavery arguments that were developed and utilized in Britain to explain and defend the proslavery position in the face of growing public and parliamentary pressure. This section explains how Britain's participation in the slave trade and the practice of slaveholding were justified by contemporaries using racially charged arguments, rational economic arguments, and paternalist, humanitarian arguments. It also provides some wider context in which these arguments could be created and deemed credible. The arguments identified in this chapter continue to be revisited and explored throughout the study.

The following two chapters delve into the sources of proslavery arguments that had the ability to permeate the urban British elite. "Proslavery in Print" explores the proslavery position as it was presented in pamphlets and treatises, scientific studies, medical manuals, travel narratives, and popular periodicals. Through the use of short excerpts from a range of publications, it becomes clear that proslavery arguments were woven into a variety of printed sources and that these arguments were framed, supported, and utilized in an attempt to influence a slightly wider audience outside of Parliament. "Proslavery Arts and Culture" looks at representations of the proslavery position in various artistic genres, including literature, poetry, artwork, caricature, and drama. These chapters support the argument that a multifaceted British proslavery culture existed among the West Indian interest in Britain in the late eighteenth and early nineteenth centuries.

The final two chapters focus on the proslavery position in Parliament as the successes and failures of the West Indian lobby in Westminster are assessed. In "Proslavery Politics and the Slave Trade," specific strategies of anti-abolitionist MPs and peers are carefully assessed to see how they shaped and hindered the process of abolition and, in particular, how the opposition to abolition attacked abolitionist rhetoric and the MPs who supported ending Britain's participation in the slave trade. This chapter highlights the importance of the parliamentary debates in the story of abolition because of their primary role in debating, crafting, and justifying crucial legal decisions about British slavery and abolition. "Proslavery Politics after Abolition" contains an examination of proslavery arguments and rhetoric employed in Parliament after 1807. This chapter makes two important claims: first, that proslavery politicians adapted their arguments in response to abolition and the pressure they now faced; and second, that anti-abolitionists clearly shaped the process and nature of the emancipation act of 1833 that officially ended slaveholding in Britain's West Indian colonies. The result is a clearer understanding of how politicians continued to defend and justify slaveholding and plantation slavery after the defeat of 1807 and in the face of surging abolitionism in the 1820s. *Proslavery Britain* concludes with a short examination of the contents of the bill for emancipation and the many clauses that financially benefited the planter at the expense of general British public and the former slaves who would remain tied to the plantations for several more years following emancipation. This section recognizes that emancipation was intended, in part, to benefit the planters.

The aims of *Proslavery Britain* are as follows: first, to demonstrate that proslavery arguments and rhetoric in Britain across this period were multifaceted and could be adapted to suit personal experience, format, and external events; second, to identify ways in which members of the West Indian interest and their supporters shared elements of a culture of proslavery with specific segments of the wider public; and third, to recognize that proslavery arguments and rhetoric were significant factors in the timing and nature of abolition and emancipation. It does so through a close reading of the parliamentary records in combination with a wide range of print and artistic sources. *Proslavery Britain* set out to explore the other side of the slavery debate and, in the process, uncovered a wealth of convincing arguments that shaped the processes of abolition and emancipation. In the end, we find that the true story of British abolition is far more complex than the traditional tale has let on.

CHAPTER 1

THE PROSLAVERY POSITION

In 1807, during the final days of debate over the bill for abolition, West Indian MPs argued their case and defended the colonies much as they had done for the prior two decades. During the discussions on 23 February following a request to read the bill for abolition in the Commons for the second time (a request that had already been postponed once), for example, George Hibbert alluded to the West Indian interest's historic successes as he attempted to explain his opposition to the bill:

> if I had been told . . . of any measure that, although it was indisputably enjoined by every principle of justice and humanity, yet that in the course of almost 20 years discussion, it had not been able to make its effective progress through the British parliament (recommended, at the same time, by the cry of the people out of doors, and by an union of the greatest talents within), until it received the protecting hand of his majesty's principle minister in either house, I should say, "it is impossible; there must be some mistake in the application of these great principles to the measure."[1]

Members of the West Indian interest and their supporters were able to delay and defeat motion and motion for abolition and amelioration in the 1790s and early 1800s despite the often-overwhelming popular support for the measure. But just how was this accomplished? Calls for abolition were repeatedly defeated through the use of convincing, clear, supposedly logical, and often pro-colonial arguments. The West Indians' successes cast doubt upon the propriety of the bill for abolition. In truth, the proslavery position significantly impacted upon the nature and timing of British abolition. This chapter will explore the ways in which this took place.

Abolition entered the political sphere in Britain in the early 1780s. The first anti-slavery petition was presented to Parliament in 1783.[2] Far from being welcomed with cheers and acceptance, Lord North declared its aims to be impossible before it was allowed to lie on the table. But this was only the beginning. In 1787 the Society for Effecting the Abolition of the Slave Trade was formed. In response, the largest and most influential West Indian organization in Britain, the Society of West India Planters and Merchants of London, formed a subcommittee to counter the abolitionist movement.[3] In 1789 they agreed on a specific plan to finance their opposition campaign. By the end of the 1780s, planters, merchants, and many others were actively responding to an organized abolitionist threat. Their funded, targeted campaigns shaped ideas about slavery and about the British Empire in the minds of the British public.[4]

Annual debates raged in the British houses of Parliament over whether or not to abolish the slave trade. Between 1783, when the Quakers presented their petition to Parliament requesting the abolition of the inhumane traffic in slaves, and 1807, when Britain abolished her participation in the transatlantic slave trade, nearly one hundred MPs defended Britain's long-standing involvement in the slave trade. Many of these men had direct links to the West Indies. For some, their family fortune had been made in the islands; others had worked on or owned plantations themselves or were involved in trading enterprises. Those who represented the major ports of Liverpool and London spoke up on behalf of their constituents regarding their respective city's need for the trade to continue. There were also many more MPs without obvious links to the trade or the colonies who chose to defend Britain's merchants, traders, and colonial interests as they sought to hold back the growing surge of popular abolitionism.

In the decades leading up to the abolition of the slave trade, members of the West Indian interest were confident that the long-established trade in slaves would continue for the foreseeable future. They presented arguments to Parliament that extolled the benefits of the slave trade for Great Britain, her colonies, and her people. These arguments justified their participation in the slave trade. To be convincing they needed their listeners to hold a number of basic assumptions, including that the trade directly contributed to Britain's prosperity and level of industrialization, that Africans and men and women of African descent possessed lesser mental capabilities and a lesser level of civilization, and that other nations would continue to trade in slaves regardless of Britain abolishing her role in the international trade. Proslavery and pro-slave trade MPs also utilized timely arguments to defend their position by alluding to or directly referring to the French revolution, war with France, and the mass uprising and loss of St. Domingo (Saint-Domingue). Finally, they stressed that the act of debating abolition and the use of inflammatory language could cause all-out rebellion in the colonies. These convincing sentiments helped postpone, reverse, modify, and throw out numerous bills for abolition and amelioration throughout the 1790s and on into the early 1800s. While the abolition of the slave trade in the British Empire was becoming increasingly likely in the first decade of the 1800s, in 1807–8 the majority of MPs discussing the ramifications of abolition publicly opposed emancipation.

In the years immediately following abolition, the focus of the slavery debates shifted to the international transatlantic slave trade being carried on by Britain's European rivals. Slave registration, the defense of the colonies, and the enforcement of abolition were pressing issues during the Napoleonic Wars. Sugar duties angered the West Indian interest and advocates of free trade. The West Indian interest in Parliament was faced with a determined, popular, organized abolitionist movement from 1823. That was the year George Canning introduced a series of resolutions in the House of Commons meant to ameliorate the conditions of the slaves on the plantations. These resolutions angered the colonists and may have further dehumanized black slaves by focusing on rationalizing slavery, improving production, and improving their breeding habits.[5] The emancipation debates of the late 1820s and early 1830s took place among a backdrop of reform and upheaval. Unrest at home, in the colonies, and across Europe troubled MPs, encouraging some to cling to tradition and others to push for reforms to prevent a full-scale revolution.[6] Parliamentary reform extended the franchise to a limited extent and changed some electoral constituencies, thereby lessening the power of the landed classes (and thus the power of the planters). In the early 1830s West Indian planters appeared more willing to agree to legislation as long as they received adequate compensation. This shift in rhetoric may have been due to financial losses already incurred, the devastation caused by natural disasters and revolts in the colonies, or perhaps a sense that, after parliamentary reform, emancipation was inevitable and, by agreeing to some elements of the plan, they would be more likely to receive a favorable settlement. As discussed later, the planters received significant compensation in the 1833 bill for emancipation.

Under close examination, two broad categories of relevant arguments emerged in the slavery debates. There were those who supported slavery and the slave trade and spoke out in favor of its continuance. This category of argument I have termed "proslavery," because it focused on the benefits of plantation slavery rather than on the negative effects of impending abolition. Several prominent MPs voiced their strong opposition to abolition and listed reasons for their position. These included the timing of the bill or motion and the potential ramifications of the bill. I have labeled these arguments "anti-abolition" arguments because they were directed at the proposed bills for abolition and the men who brought them forth. Some individuals, however, believed that the institution of slavery was necessary for the survival of the West Indian colonies but also that, if enough warning was given to the planters to secure the necessary number of slaves to work their plantations, the slave trade could (or should) be abolished. This more nuanced argument weaves through many of the proslavery arguments identified later. Over time, as a growing number of West Indians reported incidents of attacks and slander, experienced a decline in their influence, and held views that were now considered morally questionable at best, anti-abolition arguments became the more common of the two.

Before entering into a detailed discussion of proslavery argument and rhetoric, it is necessary to take note of the ways in which parliamentary speeches were recorded and shared with the British public. A small number of wealthy Londoners might have been able to attend Parliament, sit in the gallery, and watch the debates, but the majority would have had to rely on printed reports and articles for news and opinion pieces on the slavery debates. A growing number of daily, tri-weekly, and weekly newspapers, particularly out of London, reported on political news and opinions. Most of the records of the early slavery debates come from newspaper and magazine reports that were incomplete and often at odds with one another.[7] William Cobbett's *Parliamentary Debates* was first published in 1804 and the first volume of Cobbett's *The Parliamentary History of England*, which would eventually provide a record of parliamentary activity from 1066 to 1803, was not published until 1806. It has been suggested that performing rhetorical analysis on these speeches is problematic because the rhetoric recorded during these debates may demonstrate more about the audience's views than the speaker's attitudes or beliefs.[8] The reports may also have been subject to heavy or careless editing, omission, and manipulations, but despite these potential problems they remain vital records for one's understanding of the nature of the debate. They also demonstrate what the British public could have been able to learn of the parliamentary debates on slavery.[9] As such, much of the evidence found in this chapter has been drawn from Cobbett's and Hansard's published parliamentary debates. The published collections of parliamentary reports have been relied upon here because they are considered to be the most comprehensive records of the parliamentary debates of the period. They contain much of the language and sentiment of the debate (both of the speakers and of the writers and editors of the speeches) and also provide some of the best examples of the interplay of the two sides of the debate.

As will be shown, proslavery and anti-abolitionist writers, publicists, colonists, and politicians used a variety of different arguments to defend and explain their position on abolition and emancipation. Economic arguments were often advanced during the wars with France as a means of stressing the importance of the African trade to colonial production, Britain's wealth, and Britain's ability to fund her military. Strategic and naval arguments also appeared during wartime. These highlighted the important role of the slave trade in training seamen for the Royal Navy. They also stressed how Britain's European rivals and their neighboring West Indian colonies would benefit financially from Britain's abolition of the slave trade. Certain arguments were utilized in Parliament at specific times in response to internal or external stimuli. For example, the assertion that abolition was based upon dangerous revolutionary principles was put forth five times in 1793 following Louis XVI's execution and eleven times in the three years after Napoleon had been crowned emperor.[10] The number of incidences in which MPs praised the slave trade for its success as a nursery for the Royal Navy also rose during the Napoleonic Wars.[11]

Historical and legal justifications stressed the importance of relying upon precedent as a means to maintain social order. This was a particularly pressing issue during the French Revolution and when experiencing major slave uprisings in the colonies. The historical encouragement of the trade over several centuries by the British Parliament and monarchy and the right to private property were also convincing arguments that resulted in bills being defeated, delayed, or adapted to suit the planters and their fellow landowning politicians. The enslavement of Africans was defended on moral and religious grounds. Paternalist master–slave relations and examples of slavery in the Bible were brought forth to defend colonial slavery. Racial arguments drew upon pseudoscientific explanations of racial differences to justify enslaving Africans. After losing the debate over abolition in 1807, many proslavery MPs were unwilling to abandon their position. They continued to argue the failings of abolition in Parliament and in print. These failings included the government's inability to stop all other nations from trading in slaves and the loss of monetary benefits from other nations taking over their trade routes. Their confidence in the staying power of slavery, however, was shaken, and new conciliatory stances were taken up in the slavery debates in Parliament in the aftermath of the Napoleonic Wars.

The language used by proslavery MPs in Parliament changed significantly after the slave trade was abolished. After abolition every MP was expected to detest the institution of slavery; those who were interested in the institution, however, could call for gradual instead of immediate emancipation. This strategic shift in language is found both in the records of the parliamentary debates and in the print debates discussed in the following chapter. Members no longer relied on racial prejudices or Bible passages to support slavery, nor did they overtly support the institution of slavery; on the contrary, they publicly stated their dislike of slavery and the nature of their property before explaining why the institution of slavery needed to remain for the foreseeable future. Abolitionists dismissed some of the West Indian interest's arguments as being biased and self-serving, but they could not overcome the legal basis and historical support for their claims to compensation.

Economic Arguments

The British transatlantic slave trade made a significant contribution to Britain's financial prosperity and security. Money made in the plantations and through the trade was often invested in Britain, greatly improving the infrastructure of ports and providing funds for investment in other economic activities. It was central to Britain's international trade, and international trade was a critical factor in Britain's industrialization.[12] Slavery was also seen as the status quo. By the time the general British public became fully aware of the nature and the consequences of colonial slavery the institution was already being promoted as a necessary evil.[13] The transatlantic slave trade and the use of enslaved labor in the colonies also led to an increased amount of cheaper produce. Demand for plantation goods such as sugar, cotton, and coffee was growing in Britain and across Europe. MPs were skeptical that sufficient production could continue in the Caribbean without slave labor or if the workforce in the colonies was limited to the current slave population. Great numbers of men were employed in all stages of the trade, including British and West Indian merchants, plantation owners and managers, importers, shipbuilders, and sailors. The amount of money tied up in the trade was vast, as was the value of Britain's imports from the colonies and her exports to Africa and the Caribbean. Proslavery MPs could not comprehend the desire to end a profitable trade, while Britain's European competitors continued trading in slaves in the Caribbean.

Adam Smith, in contrast, believed that wealth and liberty were the two greatest blessings that could be bestowed upon the individual and the nation.[14] He opposed the prevailing system of mercantilism practiced throughout the British Empire that relied on protective tariffs, the colonial production of raw materials in exchange for manufactured goods from the mother country, and large bullion reserves. Smith's treatise, *The Wealth of Nations* (1776), encouraged a free market economy guided by an invisible hand to produce the right amount of goods at the right price for optimum competition among manufacturers. Because free labor was central to Smith's economic theory, his followers and abolitionists condemned slavery as irrational and uneconomical.[15]

Participation in the slave trade was justified by some MPs by the failure of the slaves in Britain's West Indian colonies to reproduce in great enough numbers to maintain necessary labor levels and production. Unlike in the American colonies, Britain's Caribbean planters relied upon regular slave imports to keep a sufficient workforce manning the sugar plantations. MPs and members of colonial assemblies hypothesized several reasons for the low levels of reproduction on West Indian plantations. MP Henry Dundas noted on March 1, 1799, during a discussion of William Wilberforce's motion to bring in a bill for the abolition of the slave trade, that the colonists were trying to address this problem by amassing a younger slave population: "The assembly of Jamaica, however, had adopted a regulation, by which no slaves above the age of 25, were to be introduced, because they were desirous to have such as would secure the population, and prevent the necessity of constant supplies by importation."[16] Slave women in the West Indies had fewer children than those in North America and, although Jamaica's slave population was approximately 40–50 percent female, between one-third and one-half of slave women remained childless between the mid-seventeenth century and 1833.[17] Historians have advanced a number of theories about the low birth rate among slaves in Britain's sugar-producing Caribbean colonies, including the brutal nature of plantation slavery, intentional avoidance of pregnancy, instances of infanticide and abortion, and cultural practices such as prolonged lactation and avoiding sexual intercourse after giving birth, but recent scholarship has proposed that the intensive labor demanded by sugar cultivation combined with physical discipline and the wealth of diseases affecting mother and child provide enough evidence to explain the low rates.[18] Common diseases included small pox, measles, scarlet fever, syphilis, yaws, elephantiasis, and postnatal tetanus. Sugar was also the most physically demanding plantation crop to grow and harvest.[19] MPs argued that the trade would have to continue if slave women could not produce enough children to maintain current labor levels and meet Britain's demand for sugar.

Proslavery and pro-slave trade MPs quoted statistics and emphasized the financial benefits during the debates in Westminster, helping strengthen the fight against abolition.[20] On July 5, 1799, during a debate over a bill to limit the extent of slave trading on the African coast, the duke of Clarence highlighted the importance of the West Indies to Britain's commerce. The duke stressed the significant role the West Indian colonies had played in securing Britain's present financial position:

> In 1788, the British West India capital amounted to seventy millions sterling; employing 689 vessels, 148,176 tons, navigated by 14,000 seamen. The gross duties to the British empire, 1,800,000*l.* In 1796, the trade required 350,230 tons, navigated by 24,000 seamen. If the value of the conquests from the French, Spaniards, and Dutch, amounting to at least 20,000,000*l.* be added, I may safely assert, that the present British capital on the West Indies, is equal to 100 millions sterling. A sum which demands your most serious considerations, before you consent to the abolition of the trade without which it could not exist.[21]

His statistics demonstrated significant growth over a period of eight years as the tonnage of goods doubled and the number of trained and employed men increased by over 70 percent. He insisted that these benefits would be lost with abolition because the colonies would no longer have access to the workforce (slaves), defense (provided by seamen trained on slaving vessels), and transportation for plantation produce (on vessels returning home to Britain) which they relied upon to maintain production.

Another argument put forth in favor of the slave trade was its universal nature. MPs argued that, even if Britain relinquished her large stake in the slave trade, other nations would gain financially and defensively in proportion to her loss. On June 7, 1804, before the second reading of Wilberforce's bill for abolition, Lord Castlereagh reported to the Commons:

> Demand for colonial produce was daily increasing, and would continue to do so. In the end we should find that we had deprived ourselves of the means of accomplishing our object, and that the evil must subsist till terminated by other means. He would wish the trade to exist in favour of the commercial

interest of our country, instead of being thrown into the hands of Denmark, Spain or any other country in Europe.[22]

Castlereagh stressed the slave trade's central role in several European nations' finances. He suggested that if Britons continued to demand plantation produce after enacting abolition they would be forced to rely on foreign merchants and lose more money. He argued that British merchants and producers rather than foreigners should be allowed to meet the British public's demands for colonial goods and foodstuffs.

The duke of Clarence agreed with this argument. Without a viable solution for tracking and prohibiting the transatlantic slave trade of other nations, the duke argued, he could not see how British abolition would affect the total number of slaves being transported across the Atlantic and between colonies. On May 7, 1806, during a debate on a slave importation bill that would prevent British slave merchants from providing slaves to foreign colonies, the duke presented his case:

If we were enabled to prevent any supply of slaves from being carried to the enemy's colonies, then he would agree to the policy of preventing British subjects supplying them; but this was not the case: the colonies of the enemy would be supplied with slaves from other sources; and therefore he saw no reason why the profits arising from this trade should be taken out of the hands of British subjects.[23]

He depicted the trade's financial benefits to Britain as a happy consequence of preventing enemy access to the slave trade and controlling the intercolonial supply of slaves.

Proslavery MPs braved critics in and outside of Westminster by declaring their desire to see the slave trade continued and increased. On June 10, 1806, during a discussion on Charles Fox's motion for abolition, General Isaac Gascoyne highlighted the benefits of the trade and pledged his support for its continuance:

If we had new colonies to cultivate, and he was asked his opinion, in respect to encouraging the Slave Trade, he would certainly advise it; and why? because our commerce had derived such immense sources of wealth and prosperity from it, as had proved a great means of raising the country to its present state of aggrandisement and magnificence, and enabled us to contend with our enemies.[24]

To Gascoyne, participating in the slave trade meant financial prosperity for his constituency of Liverpool and for the nation. It had increased

Britain's prestige and allowed her to defend herself in times of war by providing monetary resources and experienced sailors. From his perspective, this vital element of the nation's economy should therefore be encouraged and supported without caving into humanitarian concerns and popular pressure from uninformed individuals and pressure groups that did not understand the financial ramifications of abolition.

The abolition of Britain's participation in the slave trade in 1807 injured Britain's West Indian planters' ability to maintain plantation production levels and handed over the slave trade and slave markets to their international competitors.[25] The West Indian interest turned its attention to preventing foreign intrusion into Britain's sugar markets.[26] It used the growing abolitionist sentiment in 1814 sparked off by the Treaty of Paris to protect itself from international competition.[27] This apparent switching of sides was in fact consistent with some MPs' and planters' pre-1807 arguments about the feasibility of abolition. After 1807, then, the West Indian interest had a vested interest in persuading other nations to stop the trade because its own interests were injured by its continuance. They frequently petitioned the king to work with the leaders of other trading nations to secure an international abolition as well as the right to search and seize vessels participating in the trade in international waters. Further legislation followed which affected the slave trade, slavery, and colonial life. In 1811 participation in the slave trade was made a felony. This ended the ability of Britain's West Indian merchants and traders to participate legally in the international trade in slaves.

In 1806 Napoleon's "continental system" had banned Britain from almost every major port in Europe. This forced Britons to look to their own empire for trading opportunities. The end of the Napoleonic Wars in 1815, however, meant that trade with Europe was reinstated. Abolitionists and anti-abolitionists expressed their anger at France's reinstatement of the slave trade. France's decision reinforced anti-abolitionist arguments that Britain's abolition alone would not be able to affect significantly the total number of Africans being transported to the Caribbean colonies. They argued that Britain would lose out financially to her European neighbors who continued to participate in and prosper from the trade. France abolished the slave trade again in 1817. In 1818, however, Britain failed to obtain an international agreement to their right to search ships in international waters. This ruling confirmed anti-abolitionist beliefs that abolition would not succeed without international cooperation.

Slave produce was important to many sectors of Britain's industry in the early nineteenth century. Emancipation had the potential to affect citizens in cities and towns across the country if it caused a decline in production. On July 2, 1832, during the introduction of his motion to assess Britain's dependence on slave labor, William Robert Keith Douglas[28] reflected on the importance of slave-grown cotton: "the material for the whole cotton manufacture of this country, of Manchester and Glasgow, as well as of every little village, was supplied by compulsory slave labour."[29] Douglas reminded the House that if cotton production came to a halt because of emancipation, so too would Britain's cotton industry and the livelihoods of thousands of British workers. In 1824–6, for example, cotton imports comprised almost 10 percent of all British imports and slaves grew approximately 86 percent of this cotton.[30] In the absence of a suitable supplier of cotton grown using free labor, they would have to resort to importing slave-grown cotton from foreign nations in order to maintain current levels of production. Not only would this defeat the humanitarian goals of emancipation, but British capital would fall into the hands of foreign states and the price of cotton could rise.

One contemporary school of thought working in the West Indians' favor advanced the idea that freed slaves, or perhaps free men in general, would always choose to work as little as possible if the land was fruitful enough to provide easy subsistence. West Indians argued that the natural laziness inherent in their slaves would result in uncontrollable, unproductive plantations.[31] While Africans were considered fit to work in the hot, humid climate of the West Indies, they were not necessarily believed to be able or willing to work of their own volition. Proslavery MPs argued that a clear system of discipline was required for African laborers regardless of contemporary theories on labor and free market economics. Plantation owner Patrick Stewart employed specific examples of unproductive free labor to refute abolitionist assertions that the West Indian colonies would prosper after emancipation. On April 15, 1831, during a discussion of Thomas Fowell Buxton's motion for abolition, Stewart referred to the current state of affairs in St. Domingo and Trinidad:

> When the Americans sent cargoes to that island [St. Domingo], and were to receive timber in exchange, with which the island abounds, they were obliged to send men to cut it down and bring it to their ships . . . In Trinidad, it appeared by a despatch from Governor Woodford, in 1826, that 400 free negroes had been employed for no less than five years in building a barrack.[32]

France's loss of St. Domingo's people, land, and produce had served as a warning to other European empires.[33] The rebellion was used to demonstrate the chaos, destruction, and bloodshed that could follow any mass emancipation of black slaves. Anti-abolitionists argued that the failed attempts to conquer it were proof that it would be impossible to reestablish order in Britain's slave colonies if similar rebellions were incited by abolitionist fervor. Stewart portrayed St. Domingo as a tragic loss in order to warn against the premature granting or violent taking of freedom by a large population of black slaves. Unable to procure the necessary labor to cut down trees to pay for goods they could no longer produce themselves, St. Domingo had become an uncivilized and unproductive disappointment. In contrast, Stewart noted that Trinidad's freed slaves did take on employment opportunities, but they did not work at an acceptable pace.

According to the anti-abolitionists, colonial produce, and the management and possession of the colonies, would be endangered by emancipation. Alexander Baring, for example, argued that freed slaves would not work in the islands for any wage. On March 6, 1828, during a discussion of the impact of amelioration on the West Indies, he remarked: "Where the land was rich, and the negro could procure with a little labour enough for the supply of his wants, no inducement which the colonists could hold out would be sufficient to make him work."[34] On June 25, 1833, the duke of Wellington noted: "There always was, and there ever would be, a difficulty in getting men to work in tropical climates more than would be sufficient to provide themselves with the common necessaries of life. After they had got these, their great luxury was, to repose in the shade."[35] On July 24, 1833, Ralph Bernal advanced a similar argument.[36] Thus, laziness in the colonies was not necessarily a racial problem, but a problem that could be solved only through coerced labor. The combination of highly fertile land, a warm climate, and a situation where freed slaves could suddenly work for themselves (or choose not to work) led to a number of theories about colonial life after emancipation. The West Indian interest argued that former slaves would not work in these conditions and in 1833 agreed to an apprenticeship scheme that secured plantation labor for several more years.

Strategic and Naval Importance

Britain was at war with the American colonies between 1775 and 1783 and with France from 1778. Due to their close proximity to the Caribbean colonies of rival European nations and their great distance from Britain, the British West Indies were under threat throughout much of this period. The West Indian interest capitalized on this tension by promoting the African trade as the best training ground for seamen for the Royal Navy. British West Indians in the colonies relied on the British armed and naval forces for protection from foreign invasion and internal strife and rebellion. The colonists wanted the protection of the British Army in the colonies because of the ever-present threat of slave revolts and the growing number of African slaves in the colonies.[37]

The American Revolution also had a significant negative economic impact on the West Indies. It interrupted and stopped trade, caused higher duties, increased the need for military protection, and inflated prices.[38] In 1778 Parliament rescinded its right to levy direct taxes on the colonists. Politicians became more wary of dictating to the colonists because West Indians were now able to threaten to secede with some power behind their threats. British West Indians, however, depended heavily on their monopoly trade with Britain and Britain's naval and military protection. It is highly unlikely that they ever would have followed through on their threats to secede.[39] A strong Royal Navy was seen as instrumental in defending the colonies and maintaining Britain's vital trade links. In the 1790s anti-abolitionist MPs successfully wove the need to defend the islands into their arguments for continuing the slave trade.

To help defend its West Indian colonies Britain looked to its greatest source of manpower, slaves, and raised black regiments from the slave population. The British Army purchased an estimated 13,400 slaves in small quantities and paid between £60 and £70 for each.[40] This probably made them the largest single buyer of slaves in the Caribbean.[41] Some of these recruits were promised freedom after serving five years, but few were expected to live long enough to obtain their reward.[42] African slaves were considered a good alternative to European troops in the colonies because they were acclimatized to the tropical climate and prevalent diseases that attacked European regiments.[43] Some MPs saw abolition as a threat to the security of the colonies because it would decrease the available manpower and the supply of new potential troops. General Banastre Tarleton was one of the most vocal and well-known opponents of abolition. He had gained firsthand experience working with black troops during his military service in the War of American Independence.[44] On February 18, 1796, during a debate on Wilberforce's motion to bring in a bill for abolition, Tarleton remarked: "We ought rather to endeavour to increase the population, since it added to our defence, than depress it by stopping the importation of negroes."[45] This controversial statement directly opposed the abolitionists' warnings of the great potential for mass slave revolts as the continuing trade supported the colonies' slave population.

The proposed abolition contradicted existing methods of raising regiments and defending the colonies. On March 7, 1796, during a discussion of Wilberforce's proposed motion for abolition, Tarleton stressed to the Commons: "Ministers had given commissions to many gentlemen for raising black regiments. By the bill these regiments would be emancipated."[46] Abolition, in other words, would threaten the safety of the colonies and have serious ramifications for individuals, the islands, and the empire. General Gascoyne echoed Tarleton's concerns.[47] After years of debate regarding the legal status of black soldiers in the British Army, the Mutiny Act of 1807 granted freedom to all blacks in the King's Service.[48]

The transatlantic slave trade was an important training ground for sailors in peacetime and provided manpower for Britain's naval vessels during wartime. According to recent calculations, approximately 735,000 slaves were carried on British ships from Africa to the British Caribbean between 1783 and 1808.[49] David Eltis has calculated that the number of slaves imported into the Americas nearly doubled while Britain and France were at war from approximately 100,000 between 1781 and 1790 to over 190,000 between 1791 and 1800.[50] Richard B. Sheridan's research has supported this claim that Anglo-French conflicts in the 1790s did not hinder the overall slave trade to Britain's West Indian colonies. During the war Britain captured Trinidad, Demerara, Essequibo, and Berbice. These provided new territories for British West Indian planters and new markets for Britain's slave traders.[51] Imports to Jamaica also increased in the 1790s, peaking in 1793 with a total of over 23,000 slaves imported into the island.[52] While coffeehouses were becoming one of the trendiest places to discuss new ideas in Britain's urban centers, the coffee boom of the 1790s resulted in the transportation of more slaves across the Atlantic. An estimated 26,000 slaves worked 700 new settlements in Jamaica to meet the increased demand for coffee.[53] African slaves therefore continued to be transported to the West Indies in unprecedented numbers throughout the 1790s despite war between England and France.

The craft of sailing took years to learn and when war erupted the Royal Navy could rely upon the slave trade to provide highly skilled men who had sailed some of the longest and most dangerous oceanic journeys. MPs with connections to port cities, the military, and the West Indies reminded Westminster of the slave trade's role in providing skilled seamen to defend their colonies, protect British trade routes, and maintain the safety of the empire. West Indian merchants claimed that the African trade employed 25,000 seamen annually.[54] Tarleton was the most outspoken MP regarding the importance of the slave trade to his constituency of Liverpool and to the navy. His support for the slave trade tended to focus on its central importance to Liverpool's economy, the country's economy, and the empire's defenses. Tarleton presented this argument during a discussion of a bill to limit the importation of slaves into newly conquered and ceded territories on April 25, 1806:

> We ought to take care of the interests of our navy, and commerce would take care of itself. The African trade had been the great cause of the prosperity and opulence of Liverpool. The sailors in this trade were the best that could be found, and the greatest supplies for our navy were obtained from the port of Liverpool. Although many were of opinion that the coasting trade was the chief nursery for our marine, yet he maintained that sailors were good in proportion to the length of their voyages, and those of the sailors in the African trade were certainly long ones.[55]

He insisted that the nature and length of the transatlantic voyages demanded by the slave trade turned ordinary sailors into "the greatest supplies for our navy."[56] Britain's naval forces were critical to her strength and survival during war. Other trades, however, were also considered suitable nurseries for the Royal Navy. These included the coal trade from Newcastle to London and the deep-sea fisheries and whaling near Greenland and Newfoundland.[57] The Royal Navy drew upon all branches of Britain's strong merchant marine to gain much-needed manpower in wartime.

Two months later Tarleton again addressed the House with his concern about Liverpool's important role in supporting Britain's overall prosperity. On June 10, 1806, during a discussion of Charles Fox's motion for abolition, Tarleton reminded his fellow MPs of how Liverpool had grown from a small village to a thriving city through its involvement in the slave trade:

> It [Liverpool] was eminent for the prosperity of its commerce, its wealth, its loyalty; for the important aid it furnished to the British marine, by affording at all times a numerous supply of seamen, through its African and West Indian trade. It was equally distinguished in its spirit in fitting out private ships of war, and by contributing annually three millions sterling in revenue to the public purse.[58]

He mentioned Liverpool's experience and success in building and outfitting ships for war as well as for use in the African slave trade. Warships would have been of vital importance during the Napoleonic Wars and the number and quality would have been significantly less without Liverpool's money and shipbuilding experience. The slave trade performed the role of a nursery for seamen; this argument was seriously considered by MPs as Britain's naval power was continually tested by war during the era of abolition.

War with France ultimately proved to be a critical factor in Parliament's approval of abolition. In 1806 a bill to prevent importing slaves into foreign territories and a slave ship restriction bill were passed in response to continuing war with France and the concern that trade between the colonies was helping the enemy's finances and levels of production. Opponents of the 1806 foreign slave trade bill argued that it was in fact abolition in disguise. For the first time abolition became an election issue in some districts with the potential to hinder the West Indian interest's political prospects, security, and numbers in the Commons. As it turned out, an estimated 25 members of the West Indian interest and their supporters lost their seats in Parliament in the 1806 election.[59] In 1807 the Commons and the Lords passed a bill for abolition. Britain and the United States of America abolished slave trading from 1808.

Historical Justification

One point that anti-abolitionists raised consistently over time was that of the British government's continual support of the slave trade and African slavery in the colonies. The trade had been regulated and encouraged by generations of politicians and monarchs for economic and imperial reasons, and in the late eighteenth and early nineteenth centuries members of the West Indian interest remarked that they could not understand how public and political support had shifted so dramatically and in such a short time. As Lord Chancellor Edward Thurlow remarked on May 8, 1792, during a discussion of a bill for abolition: "As to the iniquity and atrocity which had been so largely imputed to the slave trade, he could not imagine why those crimes had not been discovered by our ancestors, and were now to be so conspicuous in the year 1792."[60] This surprise at the sudden fervor for abolition was echoed by a number of the lord chancellor's contemporaries and stirred up fears of rapid change and popular unrest.

When it came to justifying the trade from a historical perspective, some MPs reminded the House of Africa's history of supplying slaves to various nations. They argued that the prior establishment of a slave trade within Africa and to the Middle East meant that Britons were taking advantage of an existing system of trade to gain needed workers, while being able to pass along the benefits of the Christian religion and European social norms to the Africans they transported. Thomas Hughan put forth this argument on February 27, 1807, during a debate over the bill for abolition: "The slave trade in Africa was the result of slavery, and slavery was produced by the barbarism of the inhabitants. History, ancient and modern, proved the universal existence of slavery in all the countries of Africa, inhabited by negroes, and that this system prevailed ages before the commencement of the European slave-trade."[61] To Hughan, the preexistence of an internal slave trade within Africa, instituted by Africans, justified European involvement in the trade and removed any guilt, even though this involvement extended it beyond the African continent to the Americas. On April 18, 1791, during a discussion of Wilberforce's motion to bring in a bill for abolition, Thomas Grosvenor remarked that while some elements of the slave trade such as kidnapping and "other barbarous practices" were certainly immoral: "It should be recollected, that these things were the consequence of the natural law of Africa, and that instead of declaiming against it, we should endeavour, like wise men, to turn it to our own advantage."[62] He argued that the practice of slave trading and holding already existed in Africa; Britons, therefore, like their European neighbors, should take advantage of this existing internal infrastructure to maintain their stake in the profitable transatlantic trade.

The long history of government sanctions provided by proslavery MPs in Westminster typically began with the rule of Queen Elizabeth I. For example, during a debate regarding ameliorations on April 6, 1797, Bryan Edwards noted: "The government of England, in the early part of queen Elizabeth's reign, encouraged and promoted the slave trade, and the queen herself participated in its profits. In 1564 she sent a squadron of men of war to purchase slaves on the coast of Africa, and to convey them for sale to the Spanish West Indies."[63] He continued, surveying the instructions of Charles II, William III, and James VII and II to their colonial governors, to further strengthen his claims of government support for the slave trade. Edwards read part of James VII and II's directions to West Indian governor Sir Phillip Howard in 1685, which he believed were copied and issued again by William III in 1689:

> You are to give all possible encouragement and invitation to merchants and others, who shall bring trade unto our said island [Jamaica], or in any way contribute to its advantage, and particularly to the African company. And as we

are willing to recommend unto the said company that the said island may have a constant and sufficient supply of merchantable negroes at moderate rates, so you are to take care that payment be made in money or commodities.[64]

This method of listing the various acts supporting the slave trade and colonial slavery over the previous three centuries was employed by several anti-abolitionist MPs during the slavery and slave trade debates in Parliament to legitimate their argument and challenge claims of inhumanity and illegality.[65]

After the abolition of the slave trade, the West Indian interest continued to defend slaveholding by using historical evidence and arguments to legitimate the practice and deflect accusations of inhumanity. With no new legal importations of slaves reaching the British West Indies after 1807, the body of slaves was largely made up of the descendants of African slaves who worked on plantations that in many cases had been passed down through generations of British landowners. Planters argued that the current owners were not to blame for possessing this contested, inherited property. Some continued to blame Parliament, the monarchy, and British laws for the difficult position they now faced. Successive monarchs and their governments had encouraged the British people and colonists to acquire, invest in, and utilize slave labor. Planters could now point to examples of emancipated slaves in non-British territories to demonstrate the dangers of premature emancipation. Slaves were officially the private property of their masters, and thus the state could not remove or destroy this property without great difficulty, good reason, and some form of compensation. The West Indian lobby generally agreed that to consider any man to be another man's property was morally questionable, but that this was the present state of things in the colonies, long-established by law and custom, and it would probably take an equally long period of adjustment and a great amount of money to change the situation.

Abolitionist publications frequently attacked the West Indian planters to gain support from their readers. Members of the West Indian interest, who held seats in Parliament, countered these attacks in a variety of ways, including reminding the House and anyone who might read the reports of debates that the planters had not originally devised or encouraged colonial slavery. On May 20, 1818, during a discussion of Sir Samuel Romilly's motion to assess the treatment of slaves in Nevis, Joseph Marryat the elder argued:

When views of humanity were directed against the rights of the planters, and those planters were accused of being the authors of slavery, it ought to be told that they did not create the servitude which they were charged with the desire to perpetuate . . . The slavery complained of was the work of the British government, and continued under British laws; and if the rights of the colonial proprietors, acquired under such guarantees, were to be interfered with, the parties ought in this case, as in others, to be indemnified.[66]

Marryat was one of several MPs with property in the West Indies to stress his and his fellow planters' right under English law to own property in slaves as well as land. He also objected to the allegation that the planters wanted slavery to continue.

The destruction of St. Domingo decades earlier was frequently used to illustrate the dangers of prematurely granting freedom to a large population of slaves.[67] Revolutions in France and elsewhere on the continent in the 1830s impacted on the lords' willingness to tamper with the existing social order in the colonies. Lord Sandon, MP for Liverpool, emphasized a distinct lack of encouraging examples of revolution and the granting of liberty to a large number of persons, even in areas that he considered to be civilized. On June 3, 1833, while members of the House continued to discuss the plan for emancipation, Sandon reflected on the dangers they were courting: "The experiments made in Italy, in Greece, in South America, even the great experiment of the French revolution, proved that a sudden transition from political slavery to freedom was not very safe."[68] In his arguments Sandon recalled harrowing elements of the recent revolutions: the working poor rising up, killing the landowning upper classes, overthrowing the monarchy, and instituting new systems of government. In this period of great upheaval on the continent, historical precedent was dangerous to ignore.

LEGAL ARGUMENTS

The legality of slaveholding and trading was debated throughout the period under review here as individuals and organizations attempted to modify and eradicate two long-standing institutions. In 1772, the Somerset Case was interpreted as outlawing slavery in England even though Lord Chief Justice Mansfield carefully specified that his ruling only applied to the case in question and only while James Somerset resided in England. James Somerset had been bought by Charles Stewart in Boston as a slave and brought to England in 1769. Somerset escaped in 1771 but was recaptured and imprisoned on a ship bound for Jamaica, where he was to be resold into slavery. A *habeas corpus* case was brought to determine if his imprisonment was illegal. Lord Mansfield ruled that no laws made slavery legal in England. The West Indian interest responded to the Somerset Case by developing arguments that legitimated the institution of slavery and the slave trade.[69] Mansfield's decision may very well have ended the period in which the West Indian interest could be complacent because it destroyed legal precedent and recognized the slave's humanity.[70]

The Scottish high court outlawed slavery more explicitly in 1778 in the case of Knight versus Wedderburn. As a child Joseph Knight had been sold to the Scot John Wedderburn by a slave ship captain in Jamaica. Wedderburn brought Knight back with him to Scotland and after some time Knight wanted to leave his position. In 1774 Wedderburn obtained a warrant to force Knight to go before Perth's Justices of the Peace. Every justice presiding over the matter had an interest of some form in slavery and they found in favor of Wedderburn.[71] The case was then pursued for several years before being considered by the Lords of Session in 1778. Wedderburn argued that he owned Knight legally under Jamaican law and that the laws of the British Empire condoned slavery and protected his right to his property. The opposition, however, argued that their client had not willingly entered into a contract of service with Wedderburn, as Knight had been a boy and it was the ship's captain who had arranged his sale. Their decision in Knight's favor meant that all current and former slaves held in Scotland were held illegally. This decision did not free all of Scotland's slaves immediately, but it did end the open holding of slaves in Scotland.[72]

One strategy used by anti-abolitionists throughout the decades of debate was to quote existing legislation that abolition would violate. On March 7, 1796, during a discussion of Wilberforce's motion to abolish the slave trade, John Dent invoked the authority of Magna Carta, long seen as the fundamental basis of English liberty, in his argument: "the proceeding was contrary to the express declaration of Magna Carta, that 'right shall neither be sold, delayed, or denied'. Now, if this bill passed, would not right be sold, delayed and denied? What was the committee now doing?"[73] His outrage at a proposed abolition violating preexisting British laws regarding private property, enterprise, and slavery was echoed by many MPs throughout the debates on abolition and emancipation.

Legal precedent was upheld by anti-abolitionists at all stages of the debates. Nearing the end of the long fight against abolition, George Hibbert summarized his thoughts on the understanding and humanity of past MPs and insisted that Westminster had been aware of the need to regulate the slave trade and prevent abuses from occurring, but they allowed it to continue out of necessity.[74] On March 16, 1807, before the third reading of the bill for abolition, Hibbert declared:

Our ancestors indeed distinguished betwixt the trade and its abuses; that they tolerated, these they reprobated; a sufficient proof of which is afforded in the act of 23 Geo. II c. 31, which, in its preamble, authorises the trade and its application to the West Indies; but, in one of its provisions, enacts penalties upon its abuses... It is in vain then for us to say that we are not completely at issue with our ancestors upon this question, or that we know any thing which they did not know, when they gave repeated legal sanction to that which we seek to abolish.[75]

Hibbert argued that past legislation had already considered the potential for inhumane treatment during the Middle Passage and that clear penalties and regulations were already in place; prior legislation should therefore stand. After further discussion, however, the bill was read for the third time and passed.

Between the abolition of the slave trade in 1807 and the abolition of slavery in 1833 both the West Indian interest and abolitionist humanitarians viewed the slavery debate in terms of Parliament's right to dictate to the colonies.[76] This fundamental right came up numerous times in the slavery debates as members of the West Indian interest argued against further parliamentary interference with colonial life and trade. Parliament had previously encountered difficulties creating and enforcing slave legislation for the West Indies because some of the colonies had their own assemblies and the right to make their own laws. They had, however, been able to ignore the colonists and abolish the slave trade in 1807 because it had been deemed a matter of navigation and commerce.[77] Shortly after the decision to pass the bill for abolition, MP Hugh Percy moved to bring in a bill to abolish slavery gradually. His motion was quickly defeated and abolitionists immediately condemned his actions. The West Indian interest, however, used this incident to support its ongoing argument that the abolition of the slave trade was simply the first part of a secret master plan to dismantle the entire institution of slavery, an institution upon which Britain's colonies relied.

In 1812 Trinidad became the first British colony forced to institute a slave registry to monitor the island's slave population. Debate over the registry bill raised the issue of whether the British government could impose its will on colonies possessing their own legislative assemblies. Planters became suspicious that more colonies would be forced to take similar action and that the information on births, deaths, and (illegal) importations could be used against them to support the small but growing campaign for emancipation. This move by the British government also incited hostility in the planters as they resented being dictated to by Parliament. In 1815 the foreign slave trade bill failed due to the alleged crime of illegal trading under foreign flags not being sufficiently proven to exist by the abolitionists. Throughout the debate on the bill the West Indian interest maintained that no such illegal trade existed and managed to convince the House that the bill was unnecessary and groundless.

In the 1820s government ministers in London began to look more closely at colonial laws, particularly those regarding slavery, and were more willing to threaten the colonists with the use of the royal veto to reject local legislation because of increasing pressure from the abolitionists.[78] The Society for the Mitigation and Gradual Abolition of Slavery was founded in 1823. In response a West Indian counterpropaganda subcommittee spent £1000 on newspaper articles and pamphlet propaganda to defend the institution of slavery in the colonies.[79] That same year Parliament passed George Canning's resolutions for ameliorating plantation life and the slave system in the colonies. Canning had proposed a number of reforms, including provisions for religious instruction, ending Sunday markets and labor, admitting slave testimony in court, legalizing marriage between slaves, securing the slaves' property, removing obstructions to manumission, preventing the separation of enslaved families through sale, limiting corporal punishment, and establishing banks for the slaves' savings. This inspired a number of heated debates in Parliament and angered British slaveholders. They were particularly incensed that they were being asked to risk their property and prospects without there being a clearly defined system of compensation in place.[80] The resolutions also implied that British West Indians were not adequately caring for their slaves, nor were they expected to take any steps to better the working and living conditions of their slaves on their own initiative.

During the debates over Canning's resolutions and their consequences, some MPs opposed the abolitionists' claims that no man could be the property of another man by referring to existing laws on the subject. On March 23, 1824, Joseph Hume brought in an antislavery petition before asking to submit a motion asking the House not to proceed with emancipation without providing compensation to the planters. He reflected upon the legal status of the planters' property: "The property in slaves was abominable; but that property had been acquired under the sanction of the law, and the legislature of the country only was to blame. The slave proprietor had as much right to be protected in the enjoyment of his undoubted property as the fundholder or the land owner."[81] Lord Wynford was similarly concerned that emancipation or compulsory manumission would set a dangerous legal precedent. During discussions of West Indian distress that followed the presentation of a petition from the West Indian interest on April 17, 1832, he remarked: "God forbid that there should be any thing like a forcing of the master to abandon his property in the slave! Once adopt that principle, and there was the end of all property."[82] West Indian MPs echoed Lord Wynford's argument about the legitimacy of their property throughout the slavery debates. Some abolitionists also openly agreed that under British law, right or wrong, slaves were property. As such, the West Indian proprietors were due compensation if Parliament was to usurp their property.

The fact that slave ownership had been established and was protected by British law was frequently advanced in the final years of the slavery debates. According to the West Indian interest, if slaves were by law property, then the removal of said property by the state should be accompanied by a plan to compensate the owners. On March 6, 1828, Robert John Wilmot Horton used a familiar analogy to stress the need for compensation:

> In this country, if a canal were cut, or a street built, the interest of the individuals was made to yield to the public interest; but then it was well known that individuals always received a compensation. Now, the West-Indian has property which he could only work by means of slave labour; and was he not, therefore, equally entitled to compensation, if deprived of that labour, as the man in this country was, who had his property destroyed, either by the building of a street or the construction of a canal?[83]

Wilmot Horton compared the removal of slave labor to the loss of one's property due to the installation of public works and infrastructure. This familiar illustration would have likely added weight to the West Indian interest's plea for compensation.

In 1833 compensation was debated at great length. The amount of compensation initially proposed by Edward George Geoffrey Smith Stanley was £15 million; this was raised to £20 million after further calculations were made. An additional £10 million was offered as a loan to be repaid once the colonies stabilized. These changes were made amid heated debate from abolitionists, who denied that the West Indians had any legal claim to compensation, and the West Indians, who argued that the losses would be far greater and much wider-reaching than their opposition had led the House to believe.

On July 24, 1833, amid questions about the legitimacy of the planters' property, Stanley defended the West Indians' claims for compensation:

> He would tell him why the planter should be indemnified—because the principles of justice required that no man's property should be taken away without compensation—because the laws of England forbade taking away a man's property without the consent of the owner... and, lastly, because, acting on the principles of justice, that House had declared, that emancipation and compensation should go together.[84]

In the end, the compensation clause was passed, granting an unprecedented amount of money to the West Indians in return for emancipation and, by that means, legitimating their property in slaves.

Paternalist Arguments

Paternalist arguments put forth during the slavery debates stressed the benefits of transporting slaves from Africa to Britain's colonies, the supposed safeguards built into the institution of plantation slavery in the colonies, and the good work done by the planters. This category of argument was important to the anti-abolitionist faction throughout the entire period under study. Prior to 1807, proslavery MPs contrasted a dismal view of life in Africa with an idealized picture of life under British rule in the West Indies. After abolition, members of the West Indian interest argued against external legislation and interference by demonstrating that their slaves were already cared for under the existing system. They stated that slaves were treated humanely and at least as well as British workers and soldiers. These paternalist arguments invoked humanitarian ideals by emphasizing that the institution of slavery provided food, shelter, protection, and care, thus contradicting the repeated accusations of inhumane treatment.

Proslavery MPs argued that West Indian plantation owners were surrogate parents of their slaves, taking care of them in sickness and health and providing all necessities throughout their slaves' lives. Plantation owners in Parliament argued that their slaves had better living and working conditions than factory owners in Britain provided for British workers. They also provided evidence of the slaves' loyalty to their owners and to the crown to argue that the principle of humanity was fundamental to the institution of colonial slavery. Widespread paternalist beliefs and actions were central to the proslavery case for retaining British involvement in the slave trade and the postponement of emancipation in the 1820s and 1830s.

MPs with direct involvement in the slave trade and colonial slavery countered abolitionist charges of inhumanity by highlighting the material benefits of importation and West Indian slavery for Africans and their descendants. On April 2, 1792, during a discussion of Wilberforce's bill for abolition, Benjamin Vaughan relayed to his fellow MPs a list of the benefits of slave life in the British Caribbean:

> For clothes and fuel they could have little want on account of the climate; they had a house and land gratis; they suffered no imprisonment for debt, no fear of not being able to support a family to deter them from marrying; their orphans and widows were sure to be taken care of, as likewise themselves, when old, or meeting with accidents; they had medicines, surgery, midwifery, and attendance gratis; they had their private property, which no master ever took from them. They were perfectly resigned, at the time he was abroad, to their situation, and looked for nothing beyond it.[85]

He argued that life for transported African slaves in Britain's colonies was free from hardship. Here Vaughan employed a common construction of paternalist argument by backing up his claims with testimony of firsthand knowledge of plantation life. Over time, however, MPs appear to become increasingly wary of claiming firsthand knowledge through plantation ownership. This hesitation was probably due to fear of being accused of "interest" (and therefore bias) and hence incurring public condemnation.

Anti-abolitionists stressed the slaves' access to medical care on the plantations to defend the plantation system and the impossibility of the slave population maintaining itself without the continual importation of slaves into the colonies. By demonstrating the hands-on role of medical practitioners on the plantations, MPs refuted claims of inhumane treatment, excessive punishment, and torture that abolitionists insisted were familiar events on the plantations. On April 6, 1797, during a discussion of various methods for maintaining slave populations, Charles Rose Ellis insisted that proper medical care and inspections were already performed on all plantations:

> The planters cannot be accused of inattention to their duty; no estate is without the advantage of constant medical care; and the legislature has taken a very efficient step to secure a strict attention to the health of the negroes, by exacting a list of the deaths and births on each estate, accompanied by a statement of the causes of the deaths, given in by the surgeon on oath.[86]

He argued that even with constant access to medical practitioners the slave population was not able to maintain itself. According to

Ellis, experts carefully assessed the actions of the plantation owners and managers upon the death of any slave. As Alderman Nathaniel Newnham remarked on February 7, 1794, during a debate on Wilberforce's motion to abolish the practice of supplying foreign territories with slaves: "There was a mutual interest between the planter and the slave, which enforced compassion and duty."[87] According to Newnham, if the slave population was decreasing (which it was), the planters were not at fault. MPs reported that plantation owners disliked relying on the trade to maintain their slave populations, but no adequate alternative had been found.

Paternalist arguments continued to be advanced throughout the slavery debates. On December 13, 1830, plantation owner Ralph Bernal reminded the House that the slave population currently had protection, care, and job security from masters who were obliged to care for them.[88] If the role of slave master was to be taken over by the state, various laws, officials, and institutions would need to be established to protect the slaves from poverty, as well as to assist the colonists in coping with a great influx of destitute citizens. Similarly, on June 25, 1833, during the climax of the emancipation debates, Lord Ellenborough asked the House to consider the actual state of the West Indian colonies. He suggested they imagine the lives of the slaves at present compared to their hypothetical situation following an immediate emancipation:

> It would leave infancy unprotected, maturity without a guide and abandoned to debauchery and to vice, and age without a shelter and without refuge. What was the present state of the negroes? The child was reared and protected, the adult was provided for, and the aged had a sure and safe resting-place. They were as a body well governed, well protected, and happy in their station.[89]

Lord Ellenborough argued that at that point in history the slaves' working and living conditions had been ameliorated and that they were adequately cared for from birth to death. This care could not continue under the proposed scheme for emancipation, even when the years of apprenticeship were taken into consideration. Thus, emancipation would necessarily bring to an end the paternalist care shown for their colonies' slaves.

A number of slave-owning MPs produced firsthand accounts of plantation life in print and in the houses of Parliament in order to defend the continuing enslavement and transportation of Africans to their West Indian colonies. They found support from the MPs representing towns whose prosperity depended on the African trade. According to a number of MPs with an interest in the colonies, Africans did not object to the institution of slavery. This was said to be the case throughout the West Indies and particularly if the plantation was owned and governed by an English planter. As John Fuller noted on May 30, 1804, during a discussion of Wilberforce's proposed motion for abolition: "It was not, he argued, true that negroes felt themselves miserable under English masters. The very reverse was the case, for they felt themselves happy under an English master and an English govt."[90] Thomas Hughan shared a similar view. On February 27, 1807, during a discussion of a bill for abolition, Hughan declared: "he would tell the hon. members, from his own personal observation, that there did not exist a more happy race than the slaves in our colonies, if any trust was to be placed in outward appearances, which universally indicated cheerfulness and contentment."[91] With various laws and amelioration legislated by the British Parliament in conjunction with the colonial assemblies, Hughan promoted English-owned plantations as the best possible destination for an African slave in the West Indies; in Fuller's estimation, the slaves agreed. Anti-abolitionists therefore argued that if Britain withdrew from the trade while their European counterparts continued their participation, future African slaves would face lives of enslavement in foreign territories without the legal protection, caring masters, or enlightenment found on British plantations.

The West Indians in the House of Commons frequently advanced images of a happy and contented body of slaves when defending their occupations and objecting to abolitionists' claims about the hardships and oppression slaves faced in the colonies. On July 29, 1833, during a discussion on how to limit the new apprentices' working hours in order to allow them to earn and save money in their free time, William James noted that slaves in the West Indies already had sufficient opportunities to make their own money: "One slave of his alone at that moment had upwards of 200*l*... that very slave, although possessed of so much money, would not consent to receive his emancipation, if he thought it was to be at the loss of his trifling allotment of ground."[92] He argued that at least one of his slaves would object to the abolition of slavery because of the many benefits he received though this now reviled institution. Few MPs chose to advance a happy image of slavery in the colonies as emancipation drew nearer, but those who did so swore on firsthand knowledge, published reports, and commonly held racial theories that emancipation would negatively affect the slaves.

One of the most controversial arguments put forth in favor of transporting African slaves to the British West Indian colonies and continuing to use slave labor was that African slaves received better treatment and benefits in the West Indies than the poorest classes did in Britain and on the European continent. By contrasting carefully constructed images of life on Britain's colonial plantations with life in Britain's factories and cities, some MPs depicted a slave's life as preferable to that of the impoverished paid worker in Britain or Europe. Historians such as David Brion Davis have theorized that abolitionism played a role in diverting humanitarian effort and attention abroad to avoid threatening the existing social order and class structure at home.[93] Radicals were much more interested in the struggles of white factory workers than those experienced by black slaves on West Indian plantations. Influential journalist and radical William Cobbett, for example, used proslavery language to defend English workers' rights and promoted images of plantation slavery that highlighted the greater suffering that Europeans experienced in factories.[94] Pamphlets and petitions brought this argument to the masses in the 1830s.[95] Proslavery literature of this era frequently commented on prevailing harsh working conditions found everywhere.[96] These comparisons were presented repeatedly as evidence of both the preferable working conditions of the plantations and the need to focus humanitarian efforts on the people of their own country and constituencies.

According to contemporary reports and legislation, plantation slavery as instituted by West Indians in British colonies did provide some protection and care for the slaves. Evidence presented to parliamentary committees stated that African slaves received adequate medical care, shelter, food, and land on which to grow foodstuffs to supplement their own diet and sell for a profit. Britain's poorest classes, in contrast, lacked these basic necessities. On April 2, 1792, in response to Wilberforce's introduction to his motion for abolition, James Baillie, the agent for Grenada, stated: "I do declare, in the most solemn manner, that I consider the negroes in the British West India islands to be in as comfortable a state as the lower orders of mankind in any country in Europe."[97] The testimony of witnesses and firsthand accounts from the West Indian lobby contrasted two ways of life of which few had any direct knowledge: the lives of slaves on West Indian plantations and the lives of the European poor in workshops, on farms, or on the streets.

On May 30, 1804, during the discussion on Wilberforce's motion to introduce a bill for abolition, John Fuller commented on the benefits provided to slaves that were not offered to British laborers:

Mr. Fuller contended, that the situation of the negroes in West India colonies was equal, nay, superior to the condition of the labouring poor of this country. They were better fed and more comfortably accommodated. He maintained that their labour was not nearly so severe. The best of the negroes did not in general perform half as much labour as even the most indifferent of our labourers.[98]

He argued that slaves worked half as many hours and received better accommodation and food than the working poor in Britain. This controversial statement directly opposed abolitionists' assertions of the dangerous working conditions and inhumane treatment slaves received on West Indian plantations. As a plantation owner, Fuller had firsthand knowledge of plantation life and work but consequently had a vested interest in asserting the benefits of the slave trade and plantation life for the slaves in Britain's West Indian colonies.

The practice of comparing slavery in the colonies to life for Europe's peasants continued beyond the abolition of the slave trade. On May 15, 1823, during the amelioration debates, Alexander Baring remarked: "My own opinion is, that the condition of the slaves is undoubtedly, in many respects, superior to that of most of the European peasantry. They are well clothed, well fed, and, I believe, generally treated with justice and kindness."[99] Baring's comment made reference to the fact that the slaves were fed, clothed, and housed by their masters, unlike the working poor in England and abroad who had to pay for their own necessities. On July 29, 1833, William James expanded upon this idea by challenging the necessity of wages for apprentices after emancipation was enacted:

Now, he would ask, what were they to receive money for? Was it for eating, drinking, lodging—all of which they at present had, free of expense, and an allotment of ground besides?... That they were slaves it was true; but were there, he would ask, no such slaves in England—men who laboured and toiled to earn subsistence?[100]

MPs who opposed immediate emancipation often discussed the meaning of the word "slave" and its negative connotations during the slavery debates. They argued that, like "cart-whip," it was a term loaded with exaggerated tales and images of hardship and discipline and that the debates would never be handled fairly and calmly as long as abolitionists continued to define the term "slave" so negatively. Some MPs, including James, challenged the common perception of the slave by comparing their working and living conditions to those of the lower classes of the British public.

A few MPs tried to reconcile the images of paternalist planters and managers and the administration of corporal punishment on Britain's West Indian plantations. Extreme evangelicals supported severe punishments and the death penalty for murder while moderates preferred psychological intimidation rather than physical punishment.[101] Abolitionists emphasized the use of the whip to demonstrate the unnatural and oppressive regime planters maintained in the colonies. The planters and others continually contested charges that this mode of discipline was inhumane, excessive, or unnecessary. On March 16, 1824, Alexander Baring stated that it was irrational to argue that the use of the whip on colonial plantations was unnecessary when the identical mode of punishment in Britain's military was upheld by Parliament.[102] During a debate regarding emancipation on June 7, 1833, Joseph Hume argued that the whip or "lash" was used more often in their own military than in the colonies:

> The establishment of the army in 1827 consisted of 111,107 men . . . one in forty-eight received corporal punishment, and that taking 300 lashes as the average punishment, there had in that year been 687,000 lashes inflicted on British soldiers. [*No, no*] Well, then, supposing the average to be 200, it would appear that there had been 458,200 lashes inflicted during that year.[103]

Although hotly contested and subject to interpretation regarding the number of lashes allotted to each man, Hume clung to his statement that through amelioration and the existing system of enslavement in the colonies, the slaves were treated in a fairer, more humane manner than British men were in their own army. If MPs were willing to allow corporal punishment to be inflicted on their fellow countrymen, he argued, it would be hypocritical of them to label the thoroughly scrutinized system of plantation discipline as inhumane. Overall, the West Indian lobby argued that Parliament should care for their fellow British subjects first, before considering legislating for the colonies.

Moral and Religious Arguments

The morality of participating in the slave trade was frequently challenged over the course of the slavery debates. This line of argument favored the humanitarian arguments and aims of abolitionist MPs but was countered by members of the West Indian interest with firsthand knowledge of slavery in the plantations. Their most successful line of argument was that the transatlantic slave trade brought enlightenment, Christianity, and a better life to the transported slaves who ended up in Britain's colonies. During a discussion on sustaining plantation slave populations on April 6, 1796, for example, Charles Rose Ellis commented on the negative effects polygamy supposedly had on population levels: "in its best state, [polygamy] is supposed not to be favourable to population; in the West Indies, it has been found to be particularly fatal to it."[104] He suggested that instruction in the Christian faith would end this practice:

> When I say that I consider a reform in the manners and morality of the negroes to be necessary, I must explain, that I do not mean to state them to be a vicious race: on the contrary, they are in their dispositions, good and tractable; highly sensible to kind treatment, and capable of very extraordinary attachment. The point in their morality to which I allude, does not proceed from any defect in their natural disposition; it is the effect of their manners, the prejudices, and the religion of the Africans. Their religion is either a corrupt Deism or Mahometanism, and natural passion has received the sanction of this religion, in establishing a system of polygamy.[105]

His argument centered on what he deemed to be immoral cultural practices that could be countered by religious instruction in the colonies. By theorizing about how to encourage and promote natural increase over time, Ellis and his fellow West Indian MPs were also attempting to convince the House that eventually the slave trade would be unnecessary. They argued that it should therefore be allowed to come to a natural, gradual end without parliamentary interference.

Abolitionists called for justice and humanity to be instituted in the colonies and maintained that the fundamental basis for an ideal moral and humane society could be found in the Bible. Anti-abolitionists, however, were able to use passages from the Bible to defend the institution of slavery. On April 19, 1797, during a discussion of Wilberforce's motion for abolition, John Stanley, the agent for Nevis, argued: "slavery was not incompatible with christianity [*sic*] and religion, the opinions of the bishop of Gloucester, St. Paul, and several other saints, in their writings, made mention of bondsmen, without adducing any arguments against the commerce in slaves."[106] Historically, as recorded in the Bible, slavery had been a sanctioned institution; MPs could therefore argue that the West Indians were not acting in an unchristian manner by possessing slaves. During a debate on the slave trade limiting bill on July 5, 1799, Samuel Horsley, the bishop of Rochester, similarly argued that while slavery was not specifically condemned in the Bible, certain methods of enslavement were condemned. These included "man-stealing" which the bishop argued formed the basis of the slave trade: "in this text of scripture the slave-trade is condemned and prohibited by name, as a thing abominable in the sight of God, and wicked in the next degree to sodomy."[107] Lord Thurlow contradicted the bishop's argument: "He could not see that in the best system of morality and the purest system of religion which had ever appeared, the Christian religion, there was ever any prohibition against slavery like that which had been argued by the reverend prelate."[108] These arguments again defended Britain's continuing use of slaves in the colonies but not necessarily her participation in the African trade.

During a debate over abolition on June 27, 1804, plantation owner Joseph Foster Barham made an intriguing claim combining the moral benefits and civilizing power of Christian instruction with monetary gains that the plantation owners were always considering. While defending the success of West Indian missionaries, Foster Barham remarked: "Not fewer than 10,000 negroes had been converted in the island of Antigua, and their tempers and dispositions had been thereby rendered so much better, that they were entitled to an increased value of 10*l*."[109] According to Foster Barham, the calming influence of Christianity increased the value of slaves. This argument may have been advanced to encourage plantation owners to spend more money and energy on religious instruction for their slaves or to demonstrate the benefits of the slave trade and West Indian slavery for the slaves themselves. It promoted the continuance of slavery in the colonies, but it did not necessarily require the continuance of the trade. Foster Barham rejected abolitionist claims of poor treatment on the plantations. He argued that if plantation owners would make money via the spread of the Christian faith, why would they refuse to provide religious instruction to their slaves?

During a heated debate over abolition on June 10, 1806, General Isaac Gascoyne gave a thoughtful speech regarding the history of slavery. He stated that learned men throughout history had endorsed the institution of slavery: "it had been sanctioned by the authority of the wisest and most pious legislators."[110] He also provided evidence from the Bible by reading Leviticus chapter 25, verses 44 through to 46, aloud to the Commons:

"Both the bondmen and thy bond-maids which thou shalt have, shall be of the heathen that are round about you; of them shall ye buy bond-men, and bond-maids. Moreover, of the children of the strangers that do sojourn among you, of them shall ye buy, and of their families that are with you, which they begat in your land, and they shall be your possession. And ye shall take them as an inheritance for your children after you, to inherit them for a possession; they shall be your bondmen for ever." The above clearly proved, that slavery had from the earliest times, been countenanced and authorised by religion itself.[111]

In the Bible and in Westminster, owning slaves was considered to be an individual's right and a form of personal property providing a valuable inheritance for one's descendants. Gascoyne's argument combined biblical justification and historical evidence of the acceptance and encouragement of slavery.

Biblical justifications for enslaving Africans continued to be advanced as abolition became more likely. On February 23, 1807, in response to anti-slavery MP Walter Fawkes' declaration of slavery and the slave trade being forbidden by Divine law, George Hibbert shared his own research and understanding with the House:

I must say, that in the sacred books I can find no such authority. In the Old Testament, the slave trade, or the sale of men, is spoken of indifferently just as other trades... I shall mention, that in the Epistle of Paul to Philemon, Paul sends back Onesimus (whose very name bespeaks his station), who was Philemon's slave, and had run away from his master—he sends him back, I say, to resume his station without one word expressive of his disapprobation of slavery, or in vindication of Onesimus, who had fled from it.[112]

Beginning with a broad overview of the biblical acceptance of slavery, he then utilized the specific example of Paul the Apostle returning a slave to his master to argue for the divine sanctioning of the institution of slavery. Biblical justifications for slavery, however, were unable to help the anti-abolitionist cause, perhaps because of the conflicting arguments of Christian charity and humanity that were brought forth in Parliament to counter them or perhaps because of the number of other arguments available to the West Indian interest which were less controversial. They were all but abandoned following the abolition of the slave trade in 1807.

After 1807, anti-abolitionist arguments that centered on religion instead focused on efforts to provide Christian instruction to the slaves. Abolitionists frequently charged the colonists with having provided inadequate religious instruction that could have otherwise helped to ameliorate conditions in the colonies, promote a peaceful atmosphere, and allow slaves to embrace the rights, privileges, and obligations attached to freedom. The West Indian interest denied these charges and reminded its peers that the Bible did not forbid slavery. On May 15, 1823, during a debate on his motion for resolving to ameliorate the conditions of the slaves, George Canning noted: "it is not true, that there is that in the Christian religion which makes it impossible that it should co-exist with slavery in the world. Slavery has been known at all times, and under all systems of religion, whether true of false."[113] On March 7, 1826, as the House of Lords discussed the amelioration resolutions of 1823, Lord Chancellor Eldon advanced a similar view that slavery and Christianity had coexisted for centuries and noted that the wisest politicians had condoned it.[114] During the same debate Lord Dudley and Ward dismissed accusations that the planters had taken too long to provide a Christian education for their slaves: "It was to be recollected, however, that if they had never been brought from home, they would have been at least in equal darkness—slaves in body to their savage and tyrannical masters, and slaves in mind to a revolting superstition."[115] This proslavery argument about the civilizing effects of plantation slavery was advanced more often prior to the abolition of the slave trade but does emerge occasionally during this period as well, often in combination with a defense of the West Indians' actions. In contrast, during the discussion on a petition for compensation presented on December 13, 1830, Joseph Marryat the younger admitted that holding men in the state of slavery was contrary to the teachings of Christianity, but he argued that it would be morally wrong to release them onto an unprepared and vulnerable white population: "It was true that Christianity forbade slavery, but it was equally true that its doctrines forbade their letting loose a large slave-population, the inevitable consequence of which must be a general massacre."[116] Here, Marryat stressed the House's moral obligation to act cautiously while being conscious of the best interests of the entire colonial population.

In the final days of the slavery debates, the historical acceptance of slavery as illustrated in the Bible continued to be brought forth in Parliament. For example, on May 17, 1833, Lord Wynford argued for compensation in this manner:

> When it was said that these petitioners could not recognise the principles of men having the property of men, let him tell them that the Apostles had recognised slavery, and he presumed that they did not pretend to be better Christians than the Apostles. The principle had in truth been recognised from the earliest ages.[117]

He challenged the moral basis of abolition by stressing the legality of slaveholding from a biblical perspective. Following his logic, if the Apostles had recognized the slave as another's property, and they could not say that they knew better than the Apostles, it would be wrong to remove this property from its owner without compensation.

William Burge stressed the need to "civilize" the African slaves prior to emancipation.[118] He argued that their slaves required moral and religious instruction as well as a strong work ethic to handle freedom. These were elements that Burge and some of his fellow MPs believed to be lacking in the slaves due to two reasons: their race and their situation. On May 24, 1832, he advanced this proposal: "First, let them improve his moral character; impart to him the truths of Christianity... Until he acquired the habit of industry, and which he would not possess until he was further advanced in civilization, the gift of freedom would be worse than useless to him."[119] Burge and others argued that it would be immoral to emancipate the slaves before they were properly educated and prepared for their future participation in society. Immediate, premature emancipation would subject the colonies to unthinkable horrors; Westminster and the country's abolitionists would be to blame.

Racial Arguments

A number of prevailing thoughts and attitudes toward African civilization, culture, religion, and labor weave their way throughout these arguments supporting the slave trade. A lack of seemingly "civilized" behavior, political organization, and intellectual enlightenment, particularly with regards to European social norms such as monogamy and Christian practices, justified the enslavement of Africans for some MPs, while inciting empathy and paternal concern in others. Africans from across the continent were lumped together without an understanding of their individual religions, languages, and culture. As a group they were considered inferior to the European nations north of the Mediterranean. British politicians remained dismissive of African culture, civilization, and claims to fundamental rights, while arguing over whether to end what to some was simply a branch of their country's commerce. Proslavery MPs, MPs who opposed immediate abolition, and the majority of the abolitionists in Parliament who fought to end the slave trade were content to keep Africans enslaved in their colonies for the immediate future. It was the manner in which they justified their continued enslavement that varied.

Prior to the eighteenth century, theories about race stemmed from theological study, but in the late eighteenth century race began to be viewed scientifically (or pseudoscientifically).[120] Africans and Europeans were studied, measured, tested, and compared. This continued throughout the nineteenth century. Scientists, doctors, priests, and philosophers explained and examined race using scientific evidence, visual evidence, and biblical evidence as they tried to determine whether the human race stemmed from a single lineage (following the monogenesis story of Adam and Eve) or multiple lineages (polygenesis).[121] Many nineteenth-century racial beliefs, as well as the modern understanding and use of the terms "Caucasian" and "Indo-European," stemmed from the Enlightenment's scientific and philosophical developments. Nineteenth-century racial theory explained that mankind was divisible into "races" with fixed characteristics and varying moral and intellectual capacities. Because intellect and physiognomy were increasingly linked, physical characteristics were thought to reveal inner characteristics, nature, and ability.[122] It should be noted that while New World slavery did not create racism, it added a new dimension to it as multiple races suddenly lived in close proximity to each other within a distinct hierarchy.[123]

The prior existence of the slave trade and the lesser degree of "civilization" achieved in Africa as assessed by contemporaries supported the continuance of the transatlantic trade regardless of humanitarian claims and abolitionist fervor. West Indians used pre-Darwinite fixity of species theory to defend enslaving Africans.[124] On May 30, 1804, in response to Wilberforce's motion to bring in a bill for abolition, John Fuller made a number of generalizations about the African race. He first commented on their limited mental capacity: "He had never heard the Africans deny their mental inferiority. They had never hesitated to confess to him, that they could not vie with Europeans in talent or knowledge. In matters of ingenuity or calculation, they were no match for the inhabitants of the other quarters of the world."[125] He suggested that Africans were of a lower order of men and were therefore in the best situation to perform slave labor in the modern world because they did not possess the mental capacity and drive of Europeans. Even major Enlightenment figures such as David Hume endorsed claims regarding the mental inferiority of Africans.[126] The fixity of species theory ranked Africans on a scale above apes but below Europeans. Each species was suited to specific tasks and faced restrictions imposed by Providence. According to this theory Africans did not possess the ability to reason; this disadvantage helped West Indians justify their enslavement and Britain's participation in the slave trade.[127]

During his speech Fuller also discussed African civilization and progress and concluded that it was the unique situation of the continent and governance of Africa, rather than the intrusion of European powers and traders, that had sparked the slave trade:

> We had heard of the history of that country for 600 years, but we saw no rays of improvement or civilization. If the inhabitants had been capable of civilization, they could easily have been able to drive off their coasts a few African slave ships, and thus prevented the original establishment of the trade. Something in the internal circumstances of the country must then have favoured the establishment of the trade.[128]

This perspective released Britons from any responsibility regarding their involvement in the trade. He instead gave agency (and any blame) to the various participating African nations by arguing their reluctant acceptance of the trade. Fuller argued that, although Africans had been given centuries in which to match Europe's level of advancement, they were still not civilized enough to put up a resistance to this profitable trade. He said that there was therefore no reason for Europeans to dismantle it or feel a sense of ownership or guilt regarding it.

Drawing on their limited knowledge and understanding of African culture and practices, some MPs insisted that life for slaves on a West Indian plantation was better than how their lives would have been in Africa. John Henniker-Major, for example, insisted that the men and women who were now West Indian slaves would otherwise have been killed. On April 3, 1798, during a discussion of Wilberforce's motion to bring in a bill for abolition, Henniker-Major referred to evidence given to the House "that the kings of the country, instead of slaughtering their captives, now sold them to the nations of Europe. They were conveyed from a country of barbarous superstition, to a land of civilization and humanity."[129] This also reflects the moral and religious sentiments discussed earlier. Sir William Young expanded on this idea by painting a gruesome picture of African slavery on February 28, 1805:

> Are they not driven in their own country like cattle with irons about their necks? The humanity of the African master is cried up, while that of the British is deprecated. An African master, however, we are told, can coolly toss his slave, when half dead, into a ditch, and say "there is so much money lost."[130]

MPs on both sides of the debate relied on second-hand evidence, vivid descriptions, and rumors to back up their claims about life in Africa. Anti-abolitionist MPs contrasted negative images of life in

Africa with a rosy view of plantation life in Britain's colonies to stress the trade's utility in providing Africans with a better life.

The abolition debates in Westminster often became a venue for racial debates where prevailing theories about the different races' capacity to work, survive harsh living conditions, and exert themselves in hotter climates were discussed. The hot Caribbean climate differed so greatly from the British climate that some MPs argued that it was impossible to work the plantations using European labor; the assumption that Europeans could not survive and work in tropical climates persisted throughout the debates. On February 28, 1805, during a debate on Wilberforce's motion to discuss a possible bill for abolition, Sir William Pulteney insisted that an African labor force was required to work the plantations:

> The real fact was agreed upon by all parties to be this: the West Indies cannot be cultivated by Europeans, whose constitutions will not bear fatigue in that climate. It is therefore necessary, if they are to be cultivated at all, that it must be by some other class of the human species, who being natives of warmer climates, are able to endure that degree of labour and fatigue which no Europeans could do in that climate.[131]

He claimed that the slave trade would have to continue if the plantations (including his own) were to be worked and the current slave population could not naturally maintain itself. Pulteney's use of the term "class of the human species" is particularly interesting. It implies a distinct biological difference between Europeans and Africans that began to be studied during the Enlightenment.[132] Since the Caribbean climate had proven to be a threat to both the health and productivity of Europeans, most MPs accepted that African labor was the better, safer choice. Due in large part to the widespread acceptance of this theory, while the slave trade faced overpowering popular and parliamentary challenges in the early nineteenth century, Britons were allowed to keep their black slaves in the colonies.

Racial arguments were put forth less frequently following the abolition of the slave trade in 1807.[133] Most of the racial arguments advanced prior to abolition were presented to justify Britain's participation in the transatlantic slave trade. They had previously pointed to the preexistence of an internal African trade in slaves to justify shipping, trading, and utilizing African labor in the West Indian colonies. They occasionally argued that people of African descent were the best laborers because they could supposedly withstand hard labor in hotter climates. In the slavery debates of the 1820s and 1830s anti-abolitionist racial arguments emphasized the negative aspects of emancipation, warned of the superior physical strength of African slaves and their descendants, and compared "civilized" life in the colonies for the slaves with a supposedly uncivilized life in Africa.

MPs regularly questioned the African and Creole slaves' current level of civilization when debating their ability to handle freedom in the decades immediately following the abolition of the slave trade. Many MPs believed the African race to be fundamentally and unchangeably different. This belief had far-reaching ramifications. It caused great concern over whether black and white members of the colonies could live together peacefully after emancipation. The West Indian interest maintained that due to their lesser level of civilization, its slaves were comparable to children in intellect, but full-grown adults in physical strength: an alarming combination. They argued that physical punishment and discipline were necessary to control their slaves. Following the abolition of the slave trade, the West Indians stressed that its concerted efforts to remove "destructive" African practices (including native religious ceremonies and polygamy) were necessary to maintain order in the colonies and advance the slaves' level of civilization. Emancipation, in contrast, would end any hope of advancement. This became the focus of their racial defenses of slavery after 1807.

The slave as a child was a commonly advanced image in the pre-1807 debates on slavery and the slave trade and was also alluded to during discussions about emancipation in the 1820s and 1830s. This image incorporated the need to care for and instruct slaves in a paternalistic manner, but it also depicted slaves as different and as requiring special instruction to raise them up toward the level of civilization Europeans had already achieved.[134] On March 16, 1824, during a discussion of amelioration, George Canning noted that, whereas some elements of the slave might be childlike, their physical stature was not:

> In dealing with the negro, Sir, we must remember that we are dealing with a being possessing the form and strength of a man, but the intellect only of a child. To turn him loose in the manhood of his physical strength, in the maturity of his physical passions, but in the infancy of uninstructed reason, would be to raise up a creature resembling the splendid fiction of a recent romance.[135]

This allusion to Mary Shelley's *Frankenstein* (1818) is quite fascinating. In the novel Dr. Frankenstein created a monster who looked like a man but was physically larger, more powerful, and potentially more dangerous. Insurrections and slave rebellions occurred in the islands throughout this period; when the House considered the large number of African slaves and their descendants in the colonies and compared their greater physical strength and inferior civilization to the much smaller population of white colonists, freeing the slaves *en masse* amounted to a dangerous experiment. One particularly relevant interpretation of the novel is that it reflected contemporary feelings of impatience to improve human nature.[136] The West Indian interest in Parliament certainly believed that the abolitionists' impatience bordered on recklessness and had the potential to produce widespread devastation as a consequence of immediate emancipation.

The physical differences between the slaves and the white West Indian colonists caused great concern in both Houses of Parliament. Some questioned whether free black and white men could live together in harmony, or if their racial differences, most obviously characterized by skin color but also considered to include cultural practices, intelligence, work ethic, and capacity for learning, would forever result in the races living at odds with one another. Ideas of a natural hierarchy and racial superiority/inferiority infiltrated much of the discussions on human equality, inside and outside Westminster.[137] On June 3, 1833, Sir Robert Peel discussed the problem of having two races living together as equals:

> There was the distinction of colour. He did not allude to that as implying any inferiority between the black and the white—he merely alluded to it as a circumstance which threw a difficulty in amalgamating the slave population with the free, which did not exist in any country of Europe, or in any country of the East where slavery was extinguished.[138]

Peel stated that he did not believe that the African race was inferior but that the difference in skin color would likely prove to be a permanent obstacle in the way of assimilating the two groups. By this time there had been many generations of mixed-race children living and working in the colonies as free men and women and the issue of skin color had become much more complex. West Indians continued to classify their fellow inhabitants by race and color as illicit sexual relations resulted in the mixing of races and the blurring of legal rights. Hierarchies were established in the colonies that took into account the number of degrees children were from one race or the other in order to maintain the established order of rank, but these systems of classifications were mainly based on skin color.[139] The innate and unchangeable differences in the races of man were given a great deal of consideration in the nineteenth century as scientific racism developed. Racial differences and their impact on working ability, civilization, and the functioning of society continued to be debated in the halls of Westminster as well as in universities, colonial assemblies, and meeting halls throughout this period.

Across the slavery debates, members of the West Indian interest, their supporters, and those who had doubts or concerns about the speed and nature of the proposed abolition and emancipation bills could draw upon a wide range of convincing arguments to vocalize and defend their position. Some arguments were timely, whereas others were considered to be universal and unchanging. Many were advanced in reaction to the emotionally charged abolitionist arguments that accompanied a bill for abolition, amelioration, or emancipation. Certain arguments also worked well in combination. Moral, religious, and paternalist arguments asked listeners to consider the benefits of slavery for everyone involved and evoked images of both caring masters overseeing their slaves and a caring God overseeing all His people. Legal and historical arguments stressed conservatism and precedent and, along with economic arguments, appealed to a logical, rational audience. These arguments were used to fight and win numerous debates, delaying and defeating bill after bill for abolition and ultimately shaping the end to slavery in Britain's West Indian colonies.

Chapter 2

Proslavery in Print

In the January 1834 issue of the popular British periodical, *The Quarterly Review*, John Gibson Lockhart anonymously reviewed two travel narratives that centered on life in Britain's West Indian colonies. In his introduction he recalled "ignorant" speakers in Parliament, "stupid" agitators in the public sphere, and relentless arguing in the face of hard facts:

> The reflections to which the whole treatment of our colonists during the past ten years, by successive parliaments and governments, must give rise in every impartial bosom, are of a painful kind; the ignorance, the rashness, the blind audacity of too many influential persons—the mean shuffling and intriguery of others—and the hot, heavy, dogged stupidity of the perhaps not ill-meaning agitators, to whose pertinacity the present ministry has at last succumbed—are features in our recent history, on which future times will pause with mingled wonder, contempt, and pity.[1]

Lockhart was speaking of the abolitionists who had recently won the slavery debate. As the conclusion to his review demonstrates, some of the most passionate, shocking, and provocative language of the slavery debates was put forth outside of Westminster to defend the colonies and the practices of slaveholding and trading. Printed works of all types contributed to the slavery debate as authors, planters, publishers, artists, and playwrights weighed in on the slavery question. Their works express a wide range of arguments and emotions as they provided information on slavery from their own unique perspectives and to suit their own personal goals within the limits of their chosen genres. They also provide evidence of a culture of proslavery that appears to have existed within Britain among members of the West

Indian interest and one that was shared via these works to a limited audience.[2] This chapter investigates these sources.

The anti-abolitionist and anti-emancipation campaigns outside Parliament relied greatly on the printed word. West India committees made concerted efforts to funnel money and time into producing print propaganda to state their case and challenge the abolitionists' arguments. This proslavery literature has been unfairly characterized as defensive because it attempted to present a rational position on the issue of slavery and abolition when threatened by abolitionism.[3] While some of the works were clearly created in response to abolitionist attacks, authors and publishers also produced positive depictions of colonial slavery and credible reports of the economic benefits of slavery and the humanitarian efforts of colonists, some of which resulted in putting the abolitionists on the defensive. They reflect the common goals, beliefs, and opinions of the West Indian interest in Britain that were cemented and defined in the era of British abolition.[4] Anonymous individuals and authors without obvious connections to the West Indies also joined in the fight against abolition or immediate emancipation through opinion pieces, articles, art, and literature.

Abolitionists often employed sentimental rhetoric to engage their readers emotionally in order to elicit a passionate response and gain support for their cause.[5] Proslavery authors and MPs employed sentimental language less frequently, such as when highlighting the suffering of British laborers while downplaying that of the slaves, and chastised abolitionists for their dangerous use of passionate, emotive language. British reformers often appealed to the public using rational and moral arguments contained within printed materials.[6] Conservatives also employed this strategy of spreading information and gaining support. While proslavery writers often expressed their pride in avoiding the use of sentimental language in their works and arguments,[7] both sides employed a wide range of rhetorical strategies to argue their positions throughout the slavery debates.

Several important social and intellectual trends of the eighteenth and early nineteenth centuries impacted upon the potential readers of these proslavery works which could affect the nature of the pieces and the reactions that they provoked. For example, politeness had become the goal of eighteenth-century gentlemen and gentlewomen.[8] Politeness referred to an intricate mixture of behavior and manners that could help elevate one's standing in society, at least for wealthy individuals who were below the ranks of the aristocracy in Britain. Politeness could be learned and developed, unlike other denotations of rank (such as nobility) that one achieved through birthright.[9] Art and literature were central to the belief that politeness could promote both taste and morality in individuals. The educated urban elite disseminated polite values emphasizing virtue, progress, and profit to the wider society (both in urban areas and out into provincial society).[10] At the center of these values was benevolence. A polite individual was supposed to be concerned with the improvement of his or her morals and beliefs rather than just outer manners and appearance and was meant to be improving oneself for the sake of improvement rather than to climb the social ladder.[11] Sentiment and sensibility similarly stressed inner feeling, but also emphasized affections and emotions over reason and judgment.[12]

The philosophical doctrine of utilitarianism was employed by anti-abolitionists in print as well as in their oral arguments. West Indian writers used this philosophical theory, "that the aim of moral, social, and political action should be the largest possible balance of pleasure over pain or the greatest happiness of the greatest number,"[13] in combination with their happy descriptions of plantation life to justify maintaining the institution of slavery in the colonies. By the end of the 1790s they were able to point to the destruction of St. Domingo and the hardships experienced by thousands of planters and slaves as a result of the mass, bloody emancipation on the island as evidence that abolition would not bring happiness to the majority of individuals directly involved in colonial slavery. Jeremy Bentham, an early classical utilitarian thinker, was, for example, anti-slavery in his writing,[14] but he did not advocate immediate abolition and emancipation because of the need for a new social and economic system to replace the current system and because he could not be sure that the slaves would be better off once freed.[15] Numerous anti-abolitionist writers echoed this argument in their calls for greater caution and gradual emancipation. It was not necessary, however, for one to be a utilitarian to believe that the prospective end result of political or social action was more important than the principles upon which it was based.

This chapter focuses on the proslavery position in print in Britain in the later eighteenth and early nineteenth centuries. Printing grew significantly during the eighteenth century. The number of provincial presses and booksellers rose to almost 1,000 firms in 300 locations across England.[16] This was aided by changes in copyright laws, censorship, and a lack of registration. While books remained expensive at the turn of the century, newspapers, pamphlets, and serial publications reached more readers and brought them into the public, political sphere.[17] By 1780, wealthy gentlemen and artisans who made up approximately 25 percent of the population could now afford to buy books and prints.[18] There were also more opportunities to read printed works in urban centers with the proliferation of bookshops, circulating libraries, and coffeehouses. Many readers could have read each single copy of the journals and newspapers contained in these buildings.[19] London newspapers frequently provided political news to their readers and kept them up-to-date on pressing political issues including the slavery debates. Secondhand books were also available for purchase at discounted prices, making them accessible to a wider readership.

Even with the greater number of presses, recent studies of print runs and literacy rates, and known publication details such as price and number of editions, it is still difficult to assess the actual readership of the specific pieces under review later and in the following chapter. As such, this study relies on evidence of new editions, advertisements in metropolitan and country newspapers, reviews in periodicals, citations in later works, and published responses and counterarguments to assess the potential impact of these pieces. Common themes, rhetorical devices, and authorship are also discussed in an effort to connect these works to the larger efforts to defend the colonies, prevent abolition, and delay emancipation.

Literacy rates in England varied by sex, wealth, and location. Figures based on collected signatures are not very reliable, but it is estimated that by the mid-eighteenth century 60 percent of men and 40 percent of women were literate.[20] These were mostly among the nobility and wealthiest residents of urban centers, although shopkeepers and successful merchants were also more likely to be able to read.[21] Literacy rates for women were higher in London than in any other British city and urban dwellers were more likely to be able to read than those who resided in the countryside.[22] All literate Britons tended to read aloud. Public reading was seen to demonstrate one's cultivation and refinement.[23] This meant that anyone within earshot had some access to the printed word, including newspapers, literature, and pamphlets.[24]

Below is found an overview of the publicly available printed sources created or employed by anti-abolitionists and proslavery writers in Britain during the slavery debates. This chapter looks at some of the propaganda against the abolition of the slave trade, reflections on abolition, and pieces that were against immediate or indeed any emancipation. Some of these pieces were widely circulated and advertised, while others only saw one edition printed in London. They have been chosen to provide an overview of the range of proslavery and anti-abolitionist works that were printed in Britain and were accessible to the members of the West Indian interest living in Britain and Britain's urban elite who had been educated about slavery and slave trade through abolitionist works and newspaper accounts of legal and parliamentary decisions.[25] It will provide an overview of the range of published sources anti-abolitionists employed to define the proslavery position and strengthen the case against abolition. Authors would also oppose slavery in principle (particularly in publications created after the abolition of the slave trade in 1807) but still argued for its continuance.[26] Numerous types of sources were used to persuade the reader of the validity of the proslavery position. The variety of sources, the language employed in these works, and the relationships between argument or intention and genre will be highlighted below.

The first section of this chapter will focus on pamphlet propaganda. This includes a survey of firsthand accounts, replies to major abolitionist works, and religious tracts. Two major periodicals of the period are then consulted to examine briefly the popularity of major abolitionist and anti-abolitionist works in the early nineteenth century and the anti-abolitionist sentiment contained within the reviews. The third section will focus on informative works meant to instruct and educate the reader. These include histories of the West Indies and the slave trade, travel writing, plantation handbooks and manuals, and scientific studies on the nature of mankind. Anti-abolitionist and overtly racist thinking informs many of these studies, even though the authors sometimes state that their works were not necessarily created to contribute to the slavery debate. Anti-abolitionists faced countless humanitarian, moral, and religious arguments from the abolitionists in print;[27] they countered these attacks with arguments that they believed were informed by superior logic and reason in support of the trade in slaves, colonial slavery, and the colonies.

Pamphlet Propaganda

The anti-abolitionist lobby and West Indian interest used pamphlets to spread the word about the true state of the West Indian colonies and the biased nature of the slavery debates. They wrote and distributed firsthand accounts of life in the colonies to show the humanity of the planters, highlight the benefits of slavery for the slaves, the planters, and the British Empire, and counter abolitionist accusations and opinions. Detailed replies were produced to counter popular abolitionist pamphlets. West Indian authors were at an advantage when it came to providing detailed accounts of plantation slavery because of their experience and advertised their connections to the colonies as a way to gain readers and improve their credibility.[28] In some cases proslavery authors attacked abolitionist writers for their general lack of firsthand knowledge, foresight, or evidence. Other replies dissected specific pieces of abolitionist propaganda line by line to highlight the offending author's slanderous accusations and incorrect assumptions. Religious tracts and sermons were also published to support the anti-emancipation cause. These publications were an attempt to contribute to the slavery debate, counter the abolition movement, and persuade the general British public to reconsider their views on the slave trade and slavery.

Informative, persuasive works created with the expressed intention to contribute to the slavery debates were likely designed for enfranchised male readers who, through their use of the vote, could affect the outcome of the slavery debates.[29] As electoral reform became a distinct possibility in the late 1820s and early 1830s, they formed a part of the potential electorate who needed to be persuaded to keep West Indians MPs in Parliament. Proslavery pamphlets contained strongly worded arguments about the nature of slavery in Britain's colonies and defended both the institution of slavery and the colonists. They were written to contribute to the slavery debate and distributed to sway people's opinions, helping them understand the thought processes behind enslaving Africans and using slave labor on Britain's West Indian plantations. These pamphlets could be directed to specific audiences, such as politicians, enfranchised Britons, and wealthy individuals of sufficient feeling and knowledge.[30] They were also meant to correct readers' assumptions about the slave trade and slavery and counter anti-slavery propaganda with supposedly more accurate information and explanations using personal stories and firsthand experiences. They vary in writing style more than the informative works discussed in the third section here but continued to rely more on logic and reason than on the sentimental language that anti-slavery associations, speakers, and writers often used to enlist support for their cause. Their brevity and format allowed for cheaper production than most informative works and potentially wider distribution, although eighteenth-century print runs of small books and pamphlets rarely exceeded 500 copies per edition.[31] Urban British readers could have been persuaded and educated about the proslavery cause through pamphlets more than through the other genres discussed in this chapter because of the greater number and format of the works.

Strongly worded pamphlets were published during the slavery and slave trade debates that supported the colonists and called on Parliament to do the same. Thomas Maxwell Adams' concisely written piece, *A Cool Address to the People of England, on the Slave Trade* (1788), was clearly against abolition and emancipation. Adams spent the first part of his pamphlet stressing the numerous benefits of slavery for the slaves who were protected by law. He argued that the slaves were better off than Britain's beggars and former prisoners:

> Suffer your minds to contemplate coolly the number of *vagabonds* you have throughout this kingdom: contemplate also the multitudes of unfortunate men released from time to time out of prisons by acts of grace, which set them at liberty, 'tis true; but at the same time, leaves them at little better more than *the liberty of starving*. The slaves work, and are under subordination; but, on the other hand, are maintained at considerable expence [*sic*], and become *useful* to others; USEFUL TO YOU YOURSELVES. Whose condition is the most happy? By which of these is mankind most benefited?[32]

This was part of a wider trend of proslavery writers creating a hierarchy of suffering so that they might acknowledge the suffering of the slaves, but they would stress the greater suffering of their fellow Britons.[33] It is important to note that here, as he does throughout the pamphlet, Adams asked his readers rationally and dispassionately to consider the question of slavery. He was likely highlighting a difference in the tone of his language from that of abolitionist writers. He also argued that abolition and emancipation would ruin the West Indian colonies and gratify the country's French rivals.[34] Adams reminded his readers that British laws were in place to protect the slave trade and the planters' property in slaves by listing numerous relevant acts of Parliament through the centuries.[35] His words expressed great distress over the British public's and Parliament's confusion over the true nature of the slaves and slavery in the colonies because, according to Adams, despite the abolitionists' optimistic claims, emancipation would cause the slaves to lose the many possessions and security they currently enjoyed.[36] His work was only printed in one edition by John Stockdale, one of the two major publishers of proslavery works in the late eighteenth century, and would have been unlikely to influence many readers outside of London.[37]

Jesse Foot, a physician who spent three years in the West Indies in the mid-eighteenth century, wrote *A Defence of the Planters in the West Indies; Comprised in Four Arguments* to inform and convince "rational men" of his position on the subject of colonial slavery and the slave trade.[38] His work was published in three editions in 1792 by

J. Debrett, the second of the two major publishers of proslavery works in this period. Foot's use of the term "rational men" may have been implying that his work was meant for a logical, rational, male mind, whereas anti-slavery and abolitionist works that appealed to the passions were intended for sensitive female or feminine readers.[39] Male readers for whom sentimental stories were appealing and influential (such as those presented in the slavery debates) made themselves vulnerable to criticism for their emotional response because they could be deemed incapable of making a rational assessment of the situation. Foot strongly disliked William Wilberforce and his followers for, in his view, repeatedly misleading the British public. He charged Wilberforce with rushing Parliament to act because he was afraid the current support for abolition would soon wane:

> as he [Wilberforce] brings this subject forward again, he has judged right in being so speedy, lest the fountain be drained dry from whence he draws his support—lest those who have hitherto pinned their credulity on his sleeve, should have seen the light of reason, and discovered *that truth,* he has aimed to conceal and wilfully pervert. The more this cause be thoroughly searched, the less *support* he will meet in the House of Commons.[40]

Foot argued that Wilberforce had good reason to fear a dwindling level of support because his accusations and unfounded charges would be proved false over time. He also blamed Wilberforce for inciting the recent rebellions in the colonies:

> Long before that time [when Foot was there], down to the present, there has not been the least disposition in the *negroes* to *resistance* and much less to *rebellion.* Whilst I was there, so docile were their tempers, so pastoral were their habits, that the outer doors of their master's house were never fastened during the whole of the night... What the practice might now be, since Mr. Wilberforce is beating the drum of sedition in their ears, I will not take upon me to say; but this I know, that if the effect operates naturally, it will act as it has at St. Domingo.[41]

A heightened fear of violence and rebellion in the wake of the alarming insurrection in St. Domingo permeated many proslavery arguments during this period. Foot asked his readers to remain rational in their assessment of the situation so as to assist the cause of humanity.[42] His use of the phrase "beating the drum of sedition" recalled language often employed to describe a prominent radical, Major John Cartwright, from the 1780s onward. Here Foot was intentionally connecting Wilberforce's activities to popular radicalism. Foot also asked his readers to consider channeling their humanitarian concerns and efforts toward the worthy recipients at home in Britain before looking further afield:

> What are the conditions of other societies to us, if that society we live in be so wretched and depraved, as to call loudly for our direct attention? Are we not compelled by the force of reason to correct the desperate conditions of those in our own *state,* and *before our own noses,* before we are authorised in conscience to examine farther off?[43]

To support his rhetoric, Foot listed numerous areas in society where Britons could help their fellow men. Truly anti-abolitionist in his opinions and sentiments, Foot's *Defence* was a vivid piece that encapsulated numerous proslavery arguments and called upon its readers to challenge Wilberforce and focus their humanitarian efforts closer to home.[44]

In *The West India Legislatures Vindicated from the Charge of Having Resisted the Call of the Mother Country for the Amelioration of Slavery* (1826), Alexander McDonnell defended the colonial legislatures' actions (or lack thereof) in enacting the 1823 resolutions for amelioration. McDonnell suggested that the manumission clause contained within the resolutions was the main reason why the colonial governments appeared to be refusing to enact the resolutions and outlined their problems with them. He argued that the manumission clause would lead to an insufficient number of workers on the plantations, would lower the worth of the slaves, and created the need for a clear discussion and assurance of compensation for any losses the planters would encounter through enacting the clause. He also wrote that the planters were not opposed to manumission or to using free labor if free laborers could be found who would work their lands.[45] He was strongly opposed to Britain dictating to its colonies. McDonnell called on Parliament to stand up to the abolitionists and allow the public to see the real evidence on the state of slavery in the colonies:

> Ministers have never attempted to allay the public clamour, or to remove any of the misunderstanding which prevails throughout the community respecting the present condition of slavery, so greatly improved since the abolition of the Slave Trade. Possessing despatches and authenticated statements in detail, proving the systematic exertions of individual proprietors to have established a milder system of management, and also demonstrating the utter fallaciousness, in practice, of many of the plans of the abolitionists, they have suffered such evidence to repose quietly in the Colonial Office, and have allowed opinions to go forth to the world, not only unjust towards men who reposed confidence

in their impartiality, but injurious to the character and prosperity of the British empire.[46]

McDonnell was overtly anti-abolitionist and pro-colonial throughout the pamphlet. His work appears to have only been published once. Foot, Adams, and McDonnell used their pamphlets to argue for a reassessment of the planters' position and challenge the words, motives, and potential outcomes of the abolitionist movement and its leaders. Their proslavery propaganda vindicated the planters' position overall without the use of extensive firsthand accounts that might face charges of bias or self-interest.

West Indians also published their firsthand recollections, anecdotes, and observations to share their experiences and personal beliefs with the British public. These were used to counter the popular abolitionist strategy of making the slaves' struggles evident to Britons through the use of eyewitness accounts from visitors and blacks in England.[47] In the anonymously written *Sketches and Recollections of the West Indies* (1828), the author stated that he or she was providing a record of his or her own experiences in order to help others better understand the slavery question.[48] For his *Four Years' Residence in the West Indies* (1830), F. W. N. Bayley wrote an almost 700-page letter to his readers which was meant to be light and entertaining except for its commentary on the emancipation question.[49] In these serious sections he hoped to provide new information and in the process enlighten his readers to the need for a gradual rather than immediate emancipation.[50] Mrs. Carmichael drew from her experiences as a slave owner in St. Vincent and Trinidad to inform her readers in her two-volume publication, *Domestic Manners and Social Condition of the White, Coloured, and Negro Population of the West Indies* (1833).[51] She noted that, while much of her work was written prior to the agitation of the question of emancipation in Parliament, she recognized that the timing of the publication would allow it to inform her interested readers, whom she hoped would be the general public and not just "grand people, planters, and M.P.s."[52] This short wish provides a contemporary look at the likely audiences of the pieces under review in this chapter. The three accounts discussed here were all published in the final years of the slavery debates in Britain. Firsthand accounts had also been published in the eighteenth century, but these were often less political and described the author's journey to and around the colonies rather than the political atmosphere and the state of slavery in the islands with the intention of informing the slavery debate in Britain.

The author of *Sketches and Recollections of the West Indies* observed early on that any document that could provide information on colonial slavery was useful and that his or her long and intimate acquaintance with the islands had given him or her enough personal knowledge to be able to provide a "just" perspective on the subject.[53] The author's clearly pro-colonial publication began with a narrative of his or her travels to and around the islands before moving on to discussions of the work planters had done to meliorate conditions, the current state of plantation slavery, and thoughts on the emancipation question. The author included several chapters outlining the colonists' efforts toward enacting the amelioration resolutions of 1823 but also provided information on why they had not implemented every suggestion. The author's reasons included recent insurrections, the need for compensation, the prevalent belief that the abolitionists and Parliament were trying to destroy their property, and the unjustness of forcing men to adopt new methods of cultivation on their own lands. The author noted the dangers of adopting untested farming methods and questioned whether farmers in Britain would ever be forced to do such a thing:

> Should the English farmer be told, that a new mode of husbandry was about to be introduced by the manufacturers, and that they were required to adopt it, without any practical trial, or without time being allowed for experiment—would they, or could they, be expected to enter into the new measure so fully and readily, as after the requisite test?[54]

The author also argued that the colonists themselves did not believe in the perpetual existence of slavery:

> Let it not for a moment be imagined, that the colonists seek to uphold the system of slavery. No; they wish only to have *security* for their property—*compensation* for it—and they will resign it *to-morrow*. They are friendly to melioration; and *they are* the *friends*, as well as the *masters* of the slaves, not alone from interested motives, but from the ties of mutual protection and dependence—from those ties which long and reciprocal relations naturally produce between master and servant.[55]

To conclude, the author stated that he or she believed that the colonists had been unfairly portrayed and that the only way to understand the true nature of colonial slavery (and thus form an unbiased opinion on the subject of emancipation) was to witness it for oneself.[56] The author also advocated reading the works of James MacQueen and Alexander Barclay for further information on the colonies.[57] This reflects an underlying message throughout many of the works discussed here that abolitionist writings by authors with no firsthand experience could not be trusted to provide accurate information on the colonies and on colonial slavery for their readers. *Sketches and Recollections of the West Indies* was likely only published in one edition but it attracted widespread attention. It was reviewed in several newspapers and magazines across Britain, including the *Edinburgh Evening Post,* Exeter's *Western Times,* and the March 1828 issue of *La Belle Assemblée, or Bell's Court and Fashionable Magazine Addressed Particularly to the Ladies,* a monthly magazine from London.

As in *Sketches and Recollections,* F. W. N. Bayley's *Four Years' Residence in the West Indies* began with a discussion of his travels to and throughout the West Indies. Throughout his extensive letter to his readers, Bayley asserted both his impartiality and his desire to see a gradual emancipation occur in the colonies. In the sections that considered colonial slavery, he hoped to provide new information supported with excerpts of dialogue. He provided short histories of the colonies and numerous chapters on the slaves and slave life before concluding with the details of his voyage home to Britain. Bayley argued for a gradual emancipation to take place because in his opinion the slaves were happy in their current position:

> if a slave be really happy in his slavery he is by no means fit for emancipation. If he feels that he enjoys blessings and privileges of no common order—that he is provided with all the necessaries and comforts he can desire, and if contented with that feeling he exclaim "what do I want more?" I maintain that he is not prepared for freedom; but if on the contrary he say, "I am housed, fed, clothed, and nourished, but what is all this without liberty?" then I say that he is entitled to the emancipation he desires.[58]

According to his logic, if the slaves were truly ready for freedom, they would not be happy. He recalled past conversations with misinformed slaves, noting that, upon informing them that after emancipation they would no longer have their homes, land, food, clothing, medical care, and so on provided for them, they immediately withdrew any stated desire for freedom.[59] In his later chapters, Bayley noted the many ways in which colonists had improved plantation life for their slaves and provided stories of idle, destitute freed slaves to warn against premature emancipation. This work overall provided detailed information on the lives and beliefs of slaves and their owners and was constructed in such a way so as to promote a safe, gradual emancipation in the colonies. *Four Years' Residence* was reviewed in several newspapers and periodicals in 1830, including *The Standard*, a conservative London newspaper, and the *Derby Mercury*, and was announced as an upcoming publication in the April 1830 issue of the *Edinburgh Journal of Natural and Geographical Science.*

Mrs. Carmichael provided a slightly different point of view in her *Domestic Manners and Social Condition of the White, Coloured, and Negro Population of the West Indies.* First, she was a slave owner; second, she admitted that before arriving in the islands she had been influenced by anti-slavery propaganda and therefore had held a negative opinion of colonial slavery;[60] and third, most of the piece was written before the issue of emancipation became pressing. The first volume of *Domestic Manners* included her initial impressions of the colonies, with one chapter each on the white and "colored" (by which she meant people of mixed race) populations on the islands, and then the remaining chapters were devoted to descriptions of the colonies' black population. The second volume centered on the environment and various elements of colonial life. She stated that she intended to give her opinions and findings on the slaves, slavery, and emancipation, and identified numerous areas in which she hoped to correct erroneous beliefs about slavery and colonial life. In 1833 *Domestic Manners* was advertised in the *John Bull* periodical, *The Standard*, and the *Examiner*, and a lengthy excerpt was published in the August 17, 1833 issue of the *Leeds Times.*

Domestic Manners contained arguments and evidence to show that the slaves were not overworked, they were all Christians, their housing was adequate to suit the climate, and that the administering of corporal punishment was not cruel, nor did it mean that the slaves' masters did not care for them. Converting one's slaves was an essential part of being Christian slave owners, she argued, and, from a proslavery activist's perspective, demonstrated the existence and success of benevolent masters.[61] Carmichael also noted a dramatic change in her slaves' work ethic and opinions of her after colonial newspapers reported on Parliament's debates on slavery:

> Although few slaves can read, yet there are many free negroes and coloured people who can, and who do read the English newspapers; and the very memorable debates in parliament upon the subject of slavery soon found their way, in a most distorted and mangled form, to the negroes—and the effect was instantly visible . . . [the slaves] shewed in their every action that they looked upon me, being their *proprietor*, as *necessarily* the enemy.[62]

Slaves were able to gain political knowledge through newspaper articles and editorials. Information contained within the articles might have been intended to be innocuous but was likely reinterpreted many times as the information filtered through the slave masses. This flow of information to the slaves was greatly feared by slave-owning colonists.[63] Carmichael employed numerous anecdotes from her time in the colonies to explain her reasoning and views on the propriety of colonial slavery and the dangerous effects of the emancipation debate. All three of these writers drew extensively on their personal experiences to provide information to their readers in the hopes of promoting the policy of gradual emancipation. They recognized that the majority of their readers would never go to the West Indies and yet might possess knowledge of the colonies based on the work of Britain's abolitionists. In response, they stressed their personal interactions with the slaves and shared scenes of "actual" plantation life in an effort to provide an accurate and opposing point of view in support of the colonies.

A number of publications were produced in the 1820s to refute abolitionist works directly. Authors wrote that they felt compelled to contest the damaging claims being published in order to vindicate the West Indian interest, help restore the reputation of the colonists, and encourage support for the colonies. They attacked the abolitionists for supposedly spreading lies about the West Indians and highlighted specific ways in which they had intentionally misled the British public on the subjects of colonial slavery and abolition. It is not surprising that these pamphlets contained much more heated language than that found in other anti-abolitionist publications. The authors' emotional attachment to the subject (and the colonies) is evident throughout many of the responses addressed here.

In 1823 Rev. George Wilson Bridges wrote a succinct response to Wilberforce's *An Appeal to the Religion, Justice, and Humanity of the Inhabitants of the British Empire, in behalf of the Negro Slaves in the West Indies* (1823), entitled *A Voice from Jamaica in Reply to William Wilberforce, Esq. M.P.* His reply was composed in the form of a letter addressed to Wilberforce and was intended to confront him and his followers. Bridges expressed great frustration and anger that Wilberforce had published lies about the colonies for the general public to read: "Our laws, Sir, if you will read them, our habits, our religion, our common sense, will prove that your suspicions are erroneous, and your accusations unfounded, uncharitable, and unjust."[64] He also noted that Wilberforce might be accidently publishing inaccurate information because he had never been to the colonies himself.[65] Bridges was convinced, however, that Wilberforce's language and accusations would have dangerous consequences for the colonies:

> I cannot, Sir, read these passages, and think of the horrible results they lead to, and which you so calmly anticipate, without conceiving that you must be under the influence of mental delusion; and without shuddering at the fate of the thousands you carelessly doom to the scalping knife of men now harmless, contented and quiet; but whose almost obliterated African passions such language is calculated to inflame, and thus to transform our very servants into agents devoted to our destruction.[66]

Throughout this short, confrontational pamphlet Bridges was able to refute numerous specific claims made in Wilberforce's publication, using firsthand knowledge, recorded laws, and contrary evidence. In 1823 *A Voice from Jamaica* was advertised in the *Morning Post,* a daily London newspaper, and included in the monthly list of new publications of *The Scots Magazine*, a monthly magazine from Edinburgh.

Robert Hibbert Junior's pamphlet, *Facts, Verified Upon Oath, in Contradiction of the Report of Rev. Thomas Cooper, concerning the General Condition of the Slaves in Jamaica* (1824), is a concise reply that employed the sworn testimony of three men in Jamaica to disprove Thomas Cooper's report, *Facts Illustrative of the Condition of the Negro Slaves in Jamaica* (1824). Cooper had recently published this negative report of his three years in Jamaica, during which time, as Hibbert emphasized to his readers early on, he never complained or made the owner of the estate he was staying on aware of his concerns about slavery on that plantation. As a self-defined Creole who had lived in Jamaica for 12 years, Hibbert wrote that he was stunned and hurt by Cooper's accusations.[67] His goal was to produce sworn testimony that would refute Cooper's account of his time on the Georgia estate in Jamaica without having to give evidence himself. The body of the pamphlet dissected Cooper's report and provided references to specific arguments and pages that were contradicted using the testimony of the plantation's overseer, the medical practitioner, and George Hibbert Oates. This piece is a fine example of a West Indian contesting abolitionist propaganda and appealing to the putatively objective testimony of sworn witnesses. It appears to have only been published in one edition and was advertised in the *Morning Post.*

James MacQueen published two very different defenses in the mid-1820s. In his lengthy work, *The West India Colonies* (1824), MacQueen accused the *Edinburgh Review* of being a major source of inaccurate, biased information on the West Indies and of spreading misleading, harmful information to its readers.[68] He drew on a variety of sources to back up his own claims and opinions on colonial slavery, including laws, the Bible, production levels, and the known history of slavery. These were also employed to refute various claims that the *Edinburgh Review*'s writers had made. This long, detailed piece also challenged the manifesto of the African Institution and claims made by abolitionists such as Thomas Clarkson. It appears to have been published in at least two editions, as the edition advertised in the March 15, 1825 *Morning Chronicle* (a daily London newspaper) includes different publishing information from that of the edition utilized in this study. The Barbadian legislature was so pleased with his effort that it awarded MacQueen £500 for defending the West Indies in this publication.[69]

In contrast to the style and origin of his *West India Colonies*, MacQueen's *The Colonial Controversy* (1825) was a collection of letters that he originally wrote and published in the *Glasgow Courier* in the autumn of 1824. MacQueen had been the editor of this triweekly journal. His letters were edited for this publication and formed a lengthy reply to the attacks by "Anglus" on the West Indians and on MacQueen himself. Every letter was addressed to the prime minister, the Earl of Liverpool, whom MacQueen maintained should be protecting the colonies by taking a stand against the abolitionists' false accusations.[70] In his first letter, MacQueen argued that the abolitionists were having to resort to lying because they were losing the debate:

> they feel the ground they take sliding from beneath their feet, and hence they endeavour to confuse the question, by *vain* declamation: by substituting clamour, and every kind of misrepresentation and misstatement, in order to withdraw the public mind from the real point at issue, that under deception they may carry their point.[71]

As in his earlier piece, MacQueen repeatedly defended the colonies and highlighted the misleading works of other abolitionists in order to stress the fragility and dubious nature of the anti-slavery movement.

Alexander Barclay also complained about the *Edinburgh Review*'s treatment of the West Indian colonists. His work, *A Practical View of the Present State of Slavery in the West Indies* (1826), ended with a 50-page discussion of the *Review*'s errors and thoughts on two other abolitionist pamphlets but focused most of its attention on James Stephen's *Slavery of the British West India Colonies Delineated* (1824). Like the other authors noted in this section, Barclay argued that the abolitionists had grossly and intentionally misled the British public.[72] He informed his readers that, having lived in Jamaica for 21 years before returning to England, he had long been aware of the inconsistent and incorrect comments spread in abolitionist literature but was only recently inspired to publish his opinions after the slavery debates started up again in Parliament and the *Edinburgh Review* began treating Stephen's work as though it were true.[73] He was able to employ firsthand knowledge, along with an account of recent changes in the colonies, to contradict Stephen's claims and highlight where abolitionists were employing outdated information to sway public opinion. In this reply, Barclay presented his view of the current state of colonial slavery, admitted that it was not without its faults, and accepted that slaves would eventually receive their freedom, while continually reminding his readers that they were being regularly fed false, dangerous information by abolitionist propagandists. *A Practical View of the Present State of Slavery* was published in at least two editions and was sold by booksellers across Scotland and England. It was also reviewed by *La Belle Assemblée, or Bell's Court and Fashionable Magazine Addressed Particularly to the Ladies, The Ladies Monthly Museum* (a monthly magazine from London for wealthy, urban women), and the June 1826 issue of *The Anti-Slavery Reporter.* Being reviewed in *The Anti-Slavery Reporter,* an important and influential bimonthly paper that aimed to provide information on slavery and abolition to the public, implies that *A Practical View of the Present State of Slavery* was being read and considered significant by influential people involved in the abolition movement.

Alexander McDonnell's *Compulsory Manumission; or an Examination of the Actual State of the West India Question* (1827) was written in reply to the anonymous pamphlet, *Remarks on an Address to the "Members of the New Parliament, on the Proceedings of the Colonial Department with respect to the West India Question,"* in which the author attacked Britain's West Indian colonists for being inconsistent in their actions and demands. The author claimed that the West Indians were not vocal enough in their opposition to compulsory manumission, whereas McDonnell argued that Lord Seaforth spoke out in Parliament and every published West Indian pamphlet had indeed voiced its author's opposition to this proposal.[74] McDonnell was strongly opposed to compulsory manumission and employed a number of arguments to justify his position. These included the loss of property, the destruction of the positive master–slave relationship, the loss or complete stoppage of production, and the possibility of former slaves reverting to their "barbarous" ways. He stated that it directly contradicted Parliament's stated goals for ameliorating conditions as part of the preparation for their freedom:

> It has been considered, and repeatedly declared by His Majesty's ministers, that a progressive amelioration in the condition of the slaves, the diffusion of moral instruction, the just appreciation of the blessings of a pure religion, and a gradual reformation in manners and opinions, should continue to exercise their salutary influence, until slavery insensibly glided into freedom. Yet compulsory manumission proceeds in express contradiction to this principle. It teaches the slave, that the sooner he demands his freedom the easier it will be for him to succeed. It discourages the idea of delaying till the morals be improved by instruction, and it urges him to rush forward at once by the most expeditious course, by teaching him, that those only who delay incur the danger of disappointment.[75]

Like the authors of the other responses discussed here, in *Compulsory Manumission* McDonnell dissected specific arguments made by abolitionists and contradicted them by producing argument after argument in defense of the colonists. This strategy was used to question and challenge the legitimacy of the abolitionists' assertions, evidence, and ultimately their motives.

In 1824, two religious tracts discussed the nature of slavery and the current state and consequences of religious education in Britain's West Indian colonies. This is not surprising, as one of the most commonly printed genres in this period were sermons.[76] Richard Watson's sermon, *The Religious Instruction of Slaves in the West India Colonies Advocated and Defended*, promoted the efforts of Methodist missionaries in the colonies. Watson was the secretary of the Wesleyan Methodist Missionary Society and the piece's cover page noted that the profits of the publication would be put toward their West Indian missions. His sermon was published in at least four editions. In contrast, the Rev. B. Bailey's *The House of Bondage* provided readers with a history of slavery from biblical times to the present. Bailey's work was reviewed in *The Gentleman's Magazine, and Historical Chronicle* from London and *The Christian Observer*, an Anglican periodical, and mentioned under the list of new publications in *The Monthly Repository of Theology and General Literature*, a monthly Unitarian periodical from Hackney. These short tracts approached the institution of slavery from a religious perspective and promoted the study and knowledge of Christianity as a vital step in the transition from slavery to freedom.

In his sermon Watson was sympathetic toward Africans and their descendants in the colonies, arguing that they had faced more hardships than any other race, and even titled the first section of his sermon "The objects of your sympathy."[77] Both Watson and Bailey discussed the origins of African slavery in terms of God cursing

Ham's descendants, as recorded in the Bible.[78] Bailey examined this theory in detail. He argued that all of Africa had been populated by Ham's descendants and asserted that their uncivil manners and lack of intellectual progress were examples of God's eternal wrath.[79] Unlike Watson, who stated that his intention was to promote missionary work in the colonies, Bailey informed his readers that, having personally avoided reading any pamphlets on the slavery debate, he wanted to provide information from a religious perspective to educate his readers as they chose sides in the debate. He argued that European men were far more concerned with the slaves' position in society than the slaves were themselves.[80] Both men recognized that emancipation might result in much bloodshed and violence.[81] They therefore stressed the need for the continuation and extension of religious education to every slave in Britain's West Indian colonies and, throughout their tracts, advocated a gradual, cautious transition to emancipation.

REVIEWS

One method with which to assess the popularity or impact of pamphlet propaganda in the early nineteenth century is to look at those that were discussed in contemporary periodicals. Influential periodicals were closely aligned to political parties and contained reviews meant to contribute to political and popular debate, informing the reading public as well as politicians of a similar mind set. They attempted to reach and appeal to a wide audience through providing information and criticism on a wide range of topics and genres.[82] The periodicals' popularity and influence peaked at the same time as the slavery debate reached its height, allowing their reviewers to support or challenge the information contained within popular treatises on the slavery question. They could legitimize and promote one publication and carefully dismantle the information and conclusions of another. Whether sharing abolitionist arguments, crafting defenses of the colonies, or considering the best speed at which to achieve emancipation, they drew their readers into the debate and worked to undermine the credibility of their opposition.

The *Edinburgh Review* was Whiggish from the beginning, although it has been argued that the relationship between the *Edinburgh Review* and the Whigs was much more complex than this, as not all of the reviewers were Foxites or Whigs, or even necessarily unified in their personal political opinions.[83] It does appear, however, that younger Whigs were bound together against Scottish Toryism by the *Edinburgh Review*.[84] The *Edinburgh Review* sold 750 copies of its first edition in 1802; by 1814 they were printing 13,000 copies per edition.[85] *The Quarterly Review* developed out of Tory desires to challenge the *Edinburgh Review*'s "intellectual and ideological monopoly."[86] It had slightly larger print runs of up to 14,000.[87] It is likely that these two periodicals had a much larger readership and that this readership was not clearly defined by political or religious stances.[88] It included educated readers who were specifically interested in politics and those who were more interested in learning about literature.[89] These readers would have read the reviews in circulating libraries, coffeehouses, society meetings, and their homes. The politically influenced editorship and review format of the periodicals of the early nineteenth century allowed anti-abolitionists to challenge abolitionist works and opinions as well as the underlying assumptions on which their publications were based.

Reviewers presented strong opinions on the major topics related to the pieces being discussed and put forward their views in a manner that aimed to correct or confirm the contents of the works. They tended to include more information about the topic of the piece or pieces under review than about the specific titles.[90] In respect to the slavery question, contributors to the anti-abolitionist periodical, *The Quarterly Review,* prided themselves on their use of logic and temperate language and chastised the authors of the abolitionist works they were reviewing for using incendiary language, negative imagery, and unchecked facts to promote their cause. As one author noted in the July 1823 edition of *The Quarterly Review:* "The abolitionists [had] accordingly re-commenced their efforts with all the ardour of men whose imaginations are kindled by the hope of accomplishing a favourite object, and who are strangers to the coolness and deliberation inspired by an accurate knowledge of circumstances."[91] Contributors to the major periodicals wrote their reviews anonymously but have frequently since been identified. By being anonymous, the reviewers could attack authors, misrepresent works that had yet to be published, and discuss items that were strategically chosen as a means of sharing their own views and opinions on topics that were most important to them (including the slavery debates).[92] Anonymity also created interest and intrigue for the readers.[93] The reviewers wanted to impact upon public opinion, whether as a means to strengthen widely held beliefs or to create change.[94] The reviews drew readers to certain books and works and away from others, therefore influencing which works were particularly successful.[95] If a writer was lucky, they might have a personal connection to a reviewer who was then more inclined to write a longer, more flattering review.[96] With their reviews, the reviewers hoped to influence both their readers and contemporary writers.[97]

The two most important periodicals of the period, the *Edinburgh Review* and *The Quarterly Review*, have been examined here from their origins (1802 and 1809 respectively) until the end of 1834 for any article relating to the West Indies, the slave trade, slavery, and abolition. The *Edinburgh Review* contained 30 articles reviewing 42 publications and one note on these topics, whereas *The Quarterly Review* contained 12 articles reviewing a total of 31 publications. The *Edinburgh Review* cofounder and editor, abolitionist, and future lord chancellor, Henry Brougham, contributed 19 of these articles in the *Edinburgh Review*. Other abolitionists, including Wilberforce and James Stephen, a former resident of the West Indies, also wrote reviews for the *Edinburgh Review*. *The Quarterly Review*, by contrast, contained pieces by members of the West Indian interest, including slaveholders and cousins Charles Rose Ellis and George Ellis. This reflects the different positions on the slavery question and the political leanings of the two periodicals. The proslavery, procolonial stance of *The Quarterly Review* is particularly relevant to this chapter.

The two periodicals reviewed a variety of relevant works including abolitionist propaganda, poetry, histories, published travel journals, parliamentary speeches, and reports of institutions. Seven works relating to slavery, the slave trade, or the West Indies were reviewed by both periodicals: William Spence's *The Radical Cause of the Present Distresses of the West India Planters, &c.* (2nd edition, 1808); *A Permanent and Effectual Remedy suggested for the Evils under which the British West Indies now labour, in a Letter from a W.I. Merchant to a W.I. Planter* (1808); Zachary Macaulay's *Negro Slavery; or a View of some of the more prominent Features of the State of Society as it exists in the United States of America and in the Colonies of the West Indies, especially in Jamaica* (1823); Thomas Clarkson's *Thoughts on the Necessity of Improving the Condition of the Slaves in the British Colonies, with a view to their ultimate Emancipation; and on the Practicability, the Safety, and the Advantages of the latter Measure* (2nd edition, 1823); James Stephen's *The Slavery of the British West India Colonies delineated, as it exists both in Law and Practice, and compared with the Slavery of other Countries, Ancient and Modern* (1824); *Statements, Calculations, and Explanations, submitted to the Board of Trade, relative to the State of the British West India Colonies*, printed by order of the House of Commons (1831); and Matthew

G. Lewis' *Journal of a West India Proprietor* (1834). The timing of these articles and dates of publication reflect periods of higher interest in the subjects of abolition and emancipation and surges in abolitionist propaganda and popularity. Three of the works commented on in the *Quarterly Review*, John Poyer's *The History of Barbadoes, from the first Discovery of the Island in the Year 1605, till the Accession of Lord Seaforth, 1801* (1808), James MacQueen's *The West India Colonies; The Calumnies and Misrepresentations Circulated Against Them by The Edinburgh Review, Mr. Clarkson, Mr. Cropper, etc. etc.* (1824), and Mrs. Carmichael's *Domestic Manners in the West Indies* (1833), are discussed elsewhere in this chapter. The inclusion of these pieces in the periodicals indicates that these items were particularly influential and related to issues on which the editors wished to comment.

The 12 articles in *The Quarterly Review* relevant to the slavery question were published during two distinct periods of debate on the subject. The first four articles were written between 1809 (when the journal began) and 1811 as Parliament and abolitionists were focused on persuading other nations to end their participation in the slave trade and planters and other proslavery and pro-slave trade activists pessimistically watched for the negative and unforeseen ramifications of abolition. The remaining eight articles were published between 1822, when abolitionists increased their calls for ameliorating conditions for slaves in the colonies, and the end of colonial slavery in the British West Indies in 1834.

Contributors to *The Quarterly Review* included editorial commentary on the slavery debates and the issues of abolition and emancipation in their reviews. In his review of John Poyer's *The History of Barbadoes* (below), for example, George Ellis first provided an outline of Poyer's work before focusing on the issue of the slave population in the islands and possible reasons for its decrease. This would have been particularly relevant in the period following abolition as there was suddenly no legal means of acquiring new slaves beyond those born in the colonies. Ellis doubted that plantation labor, long hours, whipping, or government interference was causing the low birth rate and impeding the natural increase of slaves in the islands:

> To say that this increase has been hitherto prevented by the severity of their treatment, is to attribute to those of our countrymen whose daily emigration forms so large a part of our West Indian population, a strange and unnatural cruelty; besides which it appears very doubtful, from the experience of the severer monastic orders, whether labour, and abstinence, and stripes, and

interrupted slumbers can materially check the impulse which leads to the union of the sexes.[98]

He defended the planters from charges that they were impeding the slave population through strenuous or violent labor by comparing plantation life to monastic life and questioned how planters could possibly have control over the physical interactions between their slaves. Ellis, with his own personal connections to colonial life, had a strong interest in portraying the colonists as paternalist carers for the colonies' slaves. He was also careful to describe the colonists as "our countrymen," reminding his readers of Britain's close connections to the colonies and alluding to the humanity of their fellow Britons who happened to have ties to the West Indies.

An anonymous contributor[99] to the July 1823 issue of *The Quarterly Review* wrote a substantial review of six works including abolitionist pamphlets and a published version of the May 15, 1823 debate in Parliament on amelioration. The author began by stating his or her intention to focus on the true state of slavery in the colonies rather than the international trade in slaves. The author stated that conditions in the colonies were improving, but that abolitionists in Britain over the past year had become impatient, hence the move for government-outlined amelioration. Throughout the review the author argued that abolitionists had knowingly or unknowingly been spreading false information about life in the colonies and about the colonists through propaganda: "They assailed the public through a variety of channels, in pamphlets, reviews, magazines, constantly pursuing the plan of flinging odium on the treatment of the negroes in our sugar colonies, and of rousing in their behalf the sympathy of the public."[100] The author noted, however, that if the planters had made more of an effort to counter the wave of abolitionist propaganda and explain the situation to the British public, popular opinion might have been swayed their way and erroneous views of slavery in the colonies would have been corrected.[101]

The author then provided a three-part review for his or her readers. The author first reviewed a number of abolitionist works and then countered their information with what he or she described as "a sketch of the actual treatment and condition of the slaves in our colonies."[102] The author followed this with an examination of the ways in which the planters could improve conditions for their slaves without encountering any injury to their property. Within the review the author included a history of servitude throughout the world, made comparisons between slavery in the colonies and the working conditions of the poor in Europe and Ireland, and expressed the prevailing belief in the colonies that Africans and their descendants would not work without coercion.[103] The author argued that they did not need to stop wishing for emancipation, but that they must make Britons aware of actual life in the colonies. The author also noted that the terms "slavery" and "emancipation" had very different connotations in different locales that must be overcome.[104] In conclusion, the author stated that he or she had tried to remain impartial:

> We have done our best to conduct our researches with strict impartiality, and if the larger share of our animadversions is pointed at the abolitionists, it is only because they have been more active in the field, and have, as we conceive, communicated, in several respects, erroneous ideas to the public. Their better plan would have been to distrust all *ex parte* evidence.[105]

The planters, however, as the author lamented, had been almost silent on the subject, leading to a lack of accurate information with which to help the British public understand the true nature of slavery in the colonies.[106]

Plantation owner Charles Rose Ellis and fellow MP Robert John Wilmot Horton wrote a lengthy review for the January 1824 issue of *The Quarterly Review*. Their work began with a discussion of the published version of George Canning's speech in the House of Commons of March 17, 1824, and the related Order in Council sent to Trinidad for amelioration. While the piece initially listed a number of publications to be discussed within the review, the authors focused on Canning's speech, the issue of free versus slave labor, and defending the colonists against abolitionists' charges and MPs' assumptions. As in the previous article, the authors remained focused on explaining and defending the West Indian position and devoted little time to discussing the various titles under review.

This review was clearly pro-colonial in nature. Ellis' own connections to slavery would have encouraged him to defend his fellow planters throughout the piece. He and Wilmot Horton argued that the planters did not love the institution of slavery nor did they necessarily want it to remain:

> It is by no means the love of slavery which characterizes the proceedings or the sentiments of the West India colonies: it is the dread of the loss of property; –it is the instinctive anxiety for the preservation of life; –it is the fear of an experiment involving a radical change, which, however benevolent in its intention, may lead to results which the promoters of it did not contemplate.[107]

They argued for compensation for the planters as a means of quelling the colonists' fears of destruction and the need to move slowly forward with any changes to the labor structure in the colonies. They also disagreed with the use of Sierra Leone as a positive example of Africans providing wage labor because the colony did not produce and export sugar.[108] The authors instead pointed to St. Domingo as the most relevant example of what Britons should expect following a mass emancipation. Throughout the piece Ellis and Wilmot Horton complained that the abolitionists were promoting inaccurate and dangerous ideas and actions:

> we shall never yield to declamation, or to arguments that are not directly founded upon facts of a clear and unimpeachable nature; and—in a question of such extreme delicacy, we must beg leave to observe that those who advance facts, of the correctness of which they are not absolutely certain, allow themselves a latitude very nearly approaching to criminality. We are sometimes afraid, that there are persons engaged in polemical controversy upon this subject, so hurried on by their detestation of a state of slavery—so morbidly anxious for its extinction, that they are disposed to adopt that most dangerous of all human principles of action, that the end may occasionally sanctify the employment of means which in themselves, and abstractedly taken, cannot be justified.[109]

Their concerns again centered on the charge that abolitionists had been misleading the British public while encouraging Parliament to make dangerous decisions on colonial slavery. They stressed the need for patience and for the West Indian colonists to be given the time and the respect they deserved because no one, not even the planters, wanted slavery to continue forever. The *Edinburgh Review* and *The Quarterly Review* presented two carefully crafted sides of the slavery debate and, in the process, helped shape public opinion on the issues of slavery, emancipation, and empire.

Informative Works

Histories and travel narratives in this period gained widespread attention and gave credence to the anti-abolitionists' contentions of the importance of the colonies to Britain and her long-standing support for and encouragement of the slave trade. The works discussed in this section were not solely intended to inform the British public about the slavery debate, but rather about the nature of mankind, the makeup of the British Empire, or the workings of a colonial plantation. While any of these sources might have contributed to the debate, certain histories and studies provided useful information and evidence for later works written by authors without firsthand knowledge of the slave trade, colonial slavery, or the West Indian colonies that allowed them to promote the continuance of the slave trade and slavery. For example, Edward Long and Bryan Edwards' histories, discussed later, have been cited as sources for late eighteenth and early nineteenth-century fiction.[110] Long and Edwards also had the power and knowledge to influence politics. The two authors were cited as having provided information to the agent for Jamaica, Steven Fuller, as Fuller prepared to give evidence to the House of Commons on the West Indies.[111] Edwards also later served as an MP. Plantation manuals for the running of colonial plantations and maintaining the health of the slaves promoted the notion that plantation slavery in the colonies was normal and relatively healthy, although it was work to which Africans were better suited than Europeans. Supposedly scientific studies of the nature of mankind, including theories on the evolution of man and developments in racial theory (some of which reflect a growing interest and trust in craniology), reinforced long-held prejudices of European cultural and intellectual superiority and African inferiority. Contemporary beliefs about white supremacy helped to shape amelioration, rationalize slavery, improve productivity while debasing blacks, and demonstrate opinions about the innate animalistic nature of Africans.[112] These ideas pervaded the histories, journals, manuals, and studies addressed in this section.

These instructive works were intentionally educational and aimed at an educated audience with interests in a wide range of subjects including human history and diversity, geography, travel, the environment, and agriculture. They could also be very popular. The surviving records of the Bristol Library, for example, show that the most popular subjects among borrowers were history, travel, and geography.[113] The authors wrote with authority, clarity, and knowledge gained through personal experience or from supposedly credible outside sources to support their findings. They discussed slavery, enslaving Africans, and the nature of Africans in scientific terms, classifying, categorizing, and ranking them in areas such as physical and mental abilities (as individuals or in tribes) and level of civilization (of the entire continent). These studies were written without excessive feeling or sentiment and instead were supposedly based on logic, rationality, and facts. They reflect a growing belief in the eighteenth century that good writing was supposed to be instructive and useful, in contrast to frivolous works meant for one's enjoyment and entertainment.[114] Authors claimed that their works were contributions to or reflections on modern scientific study and research rather than having been created to inform the slave debates. These claims were not necessarily truthful. Care has been taken to note whether each author commented on the slavery debates and the place of their work within the context of these debates. The arguments contained within the works were about the innate nature of Africans and frequently emphasized their natural suitability for performing hard labor and laboring in hot environments (with the obvious subtext that they were therefore well-suited to labor on Britain's West Indian plantations). These works helped Europeans and Caribbean colonists work with Africans on their plantations and justify enslaving Africans to the wider, educated, urban elite.

Several well-known, popular histories and travel writings about the West Indies were published in the later eighteenth and earlier nineteenth centuries. These histories frequently contained extensive commentary on the slaves' lives in the West Indies and in Africa as well as providing a history of one or more of Britain's West Indian islands. The authors, only some of whom were from the West Indies, included commentary and opinions on the innate nature of African and Creole slaves (with the term "Creole" here meaning born in the colonies), their living and working conditions on the plantations, and their treatment by their masters. The writings of English historians promoted the superiority of the English or Europeans over other nations (and races), defended the existing social order and plantation system in the colonies, and singled out troublemakers in the colonies who challenged the status quo and threatened the stability of the colonies.[115] Later advocates of the slave trade, slavery, and the colonies used the writings of authors such as Edward Long and Bryan Edwards as evidence within their own works to counter abolitionist propaganda and support their own arguments.

Edward Long's 1774 work, *The History of Jamaica*, was written outside the period addressed in this study and was likely only published in one edition, but it influenced later writers and was exploited by the West Indian interest. It has been called "the most exhaustive defence of colonial slavery ever written" and a work that employed "every available proslavery argument."[116] He wrote about economic and paternal arguments, the opportunity for mission work, racial differences, freedom from African masters, and better working conditions for slaves than for Britons. *The History of Jamaica* included sections on the island's government, history, settlement, life on the island, slaves, and the environment. Long stated in his introduction that he intended to give an impartial account of all the island's inhabitants,[117] but he only examined Africans and their colonial descendants in detail. He was dismissive of African culture, civilization, intelligence, and abilities, and frequently compared them to beasts. In his ranking of men and animals, Africans were placed on the lowest rung of mankind, just above the orangutan, with whom, he argued, African women occasionally coupled.[118] By promoting this pre-Darwinite, fixity-of-species theory, Long was able to argue that all ranks of men and beasts had preordained positions in society which they were meant to fill.[119] Over time, Long became one of the most notable supporters of the polygenesis theory.

Bryan Edwards was a member in Jamaica's assembly and published numerous items related to the West Indies and the transatlantic slave trade. His 1793 study, *The History, Civil and Commercial, of the British Colonies in the West Indies,* was first published by John Stockdale in London in two types of bindings and was later published in four editions between 1793 and 1807. There were abridged single-volume versions and expanded three-volume editions that included a topical history of St. Domingo, as well as a separate published list of maps and plates that could be used to supplement the first edition. It was advertised in numerous London newspapers and noted as forthcoming in periodicals across Britain.

This highly influential and extensive work covered the histories of Britain's West Indian colonies, their people, produce, and government. Edwards stated early on that he had relied on his own experiences in the West Indies and those of his friends and acquaintances to inform his work rather than making use of other histories and published sources.[120] The cover noted that he was from Jamaica to further strengthen his credibility. Edwards thanked Long in particular for his assistance in editing and providing additional information to support and expand his study.[121] Throughout the history, he attempted to achieve two goals. The first was to emphasize the great importance of the colonies to Britain's prosperity and power. This goal is evident from the dedication dated June 3, 1793: "To the King's Most Excellent Majesty; this Political and Commercial Survey of His Majesty's Dominions in the West Indies; which, under his mild and auspicious government, are become the principle source of the national opulence and maritime power." The second was to prove the abolitionists wrong. He hoped to persuade them to stop spreading false information and apologize to the planters and the British public for their actions.[122] This goal brought his study directly into the slave trade debates. Edwards overall provided a positive view of plantation life that could be ameliorated further if left in the hands of the planters.

In his 1797 study, *An Historical Survey of the French Colony in the Island of St. Domingo*, Edwards claimed that he was now trying to stay out of the slave trade debates.[123] The evidence he gathered from personal experience and testimony, however, led him to believe that abolitionists were inciting slaves to rebel and he recorded this in his study.[124] This opinion, given within the context of a study of St. Domingo's history, was strengthened when Edwards argued that it was London's abolitionists who inspired France's *Les Amis des Noirs*, a contentious abolitionist society largely blamed for the rebellion and bloodshed in St. Domingo.[125] Like his history of the West Indies, this study began with a history of the islands. It then provided readers with a dramatic account of the rebellion from the white colonists' perspective complete with vivid depictions of violence and brutality, statistics on the French and Spanish settlements, and reports on Britain's military successes in the area. Edward's history of St. Domingo was designed to be far more entertaining than his earlier work, but it occasionally ventured into political commentary by providing opinions on slavery and abolition. He noted in the first chapter, however, during a discussion of the terms "slavery" and "freedom", that he was not defending the institution of slavery, just reporting on it.[126] The language and timing of the piece suggests otherwise. *An Historical Survey of the French Colony in the Island of St. Domingo* was advertised in a number of London newspapers including the *London Chronicle*, the *London Evening Post*, and the *Whitehall Evening Post* (all triweekly newspapers), the *True Briton* (a government newspaper), and *The Times*. It also sparked a published refutation, Colonel Venault de Charmilly's *Answer, by way of letter, to Bryan Edwards, Esq., M.P., F.R.S., planter of Jamaica, &c. Containing a refutation of his historical survey on the French colony of St. Domingo, etc. etc.*, that was published in London by J. Debrett in 1797. Edward's study was soon attached to his widely popular *The History, Civil and Commercial, of the British Colonies in the West Indies* and the two were sold together in later editions.

John Poyer's 1808 study, *The History of Barbados*, traced the entire known history of Barbados in 18 chapters. It was originally published in Barbados for a local audience and then published once in London in 1808.[127] What set his study apart from the others was his decision not to discuss colonial slavery or the slaves beyond the preface. Poyer remarked that he made this choice because Edwards had already given a thorough account of the institution and, although he believed the topic to be relevant to the study, his readers might deem his account too repetitive.[128] This decision implies Poyer's belief that the majority of his readers would have already read Edwards' account. He explained, however, that this decision would not prevent him from defending the colonists:

> It has, doubtless, been expected that I should take notice of the torrent of illiberal invective with which our mistaken, misinformed, transatlantic fellow-subjects continue to overwhelm a peaceful, unoffending community, with whose internal situation they are imperfectly acquainted; and that I should vindicate the character of my injured country, from the gross calumnies which are daily propagated, concerning the treatment of slaves.[129]

He stated that the planters were too far away to be heard and so he chose to fill much of his preface with excerpts of firsthand knowledge and testimonies as to the true nature of colonial slavery that were designed to counter the accusations being regularly made against the colonists. Between these pro-colonial excerpts, Poyer asked his readers to consider why Africans should be the only race of men exempt from work.[130] He concluded that, if Britons would not believe the testimony of the learned men presented there (including two ministers, a doctor, and the duke of Clarence), he had little chance of persuading anyone of his own views. Poyer's work was published once in London as well as in Barbados for local circulation.[131]

Unlike Poyer's study, J. Stewart's *A View of the Past and Present State of the Island of Jamaica* (1823) devoted more space to discussing the inhabitants of Jamaica than to the island's history, climate, trade, government, and defense, because he believed these topics would be more interesting to readers and were more worthy of discussion.[132] Stewart noted that he had lived in Jamaica for many years, giving him a unique, impartial outlook and the ability to provide new information for his readers.[133] He devoted several chapters to the white, colored (by which he meant mixed race), and black populations of the island; five out of the 20 chapters focused on the island's slaves. Stewart stated that he was in favor of amelioration, but against immediate emancipation, because the slaves were not yet ready for freedom and, if they were emancipated, would soon find themselves suffering under the tyrannical rule of black masters.[134] He also argued that Britain would need to provide almost £100 million in compensation to her colonists, her trade and navy would suffer, and the maritime industry would experience severe job losses.[135] All of these reasons, however, did not make Stewart an advocate of perpetual slavery; he maintained that time and gradual improvements would bring about all the changes in the colonies desired by abolitionists.[136] As in the other histories discussed here, Stewart's thoughts on slavery and the slave trade informed his views on the island's history and inhabitants, shaped the structure of the study, and was written for the benefit of skeptical, politically minded readers. His work was advertised in the *Liverpool Mercury*, several London newspapers, and reviewed in the August 1823 issue of the *Scottish Missionary Register*, a periodical published by the Scottish Missionary Society.

Plantation manuals were officially written and published in Great Britain for the benefit of West Indian plantation owners living in Britain. They also, however, emphasized and promoted the current satisfactory level of care that planters were supposedly providing for their slaves.[137] The manuals discussed here were not overtly proslavery, but rather their authors accepted and promoted the enslavement of Africans in the West Indies as necessary to the welfare and survival of the colonies. This reflected the widespread colonist mentality that, while slavery was unfortunate, it was also necessary. [138] The authors were not opposed to slavery, but to bad slave owners and managers. Both argued for the adequate care and treatment of the slaves and provided a manual for the everyday management of the slaves that was meant to benefit both the slaves (through better health, working conditions, and provisions) and their owners (through increased production, greater revenues, and less loss of life). Due to their instructional approach, plantation manuals helped West Indians argue that adequate attention could be paid to the slaves' welfare without the additional interference of Parliament or the abolitionists.[139]

James Grainger, M.D., first published his manual anonymously in 1764, but *An Essay on the More Common West-India Diseases* was reprinted under the author's name in a second edition in 1802 in the midst of the abolition debate. The author of the second edition's preface, William Wright, noted that British and West Indian readers had called for a new edition.[140] The manual was originally meant for planters and managers in Britain's West Indian islands, but the second edition notes that medical practitioners had also used it.[141] Grainger stated that he wrote the manual because hundreds of slaves were dying needlessly each year in the colonies and there was no adequate manual on how to care for them.[142] He also warned his readers that, while he had attempted to provide all necessary instructions for the adequate care of slaves, this was not a manual to be used by the inexperienced, newly arrived, British-born colonist.[143] Grainger's manual was organized into four sections: how to choose from a selection of newly arrived slaves; how to treat diseases that slaves were exposed to in the islands; which "distempers" affected the slaves; and what provisions (particularly food, clothing, and medical attention) were necessary for their survival. In the first section he provided specific information on the different tribes from which African slaves were taken and the impact that these different cultures and habits supposedly had on a slave's temper and productivity. Grainger argued that slaves should be purchased as young as possible for the benefit of the entire plantation.[144] He warned planters against overworking newly arrived slaves as in Grainger's experience it took a full 12 months for them to adjust or "season."[145] He insisted that slaves required discipline if deserving of punishment:

> As Negroes are ignorant, they must be vicious; they ought always to be attended to in their punishments. Thirty-nine is the lash of the law; half that number is, in my opinion, a sufficient punishment for any offence they can commit. Negroes must be punished for their own as well as their master's sake; but lenity should always temper justice. A Negroe should never be struck with a stick, nor ever punished in a passion.[146]

Throughout his study, Grainger placed a great deal of responsibility upon the planter to care for his slaves and see that they worked, thrived, and reproduced. In the concluding pages of the manual Grainger acknowledged the existence of inhumane planters in the colonies and carefully reminded his interested readers that, if they abused or ignored a sick slave in their care, they would have to answer to God.[147]

Practical Rules for the Management and Medical Treatment of Negro Slaves, in the Sugar Colonies (1803) was written during the slave trade debates. As such, much of this anonymously authored manual's introduction was devoted to a discussion of the slavery debate and the effects of shipping regulations that came into effect in the 1790s. The manual was specifically advertised as being applicable to the slave trade debate in the *Morning Post* in August 1804.[148] The June 1831 edition of *The Anti-Slavery Reporter* suggested that the author was a Dr. Collins, a medical practitioner and slave owner who had lived in St. Vincent.[149] They also suggested that James Stephen had taken evidence from the manual to include in his popular and influential abolitionist work, *The Slavery of the British West India Colonies Delineated*.

Practical Rules was divided into two sections. The first was a guide to managing healthy slaves from their first arrival in the colonies. The second was a guide to treating sick slaves. The author began by justifying the legitimacy and validity of his manual by pointing to his 20 years of experience directing "a pretty large gang of negroes" in whose lives he had invested and who rarely died.[150] He stated that he began writing the manual as a guide for his own manager while he was away, but then decided to expand it to make it suitable for wider distribution. Like Grainger, this author treated the institution of slavery as a necessity and stated that with humane treatment both the slaves and the planters would reap rewards. The author argued that, in fact, being a planter was an excellent way to exercise philanthropy.[151] Good planters, he argued, were able to remove every negative element of slavery from their plantations except for the name "slavery."[152] He disagreed with the abolitionists' assertions that plantations could be worked using free labor by arguing that the climate of the colonies significantly diminished the ability of men from temperate climates to work:

> I will venture to say, there is not a regiment in the service, that could have resisted the fatigue a twelvemonth [*sic*], and have had a twentieth part of their number on their legs at the end of that time. Let us hear no more then of white men working, where they have so much difficulty to exist, even without work.[153]

Like Grainger, the author of this manual examined various elements of plantation life and gave specific advice on the choosing, caring for, and managing of slaves. He discussed the defining characteristics of the different tribes from which slaves originated and also promoted the buying of young boys and girls, seeing them as an investment for a planter considering his long-term profits and labor needs.[154] He covered numerous topics, including seasoning, diet, clothing, lodging, reproduction, labor, discipline, and religion, and provided specific advice on each. He stated that, overall, if they followed his advice, the planters would find that they only lost as many newly arrived slaves as they did seasoned ones.[155] Specific numbers or statistics on fatalities were not provided. His statement implied that death was an acceptable part of plantation life and slave management.

West Indians were able to use the existence and content of these manuals to prove that their fellow planters were informed about caring for slaves, their needs, their habits, and their illnesses. The manuals' purpose and contents implied that slavery was a vital element in maintaining stability and production in the islands. Through their advice and guidance the authors highlighted the humanity of the planters and the true nature of colonial slavery. They provided numerous examples of diseases to which the slaves were exposed and which anti-abolitionists could hold up as legitimate reasons for population decline. The authors also discussed the dangers of importing older African slaves that anti-abolitionists could use to defend themselves against accusations of poor treatment being the cause of rebellion or death. Both authors commended the colonists and, to some extent, the abolitionists on meliorating conditions on the plantations and aboard the slave ships, but neither was providing a manual meant to allow for the eventual transition to freedom.

Eighteenth- and early nineteenth-century scientific studies of mankind, its origins, and its varieties from this period provide fascinating insights into contemporary beliefs about European superiority which have long since been undermined by modern study and scientific evidence. As the Bible's authority on the history of man weakened, investigators developed new theories with which to understand the differences in mankind. This resulted in new forms of scientific racism.[156] European culture, language, and appearance were placed in direct opposition to that of African nations to highlight the apparent backwardness and lack of civilization of the African people and to help justify their enslavement.[157] Planters did not have to justify slavery by overtly using biological theories and findings because it was enough to show that men were all of one species, but with Africans on a lower level than Europeans.[158] Craniologists emphasized the smaller brain capacity of African men and women, reflecting nineteenth-century racial theories that mental ability and physiognomy were linked and directly contributed to racial characteristics.[159] Some racial theorists supported the contested theory of polygenism, a belief in the separate origins of African, European, and other peoples around the world. Polygenist theory was neither influential nor was it able to satisfactorily justify the slave trade and slavery to contemporary readers. Planters appear to have resisted supporting the theory even though it had the potential to be a convincing defense.[160] Interestingly, both mono- and polygenist theories ranked Africans lower down the list of the races of mankind.[161] Proslavery authors highlighted the superior physical strength of the Africans and their ability to handle extreme tropical climates in which Europeans suffered. Others stressed the environment's darkening and thickening of their skin that allowed them to tolerate hard labor and whipping.[162] These theories directly challenged abolitionist efforts to depict Africans and black slaves as men and brothers who deserved better treatment as fellow human beings.[163] Proslavery authors, in contrast, wanted to show how people of African descent were fundamentally different from both Europeans and colonists to make it harder for the public to have empathy for them. Anti-abolitionists were able to employ these pseudoscientific findings to promote their cause and support their positions.

Three such studies that attempted to trace the history of mankind and its different races and characteristics were Charles White's *An Account of the Regular Gradation in Man, and in Different Animals and Vegetables*, originally a series of readings given to Manchester's Literary and Philosophical Society in 1795; James Cowles Prichard's *Researches into the Physical History of Mankind* (1813); and John Bigland's *An Historical Display of the Effects of Physical and Moral Causes on the Character and Circumstances of Nations* (1816). White provided his readers with a polygenesis worldview that he supported using supposedly scientific evidence. He focused on Europeans and Africans, placing Europeans at the top of his rankings of the races of mankind and Africans at the bottom, just above apes. Throughout his work, White made a number of comparisons between Africans and apes to highlight their similarities. Craniology had noticeably influenced White's study; he admitted to having been inspired by John Hunter's talk, "Remarks on the Gradation of Skulls," delivered in Manchester in 1794.[164] Early craniologists emphasized the differences and inferiority of African skulls and therefore their intellect and abilities. Hunter's ranking of skulls descended from European to Asiatic, American, African, monkey, and so on. White focused on certain elements of Hunter's findings when comparing skulls, noting that Africans had less internal capacity for a brain, a more prominent jaw, a receding chin (particularly important to White because this supposedly made it more ape-like), a less prominent nose, and bigger front teeth, which led him to conclude: "In all these points it differed from the European, and approached to the ape."[165] By relating Africans to animals, such authors and scientists were contributing to the dehumanization of the African and the slave.[166]

In his conclusion, White included a page examining how Europeans were the best of all the races and argued for at least four different species of man. He voiced his belief that Africans might be of more than one species. He justified this assessment of the African race(s), as well as their low position on his scale of mankind, through a brief, derogatory summary of their varied appearance:

> perhaps the lowest degree of the human race resides there. I am inclined to think that hair, rather than colour, ought to guide us in that quarter; and that it is not the blackest inhabitants, but those with extremely short hair, and a

most ungracious appearance, as the Hottentots,[167] who may be reckoned the lowest on the scale of humanity.[168]

Finally, White emphasized that this study was not intended to contribute to the abolition debate, but that his work might unintentionally help the anti-abolitionist cause by providing a negative portrayal of Africans; if asked, he would support abolition.[169] White's work was advertised as being available at booksellers across England in the *Bury and Norwich Post,* a weekly newspaper from Bury St. Edmond's, and was cited as a source of evidence for Robert Eveleigh Taylor's Latin text, *Inauguralis, de Hominum Varietatibus*, published in Edinburgh in 1800, and Thomas Read Rootes Cobb's *An Inquiry into the Law of Negro Slavery in the United States of America: to which is prefixed an historical sketch of slavery*, published in Philadelphia in 1858. His work, therefore, reached and influenced international readers and writers.

James Cowles Prichard was a medical practitioner who promoted a monogenist worldview and wrote his study with the intention of proving that all men came from a single point and moment of origin.[170] His extensive survey of mankind covered numerous groups from around the world but began with an in-depth analysis of African peoples. He brought together published reports and eyewitness accounts of the various African tribes to describe the men, women, and children of Africa with a particular focus on their appearance. Prichard noted in the first chapter of the first volume that his goals were to explore the different physical characteristics of the races and attempt to account for these differences.[171] He did not believe that climate explained the varied appearance of the different races of man because generations of Africans had lived in the Americas and remained black in color.[172] Climate had been the Enlightenment's answer to the different physical appearances of mankind even though all men were believed to have descended from Noah.[173] Prichard was very influential in Britain in supporting a theory of heredity to explain diversity.[174] His work was published in at least four multivolume editions and was later supplemented by additional work on the origins of Celtic groups. The various editions were advertised in London newspapers and the work was cited as a source of evidence for Theodric Beck and John Beck's *Elements of Medical Jurisprudence* that was published in Philadelphia in 1860.

As with White's reports of Hunter's findings, Prichard reported that he had also found some similarities between African and ape skulls.[175] Both White's and Prichard's decisions to emphasize innate, unchangeable physical differences in both natural ability (physical strength, brain capacity) and appearance (dark skin, ape-like features) allowed the West Indian interest to use their studies to argue that these differences were important, natural, permanent, and scientifically recognized. The permanence of the differences meant (to them) that not only would it take a great deal of time to change the natural behavior of the African slaves, but that even as former slaves they would never be able to assimilate fully into (white) colonial society.

In contrast to White's and Prichard's studies, John Bigland concluded in his 1816 study, *An Historical Display of the Effects of Physical and Moral Causes on the Character and Circumstances of Nations,* that geography and climate had been the two greatest influences on the different races of mankind. According to his findings, Africans were to be pitied because from the beginning they were exposed to an inferior landscape and climate; this affected all other aspects of their lives, bodies, and culture, as well as cementing their current position as the world's slaves. In particular, Bigland argued that Africans and Asians were disadvantaged from the earliest period because they did not have an inland sea around which to settle and become civilized.[176] In his discussion of a tropical climate's effects on the different races, he noted that Africans (as well as some Asians): "under the influence of an ardent sun, are fiery, sensual, and vindictive."[177] Bigland suggested that hot, tropical climates bred stronger, "livelier" animals as well as men.[178] He noted the great physical strength of certain African tribes, remarking: "Black men of Guinea are also robust and can handle a lot of hard work and fatigue."[179] It was with some regret that Bigland commented on the long-standing reliance of other nations on black slave labor: "Unfeeling avarice long endeavoured to propagate and establish an opinion, that the unfortunate negroes were beings of an inferior class, formed by nature, and designed by providence, for a state of perpetual slavery."[180] His findings on the natural strength and long tradition by many nations to enslave Africans supported the anti-abolitionists' arguments that African labor was necessary and that others had enslaved Africans long before they arrived in the West Indies. Bigland's work was advertised in several London and Edinburgh periodicals, including *The Gentleman's Magazine: And Historical Chronicle, The Literary Panorama and National Register, The Edinburgh Monthly Magazine* (later known as *Blackwood's Edinburgh Magazine*), and *The Scots Magazine and Edinburgh Literary Miscellany.* Word of the study traveled beyond Britain's borders. It was included in the A. M. H. Boulard's 1828 *Catalogue des Livres Anglais* from Paris.

As shown earlier, a vast number of various types of sources defended the proslavery position of the West Indian interest in Britain in the era of abolition. The existence, number, variety, and advertisement of these pieces demonstrate that the proslavery (and anti-abolitionist) argument had the potential to reach the wider British public. Their authorship varied greatly: politicians, medical practitioners, and writers; colonists, absentees, and native Britons; those with direct interests, those who wished to help the interested, and those with no discernible interest in the trade or colonies; firsthand witnesses and those who had never been to the island or witnessed slavery; and active anti-abolitionists writing to oppose abolition versus those who professed wishing to only inform the discussion or to be coincidentally writing on the topic. Even those with firsthand experience with the trade or plantation slavery in the colonies varied, from plantation or slave owners, to merchants, traders, and bankers, to members of the military, to family members of colonists who had spent much of their lives in Britain. Within these works, proslavery, anti-abolitionist, proslave trade, pro-colonial, and anti-African arguments can be discerned. By defining and rationalizing their beliefs, goals, and practices for a wider British readership, the West Indian interest, their supporters, and British publishers produced print evidence of a proslavery culture within Britain in the era of abolition.

Chapter 3

Proslavery Arts and Culture

In 1797, Sir Phillip Gibbes published the third edition of his plantation manual, *Instructions for the Treatment of Negroes.* Within the pages of his work he explained to his readers how an Englishwoman had sent him a number of poems on the subject of slavery and that he had decided to include them in his manual. Several of the poems were supposedly intended for the enslaved laborers to sing while working the plantations to remind them of the benefits of their labor:

> How useful is labour, how healthful and so good!
> It keeps us from mischief, procures wholesome food;
> It saves from much sickness and loathsome disease
> That fall on the idle and pamper'd with ease[1]

Proslavery arguments could be found in all manner of forms in the era of abolition. The arts were no exception.

The West Indian interest and their supporters employed a full range of sources to share information about the proslavery position with a wider audience both in Britain and in the colonies. The genres of art, literature, drama, song, and poetry contributed to the slavery debate and had the potential to reach many more Britons than the propaganda and studies discussed in the previous chapter. Art historians have shown that visual images and art were specifically created to sway public opinion; they could be powerful tools in the larger political debate on slavery.[2] Many of the works discussed here were intended for a politically informed urban elite aware of Caribbean slavery, the slavery debate in Parliament, and the wider anti-slavery movement (including its major players such as William Wilberforce).

Due to the nature of these genres illiterate individuals could potentially have perceived each of these genres other than literature (in a gallery, concert hall, or theater, although the common practice of reading aloud might have allowed wider access to literature), but in order to "read" the pieces a wider knowledge of the political circumstances of their creation and therefore their intention would have been necessary. These works could therefore have contributed to the slavery debate if the audience or viewer was aware of the political landscape and debate going on in and out of Parliament, but they could also claim to be simply pieces of art (or music or drama) meant to provide entertainment and enjoyment to their urban audiences. They presented proslavery images to the public (both literally, as in a piece of artwork or a scene on stage, and figuratively, within the mind of the reader or listener) by focusing on the benefits of slavery for everyone involved or disproving the abolitionists' arguments and motives. Perhaps most importantly, they are evidence of a culture of proslavery that absentee West Indians in Britain shared and promoted for a narrow audience. This chapter will focus on art and creative writing that reflected anti-abolitionist and proslavery beliefs. Proslavery art, music, prose, and drama defended the proslavery position and depicted a positive image of colonial slavery for a limited urban audience.

The proliferation of the printing press in the eighteenth century and the lack of censorship laws allowed for the reproduction and spread of artwork, scripts, music, broadsheets, and illustrated literature across Britain.[3] By 1800, London had become the center of Europe's print trade.[4] This is reflected in the publishing details of many of the works discussed in this chapter. These works were aimed at an urban public, as performance spaces and public displays centered on Britain's cities, particularly London. Approximately one quarter of England's population was comprised of the middling ranks, such as minor gentlemen and well-off artisans, making between £50 and £200 per year.[5] These men and women made up most of the new audience for the arts. They could afford to buy books, prints, and theater tickets and would do so in an attempt to gain the sought-after qualities of refinement and taste.

The creators of these proslavery pieces availed themselves of the full range of writing styles, rhetorical strategies, and creative license. They used sentiment and feeling as well as reason and logic to persuade their audiences of the benefits of the slave trade and Caribbean slavery and to warn of the dangers of the anti-slavery movement. They also used their imaginations, personal experiences, and popular beliefs about Africans and Caribbean slavery to inform their works and add drama and interest. These shared beliefs, goals, and ideologies suggest the existence of a distinct proslavery culture existing among the West Indian interest in Britain in the era of abolition. The methods and rhetorical strategies utilized in these sources caused them to be significantly different in their style, form, and intentions from the genres discussed in Chapter 2.

Art

Art became more public in eighteenth-century Britain. It was not until the latter half of the eighteenth century that artwork was displayed in public spaces in England and made accessible to the urban elites.[6] The Royal Academy opened its doors to the viewing public and numerous other galleries opened. Going out to see pictures became a fashionable pastime for people of leisure. Important pieces of art were supposed to instruct observers.[7] There were even printed guides created to help new and experienced gallery attendees understand and appreciate art.[8] Prior to this, most artwork had been created on commission for private collections and remained in family homes.[9]

People of African descent can be found in various genres of eighteenth- and early-nineteenth-century British art. As Albert Boime has explained, once the concept and color of "black" was used to describe a group of people, this group could be placed in opposition to "white" European subjects in art as well as in other genres.[10] In the era of abolition some black subjects played the role of servant or slave to the aristocratic subject of individual or family portraits, demonstrating and enforcing a clear hierarchy between the subjects,[11] while others were themselves subjects of portraits. It is noteworthy that this is the first period in which blacks were depicted as familiar rather than foreign subjects in British prints.[12] They were pictured in familiar settings, for example, or interacting with subjects of European descent.

Both pro- and anti-slavery supporters created and viewed visual propaganda during the era of abolition. Anti-slavery paintings and prints concentrated on showing the British public the hardships and abuse slaves were subjected to on the plantations and during the Middle Passage. Proslavery art was not as prevalent at the time, nor has its images made a lasting impact on popular culture, yet proslavery art did challenge the abolitionists' public image and credibility. Portraits and political prints have been examined here to assess the meaning as well as the content of the selected works. As in the analysis of any art, it must be kept in mind that any created image is already an interpretation of its subject, and thus the analysis provided is the author's interpretation of an interpretation.[13]

Portraiture was the most common genre of art in eighteenth-century England.[14] At the Royal Academy exhibition in 1787, Sir Joshua Reynolds' portrait of the Prince of Wales with a black servant was the highlight of the annual show that was regularly dominated by portraits.[15] In this painting, the servant who is already physically smaller than the prince leans forward to adjust the prince's clothing, thus making him even shorter by comparison and placing him in a servile stance. In the background are two large stone columns that might place the picture in ancient Greece or Rome. The servant is completely dominated by the prince in his formal robes, attire, sashes, and decorations. The prince looks off to his left rather than down toward his servant, thus ignoring his presence and assistance. The prince's robes and outstretched arm add to his width and heeled shoes to his height, further establishing his dominance of the scene and the portrait. Their relative positioning and size allows the artist and viewer to easily contrast the two men. While a number of aristocratic Britons had their portraits painted with black servants at their sides, this particular painting was displayed at the annual exhibition of the Royal Academy, the center of London's artistic world.[16] The image of the black servant as an accompanying figure had disappeared from portraits across Europe by about 1800.[17]

This portrait could be interpreted as demonstrating Britain's domination over its colonies (represented by the servant, a non-white British subject, being physically dominated by British royalty). Through his servant's lower position the prince is empowered imperially as well as physically.[18] Black attendants were frequently featured in courtly portraits as a means of signifying the court's grandeur.[19] As the servant in the portrait is actively helping the prince to look his best, the portrait might also be an illustration of Britain's reliance on her colonial residents to maintain her greatness and strength. It demonstrates a firm belief in white European (in this case British) domination and superiority over the rest of the world. This sense of superiority was commonly displayed in artwork with subjects of different races.[20] It also displays the servant's slavish devotion to the painting's white subject, a common image and idea in contemporary portraiture.[21] Columns that might allude to the great Roman Empire and Rome's domination over inferior tribal groups reinforce this interpretation. Britain's (and Europe's) long-established domination over "inferior" groups benefited all white Britons and legitimized slavery for many

British and colonial subjects. Images such as this helped reinforce the importance of the colonies for its viewers.

While artistic genres such as portraiture and history painting depicted idealized British or European bodies, caricatures and satirical prints showed deformities, vices, and in particular individuals who had lost control of their bodies due to their passions.[22] A print's success depended on the ability of the viewers to recognize the faces of the artist's subjects.[23] Portraiture in the eighteenth century was a key element in making an individual recognizable to the public.[24] Because initial runs of prints were usually in the hundreds, art historians have suggested that they must have been in high demand.[25] It has been difficult, however, for historians to calculate the impact of caricatures on the British public.[26] Their production centered on London, but they were widely disseminated and read.[27]

British viewers enjoyed the mocking, bawdy humor of satirical prints, but not everyone could afford to buy them.[28] There is little evidence of exposure through public displays or private circulation outside of London to British workers.[29] Political prints also often included writing that could limit their appeal and resonance for illiterate viewers. Some political prints were likely put on display in shop windows in London, but viewers required some knowledge of current political events in Westminster to understand them.[30] During this period there were fewer than ten shops with large window displays for the viewing public to enjoy and all of these were in London.[31] While caricature became an important element of the political print after 1780, the viewer still needed to have knowledge of the characteristics and actions of the individuals being portrayed in the prints to understand their meaning or meanings.[32]

Most prints probably circulated among a small circle of political elites and propertied men in London.[33] They were generally made by men for a male audience.[34] Buyers' preferences were likely taken into account in the production and content of prints; the images and opinions contained within the prints therefore do not necessarily reflect the artist's beliefs.[35] This is particularly relevant here as the proslavery sentiments found in the caricatures addressed below do not necessarily mean that a certain artist or publisher was a supporter of the slave trade or slavery. The awareness of buyer preference allowed prints to reflect public opinion and provided feedback to politicians on opinions out-of-doors.[36] Political movements used prints to promote their cause and the political elite and their supporters subsidized and encouraged print production.[37] Criticisms were made using physical distortions and by including sex, violence, wit, and pornographic imagery in the depicted scenes.[38] Graphic satires reflected contemporary issues and illustrated opinions that people might not have put into words for fear of prosecution for libel.[39] Almost all political prints were signed by the 1820s, demonstrating acceptance of this form of criticism.[40] The artists and their backers wanted grievances to be addressed rather than revolution or radical reforms; this meant that they were not subjected to prosecution or stamp duties in the same manner as the authors of pamphlets and newspapers.[41]

Little is known about the print runs, circulation, or influence of specific prints. Approximately 20,000 satirical and humorous prints were printed in London between 1770 and 1830.[42] About half of these commented on politics, whereas the other half focused on social and personal issues, including scandals, gossip, and sex.[43] Rates of production varied through the year, with most appearing in late fall and early spring to coincide with parliamentary sessions, but on average production grew from four per week between the 1780s and early 1800s to seven to ten per week between 1830 and 1832.[44] While the number of political prints increased after 1770, however, the size of the print runs for each image remained steady due to their increased size, complexity, and coloring.[45] First print runs by popular artists probably ranged from 100 to 600 copies.[46] This average number is low relative to the several thousand copies of newspapers and around 500 copies of pamphlets printed in first runs.[47] Most political prints probably sold around 500 copies.[48] Reproductions of images were popular and could be found in homes across Britain.[49] In an average year approximately 50,000 political prints might have been produced in England.[50] Again, this is low in comparison to newspapers, with 16 million printed in 1801 and 30 million annually in the 1830s.[51]

The period 1780 to 1832 saw not only a heightened awareness of and action on slavery and abolition, but also the rise and fall of the popularity of British satirical prints. Growing demand for satirical prints demonstrates both an increase in British print culture and an increase in the public's interest in politics.[52] Through satirical caricatures, artists were able to depict reformers and anti-slavery activists as dangerous, devious, and even Jacobins. James Gillray's *Philanthropic Consolations after the loss of the Slave Bill* (1796) (Figure 3.1) shows William Wilberforce and the bishop of Westminster being consoled by two women of African descent for having lost the bill. Gillray was one of the most powerful and influential print satirists of his time. Wilberforce is depicted in profile, allowing the viewer to easily recognize him visually (although the title of the print, by mentioning the slave bill, would likely link the image to Wilberforce's constant drive

Figure 3.1 Philanthropic Consolations after the loss of the Slave Bill
Source: Courtesy of the Library of Congress, LC-USZC4-8775

for abolition in the minds of politically aware viewers). He is perched at the end of a couch, enjoying his pipe with a bare-breasted woman at the far end of the couch who leans her head invitingly toward him as she smokes her pipe. The bishop of Westminster has his back to the viewer, making him harder to recognize. He has been depicted in a much more compromising position with his arms around the second woman and his lips puckered for a kiss. Hanging on the wall are a number of caricatures, including *Inkle & Yarico* and *Captn. Kimber in the Cells of Newgate*. On a small table to one side of the image lie a number of papers and books, including an unrolled scroll reading "Defence of Orthodoxy, better late than never," and a book opened to the page "Charity covereth a Multitude of Sins." On the floor lies a torn copy of the trial of Captain Kimber. The entire scene is modeled on Hogarth's *A Harlot's Progress* (1732).[53] Although it is supposedly set in a London brothel, there are numerous allusions to the Orient throughout the print.[54]

Wilberforce is depicted as a skinny, tiny man who is physically dominated by the woman beside him. The large hat on top of her turban, her overweight body, and her large, exposed breasts further emphasize their contrasting sizes. By emphasizing a black woman's sexuality (particularly when it was that of a slave's), artists and authors were able to redirect blame for illicit behavior from male colonists onto women. This countered abolitionist arguments that white male force and domination were responsible for sexual deviancy and misconduct in the colonies.[55] While the bishop of Westminster is a large man in his white robes, the woman with him has her hand around his shoulder, controlling him as much as he is controlling her. The scene depicts the men as hypocrites, driven by desire rather than humanity or reason.[56] Instead of sticking to their pre-1780 traditional roles of servant, exotic element, or toy of the elites, images of blacks in British art were becoming increasingly sexualized in the late eighteenth century as a way of emphasizing the socially compromised position of a print's subjects.[57] It also criticizes Wilberforce for being a Pitt supporter. Some radicals interpreted the support of abolition by Pitt and his government as a way to distract the public's attention from the miseries of British workers. By including the phrase, "Charity covereth a Multitude of Sins" in this print, it has been suggested that this particular argument might be being made here.[58]

Political prints that satirized or attacked individuals were often sponsored anonymously; the subjects of the prints might look foolish if they were to get upset about their depiction.[59] The two references to Captain Kimber questioned Wilberforce's credibility by highlighting the faith he and his fellow abolitionists in Parliament had placed upon the story of Captain Kimber as evidence of the mistreatment and horrors suffered by slaves on the Middle Passage, for which Kimber was later acquitted. The scene's oriental elements allude to excess: excess sex, excess money, and excessive political control (despotism).[60] Images of large, sexualized black women had become so commonly associated with the West Indies that the location of the scene did not need to be specified.[61] Black women, overall, rarely appeared in British art of the era outside of depictions of slavery, abolition, and emancipation.[62] The men here are shown to be under the dangerous influence of black women, basing their arguments on false information and stories, and driven by passion rather than reason. The artist thus questioned and satirized their motives, logic, and credibility in this one image; contemporary viewers in London would have recognized these criticisms.

Isaac Robert Cruikshank's satire, *John Bull Taking a Clear View of the Negro Slavery Question* (1826) (Figure 3.2), contains many characters and a great deal of anti-abolitionist imagery. The setting for the scene is an East India sugar warehouse on a British dock. The central figures are John Bull, representing every Englishman, and an

Figure 3.2 John Bull Taking a Clear View of the Negro Slavery Question
Source: Courtesy of the John Carter Brown Library at Brown University

abolitionist, dressed here as a Quaker. John Bull first appeared in print in the 1760s. In the late 1820s and early 1830s his image was used to represent the strengths and weaknesses of British politics.[63] Here John Bull is looking through a telescope toward a tropical island inhabited by black slaves, but his view of the island's happy slaves is blocked by an image of plantation cruelty being held up by the abolitionist in front of the telescope's lens. Kneeling below the abolitionist Quaker is a smiling overweight man searching through a box labeled, "Pictures of Negro Slavery—Box N° 3957." Behind John Bull sit members of an impoverished British family who have been left out of the recent calls for charity and humanity. A dog relieves himself on their sign asking for assistance. Young boys are forced to sign petitions against duties on East India sugar to be sent to Parliament. A stack of papers, labeled "Pamphlets against Negro Slavery," lean against the side of the sugar warehouse where another fanatical Quaker abolitionist holds up an image of cruelty as he preaches to the crowds. Near the front of the scene the artist has included a Quaker holding a sign reading, "Buy only East India sugar—tis sinful to buy any other"; as he has his back to the viewer one can clearly see the invoice for East India sugar sticking out of his back pocket. Further images of cruelties against the slaves are posted against walls in the background, as is the notice, "Just Published. Sierra Leone A FARCE as performed for the benefit of Signor Hum Bamboozle."

Cruikshank was highlighting and satirizing a number of relevant issues with this print. By wanting to monopolize the sale of sugar, he suggested that East Indians were acting out of self-interest rather than the good of the people. The image also suggested that abolitionists were intentionally distorting the average Briton's understanding of colonial slavery. Abolitionists, here dressed as fanatical, untrustworthy, business-focused Quakers, are shown having to resort to underhand means to convince Britons of the need to boycott West Indian produce and emancipate the slaves from their state of bondage. In the process, they have created an excessive amount of misleading anti-slavery propaganda as signified by the box of images and the stacks of pamphlets.[64] The abolitionists' production and use of prints in this image reminds the viewer that prints helped form public opinion rather than simply reflect it.[65] Instead of being objective or uncontaminated by outside influences, as perhaps the abolitionists wished the viewing public to believe, all prints were value-laden.[66]

Elsewhere in the image, far from being the subject of humanitarian efforts, the British poor are left to suffer and fend for themselves even though they are seated in front of the supposed humanitarians. George Cruikshank's *The New Union Club of 1819* (1819) also condemns abolitionists for ignoring the poor at home while championing the plight of the slaves abroad. Here, the slaves off on their distant tropical island are shown to be playing music and dancing, eating, drinking, and toasting their companions, but the abolitionists refuse to let Britons see this happy scene. Instead they have produced thousands of images depicting the cruelties of the plantation system. This print provides a visual demonstration of the abolitionists' domination of the slavery debate in print.[67] While the exact proportion of pro- to anti-slavery prints remains to be studied, the dominance of anti-slavery imagery in the era of abolition continues to be reflected in how little scholarship has since been devoted to pro-West Indian and pro-colonial imagery.[68] Returning to the print, the abolitionists also have to rely on the signatures of young boys and the words of fanatical Quakers to convince Britons of the slaves' plight. This multilayered caricature of abolitionist deception is perhaps one of the best visual compilations of anti-abolitionist arguments and beliefs to be created in the era of abolition. While black subjects were important to all three of the pieces discussed here, at no time were they the central focus of the work, but instead served to support or reinforce the dominance of the white figures (and therefore of Britain) in the world contained within these images.

The satirical print, *Cruelty & Oppression Abroad,* published by William Holland in 1792, also charges abolitionists with falsifying evidence and possessing ulterior motives. At the center of the image are a large number of brightly dressed African and mixed-race individuals dancing, singing, playing instruments, and laughing with one another while being watched by three European observers. The female observer holds a parasol, indicating that the location is hot and sunny. There are no clouds in the clear blue sky. Little white houses with bright orange roofs and green trees dot this picturesque landscape. On the right-hand side of the image are two men commenting not only on the happy scene in front of them but on the abolitionist movement and abolitionists' use of vivid imagery of plantation life to gain support for their cause. This print was published by Holland as part of a set of three prints relating to the slave trade six weeks after Wilberforce moved for the slave trade to be abolished in 1792. These prints are frequently attributed to caricaturist Richard Newton. The others in the set included *Justice & Humanity at Home*, in which Wilberforce ignores the issue of flogging sailors to focus on the cruelties of the slave trade for transported Africans, and *The Blind Enthusiast*, in which Wilberforce's abolitionist sentiment sets fire to the colonies. The set sold for half a guinea.

This simpler, hand-colored image contains much more text than the other two prints examined here. This text is perhaps the most important element of the piece as it clearly explains the image's anti-abolitionist argument. Filling the entire upper right corner of the image are two large text bubbles in which the abolitionist, dressed in black clothing as in *John Bull taking a Clear View*... (Figure 3.2), admits that the images of cruelty and oppression he employs to gain financial support for abolition originated in his own "wild imagination." The man in uniform argues that such happy scenes are everyday occurrences on Britain's plantations in the Caribbean. He informs his companion that, even though the abolition movement benefits from some excellent orators, slave owners and traders will be successful in keeping public opinion on their side simply by being honest: "not one half the nation believe you or your party. You have most of the good speakers on your side, the other side have relied on the justice of their cause and their own innocence, and the abuse of you and your tribe becomes daily more and more contemptible."[69] Again, this print contrasts a happy image of slavery with a false, intentionally misleading depiction created by abolitionists as a means of gaining support for the cause of abolition.

Drama

Proslavery sentiment also reached the theaters of Britain and her colonies. English playwrights often included references to topical subjects with which their audiences would have been familiar. Eighteenth-century English theater was distinct from that on the continent in that it frequently involved interactions between the audience and the performance, including verbalizing support for or against the actors, characters, and causes alluded to on stage.[70] Any political content could be cheered or booed and actors could improvise about contemporary political issues in the course of their performances.[71] Because of this interaction, if an audience did not like the content of a play, there was a distinct possibility that they would force an end to the production. As a result, a play's subject, text, and action had to be written with English audiences in mind, as playwrights and theater owners depended on a happy audience for a successful, profitable show.[72] English actor, playwright, and manager David Garrick had made significant changes to contemporary British theater in the mid-eighteenth century by moving the audience off of the stage, creating a clear distinction between audience and action, and working to focus the audience's attention to the performance.[73] Playwrights were also encouraged to provide audiences with clear moral guidance.[74] Despite these efforts, rowdy audiences continued to affect the live performances of scripted drama. These interactions, which would be particularly interesting to know about in terms of expressing the pro- and anti-slavery beliefs among audience members, were not captured within the plays' scripts considered below.

While the number of theaters in London barely increased across the eighteenth century, the size of the theaters and audience numbers grew dramatically.[75] Individuals from all walks of life, from the uppermost levels of the aristocracy in boxed seats to prostitutes and thieves in the highest stalls, could attend the theater in London, especially with such practices as providing half-price tickets for latecomers.[76] If a prospective audience member was not considered respectable-looking, however, they could be turned away at the door.[77] People attended with a purpose in mind, whether to show off their wealth, mingle and make connections, or even find a mate. Women continued to be discouraged from attending the theater due to the fear that they might be corrupted or witness something obscene (on stage or off).[78] Deciding to attend the theater was not necessarily about what was showing on stage, and even the actors could find themselves forced to adapt their acting and the scripts in response to the audience's wishes, because British audiences believed that they had a right to influence the show.[79] Live performance in this period could only be captured on paper, whether in scripts, reviews, artwork, or personal recollections, so it is fortunate that the scripts of two particularly relevant plays from this period have survived, but they do not reflect the interaction that was a central element to live performance during this period.

The two proslavery plays examined here extol the benevolence of the West Indian planter and the patriarchal, caring relationship between master and slave. J. W. Orderson's *The Fair Barbadian and Faithful Black; or, A Cure for the Gout* was performed and published at the climax of the emancipation debate and this directly impacted upon the message of the play's planter characters. In contrast, Thomas Bellamy's one-act play, *The Benevolent Planters,* was a drama performed at the Theatre Royal Haymarket in London in August 1789 and published that same year by J. Debrett. Two of the actors, Steven George and Elizabeth (Satchell) Kemble, had previously performed in other plays that dealt with the topic of slavery, including George Colman the younger's *Inkle and Yarico* and Thomas Southerne's *Oroonoko, or, The Royal Slave.* The play was advertised in numerous London newspapers, some of which included a copy of the prologue, noting that the play was intended to be a prelude to the rest of the night's entertainment. An advertisement in *The Times* from August 3, 1789, also noted, "Before the Prelude, an Address to the Humane Society for the Abolition of the Slave Trade, in the Character of a Negro, By Mr. Kemble."[80] This brought the play directly into the political sphere and the slavery debate. A song from the play, "The Negro's Complaint," was published in several collections from London, including *The new vocal enchantress containing an elegant selection of all the newest songs lately sung at the Theatres Royal Drury Lane, Covent Garden, Haymarket. Royalty Theatre, Vaux Hall, &c. &c. &c.* and *The Muse in Good Humour; or Momus's Banquet: a collection of choice songs including the modern.*[81] The play was also reviewed in the 1789 issue of *The English Review, or An Abstract of English and Foreign Literature,* where the reviewer remarked, "As a dramatic piece, the Benevolent Planters cannot boast of much merit, as it is deficient in plot, incident, and character: but its unpretending simplicity, and the moral it conveys, disarm the hand of criticism."[82] Orderson's *The Fair Barbadian* was a three-act comedy performed in Barbados in 1832 before being published in Liverpool in 1835. Unfortunately, the details of the actual performance, including the actors, the audiences, and the reception of *The Fair Barbadian* in Barbados, remain unknown.[83] The different formats, genres, audiences, and historical contexts have noticeably shaped these two defenses of slavery.

Bellamy's *The Benevolent Planters* is a short play that revolved around the efforts of three planters to make the lives of two African slaves happier through a surprise reunion. Bellamy was against slavery, but in his play he promoted paternalism in slaveholding and gradual melioration. In *The Benevolent Planters*, the planters had such a close relationship to their slaves that the slaves in question, Oran and Selima, confide in them about their heartache at having been separated from one another by the transatlantic slave trade. It was quickly noted, however, that a warring party of Africans would have killed Oran had the Europeans not arrived to save him by taking him to the West Indies.[84] The planters were thankful that, through their enslavement, Oran and Selima had received the knowledge and comforts of Christianity to help them overcome their devastating losses.[85] Oran and Selima in return were grateful slaves. The commonly used image of the grateful slave challenges the idea that slavery is necessarily cruel or evil. As a result, it calls for amelioration and not emancipation.[86] Throughout the piece, the playwright praised the benefits of religious education in the colonies and promoted kind, benevolent actions toward the slaves. As Oran declared in the final speech of the play: "for ourselves, and for our surrounding brethren, we declare, that you have proved yourself *The Benevolent Planters,* and that under subjection like yours, SLAVERY IS BUT A NAME."[87]

Orderson's *The Fair Barbadian and Faithful Black* is a complex piece with main and subplots, more than twice as many characters, and a more overt stance on colonial slavery. This was in response to the threat of impending emancipation its colonial audiences faced in 1832. According to an advertisement written by Orderson in Bridgetown in 1835, the play was meant to record real master–slave relationships before emancipation.[88] In *The Fair Barbadian,* Orderson provides a detailed record of realistic, Barbadian slave speech that results in a very different experience for the reader/audience and changes the ease with which the enslaved characters can be understood. This intentional use of Barbadian slave speech might be a reflection of the early nineteenth-century belief that the language one used revealed the workings of their mind and thus vulgar or unrefined language denoted an uncivilized speaker of a lower rank.[89]

The main storyline of *The Fair Barbadian* revolved around the impending marriage of the planter's daughter, Emily, to her evil cousin, Tom, when she instead loved Captain Carlove. As in Bellamy's work, only two slaves played a role in the plot of the story, although just one was given a name. Tom threatened and physically attacked Hampshire, the named slave character, early in the play, helping to establish him as an evil, uncaring member of the plantation family. Hampshire, the favorite slave, faced numerous threats and comedic physical abuse as his master, Judge Errington, became increasingly forgetful while struggling with gout. Despite this violence, Hampshire was happy to help solve the mysterious circumstances regarding Emily's betrothal and was eventually awarded his freedom. It is important to note that Hampshire at first refuses to accept his freedom and only does so after the Judge assures him that he will continue to work for the family in the same capacity as before, except now he will earn a wage. This may have been done to confirm that white supremacy would remain after slavery was abolished.[90]

Violence in *The Fair Barbadian and Faithful Black* is always framed by a misunderstanding. Playwrights may not have wanted to go too far toward portraying actual discipline or overly sentimentalizing slavery because their audiences might have begun to see the situation from the slave's point of view or replace the slave's emotional experience with their own.[91] This might also partly explain why, in the prologue to *The Benevolent Planters*, Oran's recollections of his time under a ruthless master was quickly countered by him recalling how thankful he was for his current owner.

Both plays comment on the negative impact abolitionists have had in the islands and on the perception of the colonies and colonists. In *The Benevolent Planters*, a short prologue was given by the same actor who played Oran but in the character of an African sailor. Prologues were frequently used as a means to convince the audience to pay attention to the following production and as an early attempt to win their approval.[92] Here, the African sailor commented on his happy life in Africa and then his awful experience at the hands of a tyrannical master before remarking that he was now in the service of a kind master and no longer experienced the hardships of being a slave. This reflects a stylistic technique some anti-abolitionist writers employed, arguing that slaves would only be grateful to their paternalist masters if they had also experienced evil, violent rule.[93] The African sailor then commented on the abolition movement in Britain. In *The Fair Barbadian*, Emily and Captain Carlove have recently arrived from England after being exposed to abolitionist sentiment. This then allows for numerous discussions of slavery to take place between the new arrivals and the planters. In the second scene of Act Two, for example, a small group visits the plantation estate and witnesses a happy, animated scene of slaves hard at work. While Emily has remained secure in the knowledge that her father was a humane planter, the Captain and his associate Major Chider are surprised and astonished at the happy image of plantation life and apologetic for having believed otherwise. Both admitted that the abolitionists had tried to mislead them as they had been misleading all Britons. As Chider confesses to the Judge's sister Alice:

> It were too trite an observation, Madam, merely to say that our own experience leads to a corrector judgement than the report or opinion of others of less information than ourselves; I will, therefore, now in honest candour confess, that I have been, like thousands of others, so deceived by the artifices and false philanthropy of Aldermanbury, as to be brought to believe that I should only see in West India slavery a race of half-starved, ill-clothed, miserable-looking, lacerated and degraded Africans.[94]

His confession provides the Judge and his sister with an opportunity to call for all those who had seen the true state of slavery in the colonies to speak out and fight back against the abolitionists. As Alice exclaims: "Yes! people will talk of things they know nothing about!—but then those that know the truth, should speak out!"[95] This could be interpreted as Orderson calling on his audience to take action. While Bellamy restricted his commentary on slavery and abolition to a few specific benefits of the slave trade and slavery, Orderson took an overtly political stance against immediate emancipation which he argued was based on false information being spread by uninformed or lying abolitionists. Through the nature of theater, both were able to share their views with a wider audience and were also able to present dynamic visual images to support the spoken dialogue.

Poetry and Song

Poetry was the most common type of literature to be printed in the eighteenth century.[96] Hundreds of poems were written about slavery between 1660 and the early 1800s.[97] Only around 5 or 10 percent of these, however, condoned or defended the institution.[98] It has been suggested that because the nature of poetry is sentimental and feminine (a direct contrast to the logical, masculine appearance anti-abolitionists tried to put forth in their writings) very few proslavery poems emerged during the slavery debates.[99] Perhaps West Indian poets intentionally focused on the land rather than the people in the West Indies in the era of abolition in order to show that the true value of the colonies was the abundant fertile land, not the slaves.[100] Contemporary proslavery poetry and verse came in a number of styles.

These included love stories, replies to abolitionist works, and songs that could be sung by the slaves or were based upon slave music. They varied greatly in form, length, authorship, and intention and portrayed an idealized vision of West Indian slavery for their British readers.

"The Field Negroe; or the Effect of Civilization" was originally published anonymously in the 1783 collection, *Poems, on Subjects Arising in England, and the West Indies,* that was advertised in the rival London newspapers, the *Morning Post* and the *Morning Herald,* in 1784. This lengthy piece told the story of a young overseer's meeting with a slave, Arthur, who had paused to take a break from working in the fields on a hot day. Arthur tells the overseer his life story that succinctly summarizes many positive elements and benefits of enslavement in the West Indian colonies. His story demonstrates contemporary thoughts on how an African could become more civilized through plantation labor and life as well as becoming stronger, happier, and more fulfilled. For example, Arthur now possessed a home, a plot of land, and a family. He could participate in games and holiday festivities. Perhaps most important for the author, Arthur continued to grow in his devotion to his master:

> Now faithful to his master's side,
> And takes his nimble course:
> He braids his hair, with decent pride,
> And runs beside his horse.
>
> And now we daily hear him sing,
> The merriest and the best[101]

By presenting a narrative of the fictional Arthur's life in "The Field Negroe," the author provided numerous examples of how to assess the slaves' happiness and was able to demonstrate the range of benefits that colonial slavery supposedly bestowed upon Africans.

The lawyer James Boswell dedicated his proslavery poem, *No Abolition of Slavery,* to the West Indian merchants and planters. He intentionally wrote this piece, as well as several other defenses of slavery, to contribute to the slavery debates.[102] *No Abolition of Slavery* is a love poem that mocks specific abolitionists while demonstrating numerous reasons why the institution of slavery should not be tampered with. Boswell was particularly hostile toward Wilberforce's efforts to achieve abolition by wooing the public and Parliament:

> Go, W—, with narrow scull,
> Go home, and preach away at Hull,

No longer to the Senate cackle,
In strains which suit the Tabernacle;
I hate your little wittling sneer,
Your pert and self-sufficient leer,
Mischief to Trade sits on thy lip,
Insects will gnaw the noblest ship;
Go, W——, be gone, for shame,
Thou dwarf with a big-sounding name.[103]

He argued that slavery was ordained in the Bible and that man could not change this fact.[104] Boswell then presented images of happy slaves who were protected and provided for, before proceeding to inform MPs that abolition would be a mistake:

Of food, clothes, cleanly lodging sure,
Each has his property secure;
Their wives and children are protected,
In sickness they are not neglected;
And when old age brings a release,
Their grateful days they end in peace.

But should our Wrongheads have their will,
Should Parliament approve their bill,
Pernicious as th'effect would be,
T'abolish negro slavery,
Such partial freedom would be vain,
Since Love's strong empire must remain.[105]

The poem was bookended by the idea that any man is susceptible to becoming enslaved by his love for a woman. Throughout the piece, Boswell attacked numerous MPs for their anti-slavery views and argued that, overall, slavery was a permanent institution that benefited all those involved.

As stated in the poem's dedication, Henry Evans Holder's *Fragments of a Poem* was published in 1792 to defend West Indian planters and merchants against the slander and accusations aimed at them by British abolitionists. The publisher noted that the work was to be sold in London, Bath, and Bristol. Holder's intention was to attempt to refute the information contained within John Marjoribanks' abolitionist work, *Slavery: An Essay in Verse* (1792). Holder's poem included a thorough introduction to the topic and Marjoribanks' pamphlet, all the while vindicating the planters, before moving onto his short fragments of poetry. Within the verses, Holder charged the abolitionists with being motivated by self-interest:

But after all, when this great work is done,
When you have fill'd this hemisphere with rage,
Against the children of the Western world,
Can you look up to GOD, and boldly say,
My motive was to serve his creatures,
And further his designs of genial love?[106]

He also argued against any outside interference with plantation slavery by reminding Marjoribanks and his readers that everything a planter had was invested in his slaves:

But who, you'll say, shall guard the wretched slave
From tyrant-cruelty and bloody scourge?
Believe me he requires no hand to guard,
No interference from your mad'ning zeal
. . .
The voice of interest will be heard aloud,
Nor yet in any state of life more loud,
Than when she teaches ev'ry master's heart,
That all his wealth is center'd in his slave.[107]

Holder claimed that the planter was constantly motivated to maintain his slaves' health and well-being and, as a result, no abolitionist interference was necessary. He argued overall that the abolitionists, caught up in the emotional rhetoric that they had created, were incorrect in their assumptions and had been misled by their own self-interest.

An Englishwoman purportedly sent five anonymously written poems to Sir Phillip Gibbes who included them in the 1797 edition of his *Instructions for the Treatment of Negroes*. Gibbes' manual was printed in at least three editions. The first three poems were meant for slaves to sing as they worked in the fields to lift their spirits. The words advise them to be grateful to their masters and God for what they had. In her untitled first poem, she reminds her readers and the slaves that God watches over them and will now be able to receive them as Christians after death:

See! The Great God sends forth his Sun
To ripen all the fields of canes:
'Tis just as if he said, "Well done
Good negroes! I'll reward your pains."

And so he will:—a little while
We have to labour here below,

And for our honest faithful toil
God will his heaven bestow.[108]

This first poem downplays the labor and demands on the slaves in the colonies and instead emphasizes the eternal rewards that await them in heaven after they die. The second untitled poem stressed the benefits of labor (as discussed in this chapter's introduction) and God's grace and redemption:

God, the master we serve, knows for us what is best:
And when life's toils are ended we sweetly shall rest;
For ev'ry good deed in God's book is recorded.
So faithful good negroes will be surely rewarded.[109]

In this poem she again depicts enslaved labor in a positive light and as a means to reach heaven.

Her fourth poem, "A Negro's Address to His Fellows," discusses how slaves are the cursed descendants of Ham:

We're children of Cham! He his father offended,
Who gave him the curse, which to us is descended.
"A servant of servants" alas! is our curse;
And bad as it is, it has sav'd us from worse.[110]

Here Ham is responsible for the enslavement of Africans in the colonies and elsewhere. As this was God's will, she argues, the planters are not to blame for the current situation in the colonies and the slaves are grateful to have found themselves in their situation. The author also informs her readers of several ways in which the slaves would be worse off in Africa had they not been taken to the West Indies, including the continued exposure to a pagan religion and tyrannical masters:

So that if to White Men now slaves you behold them,
White Men had not bought, if *Black Men* had not sold them.
Nay, were we more happy, or felt we less evil,
When snakes were our Gods, and we worship'd the devil?
A servant of servants much more were we then:
We labour'd for devils.—We now work for men.[111]

The author also argues that slaves should be thankful to their masters for the food they receive and that they must always remember that the opportunity to become a Christian is worth any amount of suffering.

Throughout the poems the author's strong belief in the benefits of a Christian education allows her to promote the slave trade's continuance as being beneficial to all African slaves. Proslavery MPs employed similar arguments of a preexisting African slave trade and the benefits of spreading Christianity during the slavery debates in Parliament.

C.F.D.'s "Bonja Song" was published in London around 1802 as a piece of sheet music. The song's popularity is reflected in its numerous reprints throughout the nineteenth century and advertisements in the *Morning Post*. The author was probably Charlotte Dallas, a woman who grew up in Jamaica, although the piece at one time was attributed to her brother Robert.[112] The author claims that the melody came from the slaves themselves, but that she added the harmony and the words. Using repetition and similar phrases, the lyrics contrast the worry-free life of the slave with the difficult life of the planter from the slave's perspective:

> He sleep all day, he wake all night,
> He full of care, his heart no light,
> He great deal want, he little get,
> He sorry, so he fret.
> . . .
> Me sing all day, me sleep all night,
> Me hab no care, my heart is light.
> Me tink not what to-morrow bring,
> Me happy, so me sing.[113]

The author emphasizes the happy, carefree life of the slave throughout the song. The lyrics also demonstrates contemporary arguments that slaves were content with their situation and either that they did not care that they were enslaved, or that they did not have the capacity to think of any alternative to enslavement (as reflected in the line "Me tink not what to-morrow bring"). Later writers would use the latter argument in their attempts to prove the slaves' mental inferiority and their incapacity to want or handle the responsibilities of freedom.[114] This proslavery song presents a very different view of plantation life to Britons from the images abolitionists were simultaneously promoting as true depictions of life in the West Indies.

M. J. Chapman's 1833 poem, *Barbadoes*, is an extended argument against immediate emancipation woven throughout a description of Barbados. *Barbadoes* was advertised in the *Hull Packet* and the *Essex Standard* (weekly newspapers from Hull and Colchester respectively) in February 1834 and reviewed in the August 1833 issue of *La Belle*

Assemblée, or Bell's Court and Fashionable Magazine Addressed Particularly to the Ladies. It was also used to help advertise Chapman's poem, *Jephtha's Daughter,* in newspapers across England in July, August, and September 1834. This advertisement quoted reviews of the author's work from *Blackwood's Magazine, Athenaeum,* the *Bristol Journal,* the *Newcastle Courant,* the *Court Journal,* and the *Berkshire Chronicle.* His work was well known and received positive reviews.

Chapman states in the introduction to *Barbadoes* that he opposes emancipation because it would ruin the colonies and the empire.[115] With his words, Chapman paints contented scenes of plantation life in the West Indies and contrasts these with images of the destruction that he argues would follow immediate emancipation. The conclusion to Part One of the poem demonstrates the author's regret at the abolitionists' actions and their consequences:

> Our island-slaves once loved their father-friend,
> Content with his their happiness to blend;
> And still would love him;—but from England goes
> A moving narrative of negro-woes;
> Of brands and tortures, only known by name—
> Of lawless power and slavery's damning shame.
> . . .
> The sound of battles, rushing through the trees;
> The hurried tramp of frantic savages!
> The slave, infuriate, pants for Freedom's smiles,
> And Hayti's fate attends our Eden-isles.[116]

In this section of his poem, Chapman blames abolitionist rhetoric and the use of stock stories of abuses and horrors on the plantations for disturbing the peace in the West Indies and creating a volatile atmosphere similar to that in which revolution had already erupted.[117] He also utilizes the familiar argument that terms such as "slavery" have been unfairly loaded with negative connotations for the wider British public that has never witnessed actual plantation life.[118]

Like the anonymous author of the poems in Gibbes' manual, Chapman argues that the slaves are far better off under the direction of the West Indian planters than if they were back in Africa:

> No more he thinks upon his Libyan skies;
> His native rites a purer faith supplies.
> He looks with gladness for the promised day,
> And horrid superstition flies away.

His life, his home, his property secure,
He knows his lot is better than before.[119]

Chapman stresses the benefits of slavery to Britain as well as to the slaves and chastises the abolitionists for threatening the stability of the colonies and destroying the benefits of their production. He stresses the important role slavery has played in spreading Christianity to transported Africans. He notes some of the ways in which enslavement, in his opinion, brings security to the enslaved. This argument is also advanced in the final slavery debates in Parliament.[120] These poets were able to present and promote positive images of slavery through their use of verse (and, in some cases, song). Their appeals to the British public, the abolitionists, and the government to halt the antislavery movement and protect the colonies are at times compelling, convincing, and entertaining. Together these pieces form a unique way of sharing the proslavery position with a wider public.

Literature

The production and distribution of novels (known as histories, tales, memoirs, and romances until the late eighteenth century) in eighteenth- and early nineteenth-century Britain was part of a wider movement in which literature changed from being produced for and read by an elite to bringing enjoyment to a much larger readership.[121] With growing literacy rates came a surge in the number of circulating libraries across Britain that served wealthier male and female readers.[122] Unlike the universities, societies, and coffeehouses of the era, women were able to attend and use circulating libraries to socialize, be seen, and find new works to read.[123] British laborers, if they could read, would have remained unable to afford literature. They could, however, come together to purchase items, buy secondhand books, or borrow items from someone's personal collection. The ability to read for enjoyment and as part of the quest for refinement required time as well as wealth and literacy.[124] This again limited the audience of the works under review here to a mainly elite, urban readership.

Two very different novels published in the 1820s reflect their authors' sympathy for the West Indian planter. *Hamel, The Obeah Man,* was published anonymously in two volumes in London in 1827, although contemporaries would have likely known that the author was Cynric R. Williams, author of *A Tour through the Island of Jamaica, from the Western to the Eastern End, in the Year 1823* (1826).[125]

Hamel was reviewed in several periodicals including the *Westminster Review*, the *London Review*, and *La Belle Assemblée, or Bell's Court and Fashionable Magazine Addressed Particularly to the Ladies* in 1827. A number of these reviews were later quoted in advertisements for the novel in the London newspapers the *Examiner*, the *Morning Post*, and the *Morning Chronicle*. *Marly; or, A Planter's Life in Jamaica* was published anonymously in two editions in Glasgow in 1828. The first edition was reissued in 1831 with a new cover, likely because the publisher had leftover copies to move.[126] These proslavery novels promoted the established system of slavery in Jamaica. While the author of *Marly* acknowledges the possibility of further melioration, *Hamel* vividly depicts the destruction and violence that can result from outside (British anti-slavery) interference. While their styles and plots greatly differ, these two novels provide yet another example of how proslavery sentiment could be shared with a wider British readership.

The plot of *Hamel, The Obeah Man* centers on a mass rebellion that erupted in the politically unstable colony of Jamaica in the early 1820s. The island and its colonists were under threat by a number of sources: nonconformist missionaries; slaves continuing to practice Obeah;[127] government interference from London; radical emancipationists in Britain; rumors of emancipation spreading through the slave population; and nearby rebellions. The revolt is led by Combah, who hopes to become king of Jamaica, the title character Hamel, and Roland, a Wesleyan Methodist missionary. As part of the uprising, Combah and Roland plan to kidnap the beautiful planter's daughter, Joanna, but Hamel, upon the return of his master and friend, Fairfax, has a change of heart and instead helps to rescue Joanna. To conclude the story, Combah is struck by lightning and falls into a ravine, Roland has to contemplate his many sins while dying of a fever, and Hamel sets sail for Africa.

Marly; or, A Planter's Life in Jamaica, is the story of a Scot, George Marly, who arrives in Jamaica in 1816 and works as a bookkeeper. Over the course of the novel, he witnesses many aspects of plantation life, reclaims his lost inheritance, and wins the hand of the woman he loves. In conclusion, Marly resolves to meliorate conditions on his plantation so as to bring about a gradual end to slavery. From the intimate details of plantation life and the island of Jamaica that he provides it is likely that the author had visited the island himself.[128] The novel overall depicts an honest, hardworking man who became a benevolent planter. Rather than remaining committed to perpetual slavery, Marly hopes that one day his slaves will be fit to receive their freedom.

The contrasting nature of these two novels is fascinating. *Hamel* is a colonial Gothic novel that emphasized the dangers and anxieties present in colonial Jamaica in order to entertain its readers.[129] It centers on a bloody, violent revolt and makes the leaders of the revolt suffer for their actions. One slave succinctly summarizes the origins of the revolt in the novel's conclusion:

> many [slaves] ... had been induced by Roland and others to take up arms in support of the rights which Mr. Wilberforce had obtained for them. "They told us so, mistress [Joanna]; they told the Negroes so, who were slaves. They preached to us that the king of England had given liberty to all, had paid for their freedom; and they read out of the big books, and little books, and Scotch books, that we should put the knives to the throats of the buckras, who then would own it was true."[130]

In *Hamel* it is mainly the misleading preaching of missionaries in the islands, who had encouraged the slaves to believe they have been freed by the British monarchy, which causes the revolt; therefore, even religious leaders in the colonies cannot be relied upon to enlighten the slaves or ensure the safety of the planters.

In contrast to the violent, passionate language and imagery found in *Hamel*, *Marly* is a calm, realistic depiction of the minute details of everyday life in the colony and presents its readers with a happy and hopeful image of Jamaica and the future of its slaves. The author even informs his readers that he wants Britons to understand better the true nature of plantation slavery in the colonies.[131] Both authors also presented colonial life as preferable to that elsewhere. While in *Hamel* the author argues that the colonists are more modern and forward-thinking than the conservative Europeans back home,[132] in *Marly* the slaves are given a far more culturally rich life than that of the planters.[133] These novels and the other forms of creative writing discussed here contributed to the slavery debate through their sympathetic portrayal of the planters as victims or as benevolent masters struggling to maintain control in a system under immediate threat from outside forces.

Proslavery beliefs and rhetoric are found within the artistic world of Britain in the era of abolition. Through the use of artistic works, the proslavery position was crafted and promoted to the wider British public. Using creative language, colorful depictions, and persuasive dramatizations of the benefits of slavery for all involved, members of the West Indian interest and their supporters created a record of a distinct, multifaceted proslavery culture of shared beliefs, goals, and opinions. This culture was then shared in print, on stage, and illustrated on the page in an attempt to inform readers, audiences, and viewers of the proslavery position. In doing so, these works contributed to the wider debate on slavery and the slave trade. Proslavery and anti-abolitionist propaganda also demonstrate the many ways in which the West Indian interest was able to reach out to the public to defend its position, itself, and the colonies. The arguments and rhetoric contained within these pieces were then utilized during the slavery debates in Parliament to hinder the legal arm of the abolitionist movement.

Chapter 4

Proslavery Politics and the Slave Trade

On June 25, 1788, a bill for shipping regulations regarding ships involved in the transatlantic slave trade faced intense debate in the House of Lords. As abolitionists fought to secure tighter regulations to ameliorate conditions for slaves on the British-built vessels, they found themselves facing wave after wave of attack from their opposition. Lord Rodney argued that it was "absurd" to think that West Indian merchants would not do everything in their power to ensure their cargos' safety when their profits depended on the slaves' survival.[1] New legislation was therefore unnecessary. Lord Heathfield presented proof that the slaves had more room in the ships than Britain's soldiers had in their tents.[2] The new legislation would therefore be inconsistent with earlier legislation and would show preferential treatment of one group of people over another. The Earl of Sandwich pointed out that the slave trade would continue regardless of Britain's involvement.[3] He stressed Britain could not control the actions of other nations but instead would lose out on the great profits from which her rivals would continue to benefit. Lord Chancellor Edward Thurlow criticized the nature and makeup of the entire bill, declaring: "[he] presumed that the wish of their lordships was to pass some bill of regulation; but as the Bill stood, it was nonsense. He therefore concluded that some amendments would be proposed to connect the nonsense of one part of the Bill, with the nonsense of the other."[4] Anti-abolitionists undertook a range of rhetorical strategies to undermine the confidence of the bill's supporters, challenge the bill's logic, and emphasize the importance of Britain's colonial interests. These strategies were undertaken repeatedly as the slavery debates raged in Parliament over the following two decades.

Anti-abolitionists in Parliament employed specific rhetorical strategies to discredit the abolition movement during the slavery debates. They attacked the abolitionists' evidence, methods of gaining support, logic, and underlying ideology to undermine their position and discredit their reasoning. An analysis of the nature and language of these attacks reveals a proactive anti-abolitionist movement unwilling passively to watch abolitionist fervor sweep across Britain and influence parliamentary proceedings. By examining proslavery and anti-abolitionist rhetoric, it is possible to discern ways in which the West Indian interest constructed persuasive defenses of its position and attacked the growing abolition movement. This perspective also reveals more nuanced shifts in arguments over time as well as the impact of outside influences. It supports existing research into the abolition debates that recognized the intentionally logical, reasoned, masculine arguments of the anti-abolitionists that achieved some success in Parliament[5] and these findings can be contrasted with the abolitionists' use of sentimental, feminine arguments for abolition and emancipation that were persuasive out-of-doors.[6] This chapter, then, recognizes that it is not just what the politicians said that is important to our understanding of the nature of the slavery debate in Parliament, but how they phrased their arguments.

Several clear rhetorical strategies were employed to discredit and halt the abolition movement in the context of war with France and challenges from reformers and radicals at home. Attacks on individual abolitionists, particularly William Wilberforce, provide evidence of a proactive anti-abolitionist segment in Parliament fighting to halt the growing support for the abolition of the slave trade. They also reacted to showings of strong popular support for abolition by ridiculing the methods abolitionists used to gain signatures and the legitimacy of their evidence. Anti-abolitionists challenged the legality and logic of abolition in the context of war with France and developed persuasive ways in which to link abolition to the infiltration of revolutionary principles. Throughout the abolition debates anti-abolitionists challenged the legality of abolition, the sentimentality and humanitarian claims of the abolitionists, and the abolitionists' reliance on abstract principles. Parliament's anti-abolitionist MPs repeatedly challenged the abolitionists' logic, morality, and motives during the debates and were in turn rewarded with the postponement and defeat of numerous abolition motions prior to 1807.

Proslavery rhetoric had its uses. Wilberforce's first successful bill for abolition was passed in the House of Commons in 1792. In 1792–3 the West Indian interest in Britain made a concerted effort to counter the wave of abolitionist propaganda that accompanied Wilberforce's bill. According to the bill, Britain's participation in the slave trade was supposed to come to an end on January 1, 1796, but the lords postponed the motion indefinitely by calling for a lengthy inquiry.[7] In the end, Wilberforce saw nine of his bills or proposed bills on the subject of abolition rejected over the decade. Below is a closer examination of how this wave of defeat came about.

ATTACKS ON INDIVIDUAL ABOLITIONISTS

MPs who opposed changes to the institution of slavery and restrictions on the African trade actively attacked abolitionists who proposed and supported these changes in Parliament. Rather than listening passively to abolitionist rhetoric or responding in a purely defensive manner, anti-abolitionists attacked the motives, evidence, and character of the abolitionists whom they opposed. As the primary proposer of bills for abolition, Wilberforce became the target of most of these personal attacks. Through these attacks, anti-abolitionists created doubt among enough undecided MPs to defeat or modify most slave trade-related bills debated in the Houses of Parliament in the 1790s and early 1800s.

Many MPs took issue with Wilberforce's method of introducing his bills with long introductory speeches that lasted several hours. On April 18, 1791, during a discussion in the Commons on Wilberforce's bill for abolition, Thomas Grosvenor used Wilberforce's lengthy introduction against him: "it appeared to him that the hon. Gentleman [Wilberforce] himself must have great doubts of the propriety of his motion; for, if it was so clear a point as it was declared to be, it could not have needed either so much evidence or so much time."[8] He questioned the validity and clarity of Wilberforce's arguments for abolition by remarking that, if their legitimacy were as self-evident as Wilberforce claimed, his bill would not have needed such a long and impassioned introduction.

On April 23, 1792, during a debate on Henry Dundas's resolutions for a gradual abolition, Lord Sheffield attacked Charles Fox's assertion that popular support was with the abolitionists: "He believed he had conversed with as many persons on that subject as any man; and he declared that he found an immense majority against an immediate abolition."[9] Fox had used his views on public opinion to support his argument for abolition, but Lord Sheffield was easily able to counter the claim with a similar one of his own, thus negating the ability of his opponents to use public opinion as a powerful motive to vote for the bill. Lord Sheffield also highlighted Fox's "enthusiasm" for abolition as undermining his ability to speak honestly about the public's views on the topic.[10]

On February 1, 1793, France declared war on Britain. Finding themselves reliant upon the colonies for raw materials, foodstuffs, and trade, MPs were increasingly wary of upsetting the colonists. By the mid-1790s the French Revolution was clearly hindering abolitionist efforts in Britain. When France outlawed slavery in 1794 and extended citizenship to all men, anti-abolitionists were able to draw clear connections between abolitionism, dangerous revolutionary principles, and Jacobinism. British abolitionism declined over following decade because of fears of change, hostility to Jacobinism, and alarm over the slave revolt in St. Domingo.[11] West Indians and Britons tied abolitionist rhetoric to the revolution in France and emancipation to large-scale violence. When Napoleon Bonaparte reinstated slavery in France's colonies and France's participation in the slave trade in 1802, British anti-abolitionists confidently declared that France's dangerous experiment had failed and should serve as a warning to them all.

The duke of Clarence voiced his opinion of the abolitionists, and of Wilberforce in particular, to the House of Lords on April 11, 1793, during a discussion of the Commons' vote for gradual abolition:

> His royal highness asserted that the promoters of the abolition were either fanatics or hypocrites, and in one of those classes he ranked Mr. Wilberforce. That French politics did interfere with the opinions and arguments of British senators, he should be able to prove by a letter from lord Stanhope to citizen Condorcet.... It contained congratulations to the French republican on the turn which the slave trade was likely to take, and the victory obtained in the House of Commons over the opponents to freedom.[12]

The duke's efforts to link abolitionists to radicals and revolutionaries were unfair but effective. He insulted and demeaned Wilberforce and his fellow abolitionists by stating that they were all fanatics or hypocrites. He then directly linked British abolitionists to dangerous French revolutionaries through the use of a letter, as well as through ideology, by showing that anti-abolitionists were being referred to as "opponents to liberty."

Colonel John Fenton Cawthorne openly questioned the abolitionists' motives during the slavery debates. On February 7, 1794, during a discussion of Wilberforce's motion to stop supplying foreign territories with slaves, he remarked: "Whatever were the pretended motives of religion, justice, and humanity, he suspected the real motives of the abolitionists were attributable to their disaffection. Long had that party betrayed symptoms of their hatred towards the constitution of this country. It was our duty to counteract the premeditated evil."[13] By challenging the professed motives of the abolitionists, Cawthorne promoted anti-abolitionism as a way to protect the constitution. This was of prime importance for conservatives because for them the British constitution confirmed the role of the monarchy and upheld the existing social order.[14] After the French Revolution began, conservatives argued that if the constitution was successfully attacked, the fabric of society would be destroyed because social distinctions would be destroyed.[15]

Lord Abingdon voted against abolition in 1792 and 1799, seeing it as a dangerous form of Jacobinism.[16] On May 2, 1794, as the House of Lords debated whether to abolish the practice of supplying foreign territories with slaves, Abingdon discussed the impropriety of casting aside 250 years of Parliament and common law sanctioned trading and feared the destruction of Britain's colonial possessions: "And for what? Is it to obtain the votes and interest of any description of men in this country, in order to secure the seats of individual members in another house of parliament?"[17] He charged the abolitionists in the House of Lords with supporting popular issues as a way of swaying voters and patrons to achieve a House of Commons favorable to bills that they wished to see passed. The debate continues as to whether anti-slavery was a means to help the classes to which the reformers belonged.[18] Abingdon supposed that this was the real reason that modifications to the slave trade were being deemed safe and favorable by some of his peers.

A number of MPs with West Indian connections suggested that the abolitionists were hiding their true intentions behind the guise of abolishing the slave trade for humanitarian reasons. As Bryan Edwards remarked on April 3, 1798, during a discussion on allowing Wilberforce to bring in another motion for abolition:

> either that the hon. gentleman [Wilberforce] is determined that, unless the measure of abolition is carried into effect by himself only, and upon his own terms, it shall not be carried at all; or that he has some other object in view,

which he does not think proper in the present stage of the business, to openly avow. That object, Sir (as the planters suspect) is nothing less than to abolish not only the Slave trade, but the system of servitude which is established in the West Indies in consequence of it. The hon. gentleman thinks perhaps, that the planters have had the staff long enough in their own hands, and he now proposes to make them change situations with their negroes.[19]

He asserted that the abolitionists' true goal was likely to be the total emancipation of the slaves and the consequential destruction of all the power and land of the West Indian planters. Edwards charged the abolitionists with putting the interests of the slaves ahead of the safety of the colonists. He also implied that the abolitionists' true intention was so dangerous and so unpopular that it was intentionally hidden. Such ulterior motives continued to be discussed by anti-abolitionists throughout the abolition debates and were partly realized on March 17, 1807, when, immediately after achieving abolition, Hugh Percy requested leave to bring in a bill for gradual emancipation.[20] Sir Charles Pole declared that this motion was proof that the planters' suspicions had been correct: "he rejoiced that it had been brought forward thus early, because it shewed the cloven foot, which had been attempted to be concealed: he believed that this was one main object in view by the abolitionists. It was fraught with much evil, and he trusted it would open the eyes of the public, to the intentions of the promoters of those measures."[21]

The anti-abolitionists frequently attacked Wilberforce's knowledge and motivation. After the French abolished slavery throughout their empire it became easier for anti-abolitionists to connect British abolitionists with the resulting destruction that followed the implementation of French revolutionary principles. On April 3, 1798, Bryan Edwards made such a connection: "I should not have suspected the hon. gentleman [Wilberforce] was any great admirer of French politics or French principles. Perhaps he considers their proceedings in emancipating the slaves, as an exception to their general conduct. If so, I can satisfy him that he is grossly mistaken."[22] He directly linked Wilberforce's motion for abolition to the application of French revolutionary principles and activities. He also challenged Wilberforce's knowledge of actual plantation conditions:

I blush for the hon. gentleman [Wilberforce] more than for the objects of his defamation, when I hear him quote two or three solitary instances of improper treatment of the negroes in a single island, and dwell on them as a just representation of the general behaviour of the planters throughout all the West Indies.[23]

The belittling of Wilberforce's argument for abolition by one of the most famous planters in and authors on the West Indies must have inspired doubts as to Wilberforce's motivation for pushing abolition on the House year after year.

Other abolitionists in and out of Parliament faced attacks by anti-abolitionist MPs during this period. Their knowledge and motivations were questioned, as was the appropriateness of anyone getting involved in the matter who did not have a stake in the trade or first-hand knowledge of life in the West Indies. On June 12, 1804, during a debate on Wilberforce's motion for abolition, John Fuller declared:

> Those who were the most violent in their outcries against the slave trade were the haters of the West India colonies. They hated them because they were the means of bringing such a mass of opulence into the mother country. They hated that opulence, because it tended to promote the dignity of the monarchy, and to uphold the constitution, the strength, and the glory of the country.[24]

Fuller classed the abolitionists as anti-monarchy, anti-British, and anti-empire. He accused them of basing their opinions upon personal distaste for the monarchy and wealth rather than on facts and reason. This dislike for the colonies and colonists, the anti-abolitionists argued, was not enough of a reason to destroy a branch of Britain's commerce and risk their colonial possessions.

The evidence used to justify abolishing the slave trade (or lack thereof) was regularly scrutinized and challenged by anti-abolitionists during the slavery debates. On February 28, 1805, during a discussion of Wilberforce's motion for abolition, General Isaac Gascoyne commented on Wilberforce's change of strategy:

> he supposed the hon. mover [Wilberforce] to have great confidence in the measure, but that he now found himself absolutely deficient in the sources of those appeals to the feelings of the house, which he was wont to use on former occasions. He seemed to have nothing new to urge on the score of humanity and benevolence; nothing to say about the cruelty and oppression of the trade, and the inefficacy of all regulations concerning it.... Since the last regulations were passed, not a solitary instance of their violation could the hon. gent. produce.[25]

He challenged Wilberforce to bring forward evidence of any remaining faults in the current state of the slave trade. As Wilberforce had regularly introduced his motions for abolition using grave examples of death and mistreatment suffered by the African slaves,

Gascoyne was able to use the absence of these emotional examples as evidence that the trade had been sufficiently and humanely ameliorated.

Abolitionist rhetoric made great use of the term "humanity" to serve their cause and gain support both in and out of Parliament. Members of the West Indian interest in Parliament, however, were not only able to refute charges of inhumane conditions and actions on the slave ships and the plantations but were occasionally able to turn them against the abolitionists themselves. On February 28, 1805, for example, John Fuller compared his own humanity to that of Wilberforce's:

> I have given permission to my own negroes to cultivate considerable spots of ground for themselves, and ample time for this purpose. I have lodged and clothed, and have engaged a physician to attend and prescribe to them. I have done every thing for their comfort. Can the hon. gent. [Wilberforce] say that he has done so much, with all his talk and noise about humanity, for the peasantry of Yorkshire?[26]

Fuller's mocking description of Wilberforce's calls for abolition as simply "talk and noise" (all talk and no action one might say), contrasted with the actual actions he had taken to ensure the men and women in his care (possession) were looked after, made a striking comparison. No one doubted that Wilberforce was at least partly motivated by humanitarianism, but Fuller attempted to challenge his credibility by favorably comparing the state of slaves in the colonies to the lives of Wilberforce's own Yorkshire poor.

Attacks on the Abolitionists' Evidence

Anti-abolitionists employed specific facts, statistics, and anecdotes to show the importance of the slave trade to Britain's commercial and manufacturing interests as well as highlighting the improving or "reasonable" death rates for the voyages and in the plantations, as demonstrated in Chapter 1. They also declared that the abolitionists' anecdotes were falsified, exaggerated, impossible, or out-of-date and used their knowledge to prove this point. They drew comparisons between living conditions and mortality in the colonies and on the slave ships with life in Britain and on other ocean-going vessels. By attributing the emotional dependence of the abolitionists' arguments on exaggerated or falsified evidence, anti-abolitionists were able to discredit the abolitionists' stance and convince undecided

MPs that they were being given damaging, inaccurate descriptions of the state of the slave trade and the lives of the slaves in the colonies.

The dangers of the Middle Passage and the need to regulate it were questioned by anti-abolitionists during a number of debates in the 1780s and 1790s. On June 25, 1788, during a discussion in the House of Lords on a bill to limit the slave trade, the Earl of Sandwich noted:

> He had heard it declared, that the African Trade was the bane of British seamen, and that Africa was their grave. He knew, from experience, that a voyage to Africa was not less healthy than any other voyage. It was not the African climate that killed the seamen, but the spirituous liquors with which the captains of the merchant ships supplied them.[27]

He maintained that if sailors did die more frequently on ships participating in the African trade, it was the fault of alcohol and their superiors, rather than the nature of the voyage, the weather, or the ship's construction. This was a problem, therefore, that was unrelated to the trade, the merchants and traders, and the colonists. It was also an argument being presented by those without direct knowledge of the trade. He attempted to appeal to the logic of his audience by demonstrating that the passing of the bill would not solve the specific problem under consideration.

Anti-abolitionists also refuted the specific anecdotes of inhumane and unimaginable horrors advanced by abolitionists used to introduce and support bills for abolition. On April 19, 1791, during a discussion on Wilberforce's motion for abolition, John Fenton Cawthorne challenged the legitimacy of William Smith's story of a ten-month-old baby, who was flogged, killed, and thrown overboard from a slave ship heading for the West Indies:

> the story of the child, from its enormity, was impossible, and many other parts of the evidence might be refuted on the same ground. Of this there were many instances; one man said that the captains of French slave ships, when they had not a sufficient quantity of water for the number on board, preferred giving them arsenick [*sic*] to throwing them into the sea; another believed that the religion of Angola was the Roman Catholic. Did evidence so absurd deserve the least attention?[28]

The Abolition Society based many of its arguments on moral and humanitarian grounds throughout this period. Their publications were often devoted to sharing information on the inhumane treatment of slaves and the terrible conditions aboard slave ships and on the plantations. They also stressed the impolicy of the trade. Cawthorne argued that it would be foolish to believe everything the abolitionists said and published on the topic as much of their evidence appeared to be so exaggerated and outlandish that it could not be true.

On February 7, 1794, during a debate on Wilberforce's motion to stop supplying foreign territories with slaves, Alderman Nathaniel Newnham commented on the abolitionists' use of overly dramatic evidence in his defense of the colonies:

> Much had been urged of the shameless barbarities of their inhuman masters. History had been traced back for more than a century to select the records of these abominable crimes; and what had been thus diligently searched for, was aggregated and exaggerated, to serve the purposes of enthusiasm, and delude the weak and pitying multitude.[29]

He argued that the abolitionists constructed and presented these stories in such a way as to persuade the wider public to join their cause. Newnham depicted the public as the "weak and pitying multitude," presumably uninformed and uneducated, which was in direct contrast with the wise and critical MPs in Parliament whose duty it was to act according to facts and from evidence rather than on emotion and exaggerated tales. Anti-abolitionists continued to challenge the legitimacy and accuracy of the abolitionists' evidence throughout the slave trade debates. Those with firsthand knowledge of the trade and of colonial slavery were able to do so in detail.

Anti-abolitionists also defended themselves and the West Indian planters and merchants in reaction to abolitionist arguments. The personal attacks on the humanity and practices of the planters and merchants were difficult to refute without invoking a defensive tone and specific evidence to contradict the abolitionists' assertions. On March 15, 1796, during a debate on Wilberforce's motion for abolition, General Richard Smith noted: "Much abuse had been thrown out against the planters for their cruelty, &c."[30] The term "abuse" implied that the abolitionists were taking unnecessary and harmful actions against the West Indians; the abolitionists were frequently charged with this during the debates. On May 15, 1797, during a discussion of Wilberforce's request for the Commons to go into a committee to discuss abolition, Isaac Gascoyne challenged the stereotypes the abolitionists had been presenting:

> the merchants who had been stigmatized with the epithets inhuman, cruel, &c. had conducted themselves in a very different manner; for at Liverpool

a meeting had been called at which it was resolved, that no ship should be allowed to clear out, whose captain and owners had not entered into an engagement under a penalty of 1,000*l*., that they would fulfil every part of the act that had been passed for the regulation of the middle passage, even after that act had expired.[31]

He argued that the image of the West Indian merchant being advanced was false and was able to demonstrate an instance of humane self-regulation. The need for new standards, of course, implied that previously there had been a problem. With such self-regulation and enforcement being undertaken by the merchants themselves, parliamentary interference might be deemed an unnecessary or improper interference with private business activities. Following this logic, abolition was unnecessary.

Anti-abolitionists also denied the assertion that the slave trade was immoral or against God's will, as demonstrated in Chapter 1. Some abolitionists, however, promoted the view that Britain had lost the American colonies because they participated in the evil practices of trading and holding slaves. With belief in Providence being widespread, if Britain had lost her American colonies due to a failure in God's eyes, the slave trade could be considered a liability for the nation's future success.[32] Abolition was then endorsed as the principal means of atonement. Anti-abolitionists, however, highlighted the flaws in this logic. On March 16, 1807, during the third reading of the bill for abolition in the Commons, George Hibbert disproved the connection Lord Henry Petty had drawn between the slave trade and God's wrath:

The hon. member has intimated a conjecture, that the crimes attendant upon the Slave Trade in the West Indies have provoked the judgement of God, and that the hurricanes to which those climates are subject are the signals of his vengeance. Sir, there is much moral and physical evil in the world, but it is a bold and rash attempt by any mortal to impute that evil as a judgement of Providence upon the heads on which it may chance to fall.[33]

He went on to argue that, following Henry Petty's logic, Jamaica should be continuing to face an onslaught of destructive weather due to the increase in the trade, but instead she had experienced two decades of relative peace. Anti-abolitionists such as Hibbert continued to undermine the abolitionists' arguments throughout the era of abolition and were frequently able to cast doubt upon the evidence put forward in favor of abolition.

Attacks on the Abolitionists' Methods

Anti-abolitionists and supporters of the slave trade and slavery took issue with the methods abolitionists used to gain popular support for their cause. They questioned the propriety of making long speeches and presenting numerous petitions signed by thousands to both Houses of Parliament, the practice of making abolition an issue in elections, and the intentional spreading of abolitionist propaganda to the wider public through the use pamphlets, newspapers, and sermons. Anti-abolitionists did produce their own petitions and propaganda but never to the same extent. Their petitions focused on policy and concerns for the welfare of Britons, in contrast to petitions for abolition that listed humanity as the first ground for their argument.[34] They wished the issue to be kept out of the churches, elections, and the wider public's consideration. Throughout the abolition debates anti-abolitionists attacked these practices in order to discredit the abolitionists in Parliament and their supporters out-of-doors.

The number of petitions submitted to Parliament that related to national issues rose dramatically in the late eighteenth century.[35] Both abolitionists and anti-abolitionists used petitions to provide evidence of popular support for their respective sides. The abolitionists' methods of gaining signatures were challenged and even derided in the Commons during the slavery debates. On April 25, 1792, during a debate on Henry Dundas's resolutions for a gradual abolition, Lord Sheffield remarked:

> As to the petitions, they rather disinclined him to abolition . . . He knew they were not the voluntary expressions of the people, but far the greater part had been procured by associations, and he should ever condemn such attempts to control the deliberations of parliament, as he thought them highly unconstitutional.[36]

Sheffield argued that because the petitions had been organized by abolition societies, rather than being an autonomous expression of public support for the issue, they could not be trusted and might actually be illegal. Shortly after this statement, Colonel Henry Phipps commented on the specific practices abolition societies reportedly used to collect signatures:

> it was evident that gentlemen were not influenced so much by their own reason, as by the petitions on the table; petitions, which he would not hesitate to call ridiculous and contemptible . . . . many knew not what they signed, nor were they capable of judging in a case of so much importance. Many of them

> were poor ignorant people; many others were just school-boys, and almost all deluded by persons who went about in search of signatures, and put these questions to the people: as freemen can you be friends to slavery? As christians [*sic*], can you wish to tolerate murder? As Englishmen, must you not wish for the abolition of a trade which is attended with both?[37]

The exact language used in petitions was important in the late eighteenth century as politicians attempted to decide who was worthy of influencing decisions taken in Parliament.[38] Petitions calling for universal suffrage were regularly thrown out because of their informal language. This may have been an intentional method of preventing commoners from having an influence on Parliament.[39] It is interesting to note that Wilberforce was one of many objectors to the "disrespectful language" contained within petitions for extending the franchise.[40] Here Phipps was concerned that the petitions were making too great an impact on the undecided members of the House. He wished to remind members of the emotionally charged, potentially misleading language abolitionists used to procure signatures, as well as the uninformed, uneducated, and possibly underage individuals whose signatures were now playing a role in the debate. Both men argued that, instead of demonstrating the true wishes of the people, the petitions actually exposed the underhand methods that abolitionists employed to gain support for their cause.

The issue of the appropriateness of petitioning was frequently questioned during this period. Anti-abolitionists challenged the legality of the anti-slavery and anti-slave trade petitions presented to Parliament. On April 11, 1793, during a discussion on abolition in the House of Lords, the Earl of Abingdon noted:

> the ground of every petition to the king, or to either House of parliament (legal ground I mean) is and can only be for two causes—either against the infringement of a constitutional right by the legislature, or by any branch of it; or, that right being so infringed, for a redress of grievances .... let us see whether the petitions that have been and may be again presented, for the abolition of the slave trade, are founded upon the infringement of any of those rights; and if not, whether they are not consequently illegal?[41]

Abingdon argued that because the issue was not related to any infringement of a constitutional right it was not an issue on which Parliament or the monarchy could be petitioned. The petitions brought forward by the abolitionists, he argued, should be deemed unconstitutional and those that had been laid on the table should not have been accepted. He stated that the abolitionists were acting improperly if not illegally by seeking and demonstrating this type of support for their cause.

Anti-abolitionists also objected to the nature of the abolitionists' speeches in Parliament during the slavery debates. On April 27, 1792, as debate continued on Henry Dundas's resolutions, Lord Carhampton first commented on the abuse being hurled at West Indian merchants and planters in Britain and in the colonies, before questioning the abolitionists' notions of humanity:

> Gentlemen might talk of inhumanity, but did he not know what right any one had to do so inhumane a thing, as to inflict a speech of four hours long on a set of innocent, worthy, and respectable men. Gentlemen had continued this abuse day after day, both in their long and short speeches, some of which would have been equally proper for a House of Commons, a pulpit, or a conventicle. If there had not been a back door behind the Speaker's chair for infirm gentlemen to escape, he did believe, they would have died on the spot.[42]

His somewhat sarcastic description of inhumanity challenged the supposedly humanitarian actions of some abolitionists by pointing to the negative impact of the slave trade debates on the politicians.

Abolitionists (Wilberforce in particular) introduced bills for abolition with speeches that could last up to several hours and the resulting debates could continue until three or four in the morning. In 1796 these practices were used against the abolitionists to defend Parliament's decision to reverse their May 1792 decision to abolish slavery. On February 26, Edward Hyde East recalled the specific circumstances of their 1792 vote:

> it had been passed at a very late hour of the night, after the original motion had been negatived by a great majority, and after several other intermediate motions for a speedier abolition had also been negatived. Several gentlemen had also given their vote for that resolution from a sort of implied compact, that by doing so, they should avoid the mischief of having so dangerous a question agitated in the interval; and therefore chose the less of two evils. Instead of fulfilling this engagement, he [Wilberforce] had brought forward the question every session since that period.[43]

He was able to show that the nature of the debate, its late hour, and the "implied compact" had affected its outcome. East argued that it had been unfair to ask men to make such an important decision while deprived of sleep and confronted with many different motions. He stated that sense had since prevailed and, in the current climate of war, unrest, and financial strain, the House had decided it would be unwise to uphold its prior decision. He also pointed to Wilberforce's continual motions regarding the slave trade as possible contributors to unrest in the colonies. Parliament was concerned about the growing number of newspaper reports on parliamentary proceedings. Members were afraid that their speeches, while acceptable within the Houses of Parliament, might be interpreted as seditious or dangerous by the lower classes that were outside the political arena. These fears could be extended to include slaves in the West Indies who were able to get news from English newspapers and by word of mouth.[44] The rhetoric contained within newspaper reports was also affected by each newspaper's rhetorical practices and political beliefs; this could lead to further confusion and misrepresentation.[45] In this case Parliament chose not to uphold its decision and, much to the anti-abolitionists' satisfaction, abolition would take another decade to be enacted.

Abolitionists frequently used descriptions of the terrible conditions and unimaginable hardships experienced by slaves to introduce and support their bills for abolition. Anti-abolitionists attacked these appeals to the passions of the Houses and called on the abolitionists to speak openly about the probable outcomes and practical solutions needed to enact and enforce abolition. As the Earl of Westmorland noted on July 5, 1799:

> It has been the practice upon this occasion to endeavour to work upon your lordships passions, by animated descriptions of the miseries of the slave trade and slavery, paying no great respect to your lordships—by insinuating that such pictures were necessary to rouse your feelings. But, in my judgement, the time would have been better spent if it had been employed in showing in what manner the bill before us would tend to remedy any one of the enormities complained of.[46]

He argued that by relying on this method of appealing to the emotions of the peers the abolitionists were actually insulting their intelligence and underestimating their level of understanding. His statement also implied that the bill would be unable to achieve its stated goals, hence the abolitionists' unwillingness to expand upon the likely outcomes of the measure.

Anti-abolitionists also charged the abolitionists with inappropriate timing. After France declared war on Britain on February 1, 1793, anti-abolitionists and abolitionists alike commented on the dangers of discussing such an emotionally charged topic as abolition when the country was engaged in defending its colonies and trying to preserve its vital trade routes. On February 26, 1793, during a discussion of Wilberforce's request to address abolition, Sir William Young suggested that the issue should be postponed:

> Men's minds, both at home and in the West-Indies, were at this moment too much heated for sober and cool deliberation. In England, and in that House, many exaggerated accounts had been given of the situation and treatment of the negroes... by these accounts the passions of the House had been excited against the dictates of judgment and sound policy.[47]

Young argued that the current state of war, in combination with the exaggerated accounts of ill treatment of the slaves aboard their ships and on their colonial plantations, would impact on the House's judgment. Lord Harrowby expressed a similar concern about the timing of an abolition bill in July of 1804, but his focus was the point in the session in which they found themselves discussing it:

> he was apprehensive it had been introduced too late in the session, to afford reasonable expectation that it could be passed before the rising of parliament. He thought some blame was imputable to those who introduced it, for having delayed it to so advanced a period of the session. He did not see how it could be pressed through the house, keeping in view that rigid impartiality which it was the duty and the practice of their lordships to observe, whenever the fortunes of individuals were concerned.[48]

Harrowby was concerned that the Lords could not give the bill the time it required when it dealt with complex issues of property and wealth. He stressed the need for "impartiality" and time to calmly reflect upon the matter. This need for cool-headed thinking was frequently stressed by anti-abolitionists in opposition to the emotionally driven arguments of the abolitionist lobby in Parliament. Harrowby blamed Wilberforce for bringing in his bill for abolition at such a late date and forcing the lords either to postpone the matter or to abandon the bill. Earl St. Vincent shared this view: "To pass such a measure as the present hastily, might, he said, eventually lead to consequences equally dreadful with those which had taken place in St. Domingo, and even to the extirpation of every white in the West India islands."[49] He employed images of revolution and destruction to stress the need for lengthy discussion and deliberation on a bill of such importance; this could not be accomplished at this late stage in the session. The bill was consequently lost.

On April 25, 1806, during a discussion of a bill to prevent Britons from importing slaves into newly conquered territories in the

West Indies, Banastre Tarleton challenged Wilberforce to declare his intentions to bring in a motion for abolition in the current session: "Ever since he had a seat in parliament, we had an annual debate on the subject, and as the measure could not be carried in its general form, they were now coming by a sidewind on the planters."[50] He accused the abolitionists of using an underhand method to attack the livelihoods of the planters. He argued that the bill under consideration was actually an attempt to enact abolition in the colonies because there was no other reason for Wilberforce to have refrained from bringing in his annual motion for abolition.

Anti-abolitionists in Parliament also attacked the methods abolitionists used to influence voters and elections. On February 18, 1796, during a debate on Wilberforce's motion for abolition, Sir William Young lamented the "solicitations and undue influence that had been used to make a bad impression on the minds of gentlemen":

> It had been custom to send a circular letter to the patrons of boroughs, to try to prejudice their minds, against the slave trade; and to corporations . . . to instruct their members to vote for abolition. To counties and places where election was more general and in the hands of many, this circular was sent to leading characters, to influence the multitude, and induce them to petition against the trade.[51]

He argued that abolitionists were intentionally influencing rotten boroughs and the uneducated public to promote their cause. By directly encouraging the wider public to petition Parliament for abolition, he argued, they were underhandedly influencing political debates and MPs' opinions. Isaac Gascoyne shared these concerns. On February 10, 1807, as the Commons debated the bill for abolition, he complained:

> The attempts to make a popular clamour against this trade were never so conspicuous as during the late Election, when the public newspapers teemed with abuse of this trade, and when promises were required from the different candidates that they would oppose its continuance. There never had been any question agitated since that of parliamentary reform, in which so much industry had been exerted to raise a popular prejudice and clamour, and to make the trade an object of universal detestation.[52]

He highlighted the abolitionists' unfair requirement that politicians state their stance on the topic, the abuse and slander thrown at the planters to discredit their position and evidence, and the sheer amount of work and energy put into raising support for abolition and into demonizing the African trade. Gascoyne's remarks emphasized how much work abolitionists had to perform in order to gain support for their cause. He suggested that this was perhaps a sign that, rather than being an obvious logical decision, Britons needed some convincing to take up the abolitionist cause.

Attacks on the Abolitionists' Logic

The logic and reasoning behind the call for abolition was charged with containing fatal flaws by anti-abolitionists throughout the debates. Anti-abolitionists challenged the legal basis for the bills, the absurdity of the abolitionists' accusations and evidence, and Britain's inability to enforce abolition. In contrast to the abolitionists, who focused on humanitarian aims, anti-abolitionists emphasized the likely outcomes of abolition in order to discredit abolitionist logic: they foresaw economic losses, weakened national defenses, and great benefits for other trading nations to their own detriment.[53] They also attacked the supposed benefits for Africa that the bills were intended to produce. The anti-abolitionists were able to attack the logic behind abolition in a variety of ways; this helped them postpone abolition and defeat several abolition bills.

A number of anti-abolitionists emphasized the absurdity of the abolitionists' logic and evidence. On May 26, 1788, during a debate on William Dolben's slave-limiting bill, Lord Penrhyn remarked: "It was absurd to suppose that men, whose profit depended on the health and vigour of the African natives, would purposely torment and distress them during their passage, so as to endanger their lives."[54] Penrhyn's argument, that the Middle Passage was not intentionally difficult or dangerous for the slaves, was deployed to oppose the need for further shipping regulations. He reasoned that no one would intend a voyage to be particularly challenging or deadly for a ship's occupants. He also argued that the very nature of the master–slave relationship ensured that slave owners would want to take care of their slaves as their livelihoods directly depended on them remaining healthy.[55] The way in which Penrhyn phrased this defense, however, attacked the reasoning behind the abolitionist argument and claims that the Middle Passage was particularly difficult or inhumane. On April 19, 1791, during a debate on Wilberforce's bill for abolition, John Stanley also argued that it was in the best interest of the planters to care for their slaves.[56] This reflects the widely held belief that by holding property men would take an interest in their workers' welfare and in their communities, providing relief and necessities as needed.[57] Anti-abolitionists argued that slave owners were passing on this paternalism in the West Indies.

The absurd nature of the abolitionists' logic was also emphasized by Henry Dundas on March 15, 1796: "it was absurd to talk of a wish to serve the cause of humanity, by throwing the trade into the hands of those who would not carry it on with so much mildness as we did."[58] Not only did Dundas call the assumptions of the abolitionists "absurd," but he advanced the claim that a likely outcome of abolition was that enslaved Africans would face greater hardships on the increased number of foreign trading vessels which would undoubtedly step in to replace Britain's role in the trade. Both Penrhyn and Dundas focused on the innate paternalist nature of Britain's West Indian colonists and plantation owners, the master–slave relationship, and the shipping regulations already in place to weaken the abolitionists' accusations and challenge the likelihood that abolition and additional trading and shipping regulations would benefit the slaves.

Anti-abolitionists argued that West Indian planters, as members of the landed class, shared the governing class's paternalist beliefs that society was naturally hierarchical. Wealthier men (such as the planters) were required to care for and guide the poorer classes (such as their slaves) and the poor were bound to serve the rich for their own advantage.[59] Paternalists promoted the idea that workers should be treated fairly, with respect, and with kindness; not all paternalists, however, believed that workers should be considered as equals.[60] As John Stanley emphasized on April 19, 1791:

> If slavery was abolished, the negroes would suppose themselves on a footing with their masters, and then an end would be put to all order, management and safety. If the measure was carried into execution, he thought we might as well give up our colonies and islands entirely in the same moment.[61]

In order to undermine the abolitionists' position, he questioned the logic of modifying existing institutions that encouraged stability in the colonies. Stanley argued that abolition would endanger the colonies and damage the empire. Although emancipation was not the main issue under discussion, Stanley and others believed that this was the abolitionists' true goal. They advanced these suspicions in the debates.

Anti-abolitionists emphasized wider-reaching effects of abolition to demonstrate the great number of negative consequences it would have on the country and the colonies and to refute the abolitionists' claims about its benefits. On April 2, 1792, James Baillie presented a question to the House:

> how could compensation be made to the many thousand manufacturers, who at present find employment in providing the numberless articles that are daily wanted for use and consumption in the West India islands, and who must sooner or later experience the distress that will result from the present phrenzy, if the colonies should be suffered to go to ruin?[62]

He implied that the abolitionists were not providing them with sufficient information and were promoting a misleading image of abolition that emphasized its benefits for enslaved Africans instead of the hardships for their own colonists. The term "present phrenzy" showed his distaste for abolition's popular support and also implied a belief that the support might be fleeting.

General Richard Smith stressed the House's duty to care for the West Indian interest as well as for the African people. On March 15, 1796, during a debate on Wilberforce's bill for abolition, he noted:

> It had been said, that the continuation of the slave trade was contrary to justice and humanity; so was the act of pressing seamen; but if he attempted to abolish it, it would be defended upon the plea of necessity. Upon the same plea, then, he opposed the abolition of the slave trade. He wished to have justice and humanity shown towards the proprietors of lands in the West Indies, and to persons interested in the prosperity and cultivation of those lands in our own country, as well as to the negroes on the coast of Africa.[63]

His statement contained two important points that contradicted the logic of abolition. The first was that other practices, such as impressing seamen, were condoned and upheld by Parliament yet might also be considered "contrary to justice and humanity"; these principles on their own were therefore not enough to abolish long-standing, necessary practices. His second point was that abolition would not promote the cause of humanity because it would benefit only one group of people while injuring several others. The underlying logic of abolition was therefore flawed. On March 1, 1799, during a discussion on whether Wilberforce could bring in a bill for abolition, Isaac Gascoyne also used the analogy of impressing seamen to demonstrate that unjust or inhumane practices sometimes needed to be continued.[64] As Tarleton remarked on May 30, 1804, during a discussion on Wilberforce's motion for abolition: "Evils were to be met with in every direction; war was an evil of the greatest kind, and yet we were obliged to endure it. Many things were tolerated which could not be justified on strict principle."[65]

The legality of abolition was also challenged in Parliament.[66] Some MPs stressed that the British government could not prescribe to the colonists or the colonial legislatures whether plantation labor should be free or enslaved. On May 12, 1789, during a debate on Wilberforce's resolutions, George Dempster remarked: "The House might, if it pleased, prevent any British subjects from becoming slaves, but they could not, with any pretence of right, prescribe to the gentlemen of the West Indies by what hands their plantations should be cultivated."[67] He argued that abolition would be an unjustified and unenforceable interference in the private practices of plantations in the colonies (including on the plantation owned by his father-in-law) because of the jurisdictional limits of the House's authority and the rights of the colonists. On May 2, 1794, during a debate on supplying foreign colonies with slaves, Lord Abingdon argued that abolition would directly violate the right to private property.[68] This was a very important point to consider, as conservatives believed the defense of private property was the legislature's most important task. This right was considered so important that even civil governments could not violate it for the greater good.[69] Slave merchants and planters were able to use this argument to appeal to their fellow property owners for protection and depicted abolition as the first in what would be a dangerous chain of events leading to Britain's downfall.[70] On March 15, 1796, George Rose challenged Britain's right to interfere with the trading practices, and therefore the property, of other nations:

> If a Dane or a Swede, for instance, chose to carry on this trade, his ship and cargo were by the provision subjected to confiscation, and he himself to the punishment of transportation, inflicted on him be an English jury, and an English judge. Would not a measure of this kind be an unjustifiable interference with the legislature of other powers, and expose us to difficulties, and even war with neutral nations?[71]

He argued that it would be unjust to confiscate the property of foreigners and subject them to trial and punishment according to British laws. This meant that Britain could not stop the transatlantic slave trade. He also foresaw the danger of retribution that could result from such attempts. By advancing various legal reasons to support their position, anti-abolitionists were able to attack the logic of the bill and cast doubt on its legality and effectiveness.

Finally, anti-abolitionists used the intra-Africa slave trade to challenge the notion that abolition would make a difference to the African people. On June 27, 1804, during a discussion of Wilberforce's motion for abolition, Rose noted:

Many of these slaves were brought by the dealers from a great distance in the interior parts of Africa. Did the hon. gent. who supported this bill suppose that the slave dealers or merchants in that country would march these poor creatures back to the different places where they were born, or had been brought, and deliver them again to their parents or relatives?[72]

He argued that it would be impossible to return to their respective homelands the men, women, and children who had already been taken to the coast. His depiction of this sad group marching all over the continent trying to find the slaves' families was both ridiculous and disheartening. He certainly cast doubt on the logic of the abolitionists' demand for an immediate end to the transatlantic trade in slaves. Sir William Young also questioned the logic of leaving men and women who were already slaves at the mercy of their African masters during this debate.[73] He disagreed with the abolitionists' position that abolition would serve the cause of humanity and that this humanity would stretch to Africa. His use of vivid images and examples of barbaric practices in Africa countered the abolitionists' common practice of telling stories of abuse on the plantations to support their bills for abolition. He argued that, overall, abolition would in fact prevent West Indians from saving the slaves from a worse fate and thus defeat its supposed humanitarian goals.

Attacks on Abolitionist Ideology

Anti-abolitionist MPs were quick to attack abolitionist rhetoric that focused on abstract principles such as liberty, equality, and humanity. In the era of the French Revolution they were able to link calls for liberty and equality with the dangerous uprisings and revolts in France and the West Indies. War with revolutionary France and Napoleon was different to earlier conflicts, in part, because it was based on ideological differences.[74] The link between abolition and revolution was made clearer after February 1794 when France abolished the slave trade and slavery in her own West Indian colonies. Some MPs argued that small concessions such as abolition would be the first step toward revolution.[75] They also argued that the abolitionists' humanity was misplaced: other groups needed their attention more than those slaves who were already in the hands and supposedly under the protection of British masters. Overall, anti-abolitionists argued that the ideology upon which abolitionism was based was dangerous to Britain and her colonists: it had the power to destroy a profitable trade, destabilize life in Britain and in the colonies, and threaten their very systems of government. The British people had to look only across the channel for proof.

Anti-abolitionists attacked the abolitionists' narrow view of humanitarianism during the slave trade debates. On February 4, 1791, during a discussion of Wilberforce's request to address the slave trade, Banastre Tarleton remarked:

> If gentlemen were anxious to exercise their philanthropy, there were a variety of other objects to display it upon. He should suppose the poor laws would afford them sufficient scope for their humanity; or the state of our infant settlement in [New] South Wales. He was as warm an admirer of humanity, and its benign influence, as any man, but he thought that gentlemen might better apply their beneficence.[76]

He noted that there were many pressing humanitarian projects affecting Britons at home and abroad that were equally (if not more) deserving of their efforts and concern and argued that the abolitionists' humanity was selective. On July 3, 1804, during a debate on abolition, the lord chancellor, the Earl of Eldon, commented on the dangers of the House passing bills on the basis of their humanitarian objectives:

> It might be a very snug thing for a Chancellor, seated on the woolsack, a right rev. prelate, seated there in virtue of a wealthy diocese, or a noble earl with a great estate, to sit and indulge their benevolence and humanity, in voting for a bill of this kind, for the relief of one description of persons; but all he would ask of right rev. and noble lords, was, to exercise their benevolence and humanity upon universal, not partial principles, and not to indulge their zeal for promoting the comforts of one set of men at the expence [*sic*] and total ruin to other classes, equally entitled to consideration and to justice.[77]

He urged his fellow peers to think about the consequences of the proposed bill for all those involved, instead of just the oppressed slaves on whom the abolitionists were focusing. Rather than attacking the bill as being based on abstract principles, Eldon emphasized that as it stood the bill would only benefit one group while injuring others who were equally entitled to their care and consideration. His use of the term "zeal" reiterated the anti-abolitionists' argument that popular pressure was not a sufficient reason to pass such a bill. He argued that the selfish thing to do would be to go along with the supposed humanity of the bill; they must not be pressured by outside influences or tempted to take the easy and popular route that led to abolition.

French patriotic rhetoric was often universalist, appealing to universal natural rights and liberty, in contrast to the historic focus of Britain's patriotic rhetoric that emphasized the need to protect traditional English values and British liberty.[78] Anti-abolitionists in Parliament frequently highlighted the dangers of acting on abstract principles and allowing popular pressure to affect parliamentary decisions. MPs increasingly feared mass revolts in the colonies because the abstract concepts of liberty, equality, and fraternity had much more obvious significance for slaves in the West Indies than for free men at home.[79] In this spirit, on April 11, 1793, during a debate on abolition in the House of Lords, the Earl of Abingdon commented: "your lordships are aware of that new philosophy on the principles of which these monsters in human shape, this savage nation, have declared war, not only against man, but against God himself."[80] He then proceeded to ask the House, if it agreed that abolition was founded on these principles, whether it would not be more appropriate for members to postpone the matter to a time when "mankind may be restored to their senses, and this enthusiastic madness no longer shall remain."[81] Abingdon stated that passing a bill for abolition would mean acting on the same dangerous revolutionary principles that had caused mass upheaval and destruction in France. He then reiterated the connection he had made between abolition and revolutionary ideology:

> For in the very definition of the terms themselves, as descriptive of the thing, what does the abolition of the slave trade mean more or less in effect, than liberty and equality? what more or less than the rights of man? and what is liberty and equality, but the foolish fundamental principles of this new philosophy?[82]

Anti-abolitionists were able to use the enthusiastic embrace of these abstract principles to discredit the abolitionists' arguments and the philosophical basis underlying their cause.

Abingdon made a further connection between the application of the principles of liberty and equality and the internal upheaval that France now faced:

> I have said, not only that this proposition is founded on this new philosophy in speculation, but that it has, on its very principles, been reduced to practice; and of this neither are the damning proofs deficient: for, look at the state of the colony of St. Domingo, and see what liberty and equality, see what the rights of man, have done there.[83]

St. Domingo became a common illustration of the destruction that followed the embracing of revolutionary principles.[84] Its descent from a profitable colony envied by all Western powers to that of an island revolting against French control, claiming freedom for its slaves, and leaving the relatively small white population dead, shocked Britain. Anti-abolitionists argued that the principles of liberty and equality had caused the men and women of St. Domingo to revolt on an unprecedented scale. These radical principles would therefore have to be considered as equally dangerous to Britain's West Indian possessions.

Anti-abolitionists also alluded to the overthrow of the French monarchy and other established institutions to demonstrate the dangerous nature of the abolitionists' ideology. On March 15, 1796, during the second reading of Wilberforce's motion for abolition, General Richard Smith asked for the ninth act of Queen Anne to be read aloud to compare the actions of Parliament in 1709–10 to that day's deliberations. He argued that, although the trade might have violated the principles of justice and humanity nearly 100 years earlier, Parliament had still found the policy of the measure reasonable:

> He admitted the preamble of the bill to be true, but then it was true one hundred years ago as well as at this time; and yet the parliament at that time gave preference to the policy of the measure, and by that means encouraged our trade, our commerce, and our shipping. We were grown wiser than our ancestors, and now we said that they were wrong in the principle upon which they acted, although we felt the good effects of their proceedings; for who would presume to say, that it was not owing to the wise regulations he had just referred to, that our commerce was at present so extended?[85]

This argument reflected a widely held belief that the current law came from ancient English custom and, as a result, Parliament should only clarify and confirm existing laws.[86] Matthew Montagu, however, challenged Smith's logic: "Montagu considered it as no argument in favour of this trade to say, that it was permitted or encouraged by our ancestors; for if they were wrong, it was no reason why we should persist in this error. The antiquity of a bad system was no justification of its continuance."[87] Henry Dundas defended Smith's comments on the long life of the British slave trade:

> Ought we, in justice to the memory of our ancestors, to testify so much eagerness to throw upon them the stigma, of having so long encouraged a trade of inhumanity and justice? . . . certainly, the long duration of any system, was an argument why it should not be abruptly exploded.[88]

The use of the word "exploded" strengthened the anti-abolitionist position that abolition was dangerous and revolutionary, not to mention an irreversible act. Dundas objected to the abolitionists' opinion that, because the slave trade had existed for so long, it ought to be abolished. George Rose concurred using a pro-colonial argument:

> Positive acts of parliament in favour of the slave trade, which decidedly pronounced, that without this trade our colonies could not exist, were to be found in our statute books. He was therefore against its being abolished abruptly, violently, or unseasonably, and without giving a fair trial to other modes by which the same object might be accomplished with equal effect, and infinitely less danger.[89]

Like Dundas, Rose incorporated the language of abrupt change, danger, and violence into his argument to warn the House against enacting rash measures to the detriment of their colonies. In the context of the French Revolution anti-abolitionists could credibly argue that the hasty overthrowing of traditional institutions could have dangerous and unpredictable consequences. Edmund Burke had warned of these dangers in his *Reflections on the Revolution in France* (1790), in which he stressed the need to secure property, respect social status, and maintain a stable government; all of these had been overthrown by the French revolution and were threatened by abolition.[90] In contrast, a key point of Thomas Paine's *Rights of Man* (1791) was that historical precedents should not hinder the rights of the living.[91] Conservative propagandists emphasized the difference between France's revolutionary order, based on abstract principles and speculation, and Britain's relatively stable political and social order that was the result of history, experience, and common sense.[92] Anti-abolitionists were able to use Burke's warnings and the destruction that followed the revolution in France as further evidence of the dangers of abolition. The bill was subsequently lost.

The conservative reaction to the French Revolution greatly hampered not only abolition, but the entire reform movement.[93] Fears of Jacobinism in Britain led to the suspension of habeas corpus, the shutting down of radical presses, and an increase in popular loyalism. Loyalists viewed British Jacobins as "traitors and potential insurrectionists."[94] Reformers of all kinds were labeled Jacobins and humanitarians were viewed as enemies of the state.[95] William Pitt and his followers rejected anything French or Jacobin-inspired in the late 1790s and the fear remained during the peace of 1802–3.[96] These fears were exploited by anti-abolitionists who portrayed themselves as expressing their loyalty to the British crown by seeking to oppose abolition.

On February 28, 1805, during a debate on Wilberforce's motion for abolition, Banastre Tarleton remarked:

> This measure, sir, is certainly founded on the opinions respecting the rights of man, which have produced such horror and devastation all over the world. It is a remnant of Jacobinism. I am sure that the hon. gent. who urges it [Wilberforce], is not in his heart a Jacobin, but still the effect of his conduct is the same as if he were one.[97]

While being careful not to label Wilberforce an outright Jacobin, he depicted abolitionism as a measure that was greatly influenced by Jacobinism and one in possession of the same power to inflict devastation on the British as Jacobin-inspired principles had achieved in France. The political demands of the poor were feared by Britain's upper classes in the wake of the French Revolution.[98] It was the slaves in the West Indies who were perhaps the most feared because of their great numbers, strength, supposed savagery, and lack of education.

By tying abolition to such abstract principles as liberty and equality in a pejorative manner, anti-abolitionists were able to demonstrate that abolition would set a dangerous precedent. On February 5, 1807, during a debate on Lord Grenville's motion for abolition, the Earl of Westmorland noted: "if such a system were acted upon, no property could be reckoned safe which could fall within the power of the legislature; upon such a principle as this the tithes of the clergy, and the very freehold estates of the landholders might be sacrifices to field-preaching and popular declamation."[99] He argued that abolition threatened the fundamental right to possess private property. Once abolition was passed, therefore, any other kind of private property might plausibly be threatened by public pressure. On February 23, 1807, when the Commons debated the bill for abolition, George Hibbert questioned the consequences of basing their decisions on the principle of humanity.[100] He doubted that the House was willing to suppress the selling of alcohol or the lotteries and as such they should not be passing any bill based on the same abstract principle. Anti-abolitionists such as the Earl of Westmorland and Hibbert were able to argue that abolition, a measure based on abstract principles, would set a dangerous precedent which would threaten the rights of individuals and their businesses while encouraging the masses to continue pressuring Parliament.

Anti-abolitionists were able to tie abolition to the abstract principles that were firmly entrenched in French revolutionary ideology. The strong arguments for reform in the 1780s mostly disappeared in the 1790s and significant reforms came to be seen as unnecessary.[101] The revolution boosted popular conservatism and encouraged Britons to preserve their existing political and social order. This growing sentiment allowed anti-abolitionists to attack the propriety of the timing of the bills, their ideological basis, the character and true intentions of the abolitionists, and the likelihood of a positive outcome. After making these connections they then reminded their fellow MPs and peers to focus on the legal basis of the bills and the potential disasters that could result from passing them. As William Windham observed on March 16, 1807, during the final debate in the Commons on the abolition bill: "on such a question, the house ought not to go upon abstract principles of right, but upon the consequences of the measure, and of the possible ruin of the British empire resulting from it."[102] The anti-abolitionists found ample support for their arguments in the dangerous consequences of the French revolution and were able to advance these comparisons very successfully in order to attack abolitionist ideology, show support for the colonies, and prevent abolition from being secured in the 1790s.

Prior to 1807, anti-abolitionists stood on firm ground from which they were able to attack numerous aspects of abolition. They charged abolitionist MPs with intentionally misleading the public and their fellow politicians. They accused them of using underhand strategies to gain and demonstrate support for abolition and to push through reforms in Parliament. They dissected abolitionist arguments to show they relied upon speculation, dangerous revolutionary ideology, out-of-date information on the colonies and the trade, and persuasive sentimental language. Their confrontational, proslavery language helped defend the West Indian position on maintaining the institution of slavery and Britain's participation in the slave trade during periods of growing and waning support for abolition in the 1780s and 1790s. During war with France, however, abolitionists were able to convince Parliament that the logical route to preventing their enemies from prospering from Britain's participation in the trade and gaining the moral upper hand was to abolish their participation in the slave trade in 1807. This decision would have a lasting impact on the West Indian interest, both in and outside of Parliament. Slavery's supporters would soon find themselves relying on legal defenses, defending their property and themselves, and publicly denouncing the institution of slavery as they worked to retain their use of slave labor in the colonies.

Chapter 5

Proslavery Politics after Abolition

In 1823, the Houses of Parliament channeled popular anti-slavery sentiment into a number of proposed plans for amelioration (both as a means of eventually achieving emancipation and as an individual goal). On May 15, William Wilberforce spoke to the Commons following the presentation of two plans for amelioration. Charles Rose Ellis then rose to speak "on behalf of the planters of the West Indies, and as one of that body" but clarified that he should not be seen as a "champion of slavery":

> As a West-India planter, I do not hold myself in any degree responsible for the establishment of the system. The planters of the present generation, most of them at least, found themselves, by inheritance, or by other accidental causes, in possession of property the fruit of the industry of their ancestors or other predecessors, and of capital vested in the West Indies by them, under the sanction of the government and of the parliament of this country, through their encouragement and in reliance on their good faith.[1]

Even in the act of defending slaveholding while self-identifying as a planter, Ellis felt the need to stress that he was not a supporter of slavery. James Wilson shared a similar viewpoint with the Commons on March 6, 1828:

> He had laboured as much as any man for what he possessed; and though he did happen to be one of the masters of that portion of his Majesty's subjects who had dark complexions—although he was one of those unfortunate masters—he had always been disposed to act by them conscientiously.[2]

Ellis, Wilson, and their fellow MPs were able to utilize a number of proslavery arguments (including paternalism, historical precedent, the legality of slaveholding, and the universal detestation of slavery) and combine them with examples of personal experience in their attempts to create persuasive defenses of the colonies. They solicited sympathy for the position that they, as planters, found themselves in as a result of the British government's historic encouragement of slaveholding and the slave trade. This chapter will explore how specific rhetorical strategies were utilized to defend the West Indian colonies and the practice of slaveholding under the British flag.

After the abolition of the slave trade, proslavery language all but disappeared from the parliamentary debates on slavery outside of early discussions of Britain's rivals benefiting from continuing the trade and the advantages of plantation life for the slaves. The West Indian interest also used less provocative language as it began to agree openly to amelioration in return for maintaining the institution of slavery and gaining favorable concessions as the blueprint for emancipation took shape in 1832–3. Passionate, angry language was confined to defending planters against charges of inhumanity, warning against impending insurrections, and expressing frustration with their inability to convince fellow MPs of the "true" state of plantation life in the colonies. This was a significant shift in the nature and language of proslavery arguments from the debates prior to the abolition of the slave trade.

The West Indian lobby's credibility came under regular attack after the abolition of the slave trade, forcing the planters and colonial representatives to defend their positions and insist on their humanity. The West Indians' credibility was challenged when the mass insurrections and bloodshed they had predicted failed to occur. For example, James Stephen verbally attacked Joseph Marryat the elder and the West Indian interest in the House of Commons on June 15, 1810, because cities had not been destroyed in the aftermath of abolition.[3] The West Indian interest in Parliament, in contrast, halted their attacks on abolitionist MPs and their ideology. Instead, they spent much time defending its members, their businesses, the colonies, and their property. Members of the West Indian interest in Parliament continued to show their support for the colonies by reminding the Houses of Parliament of the planters' humanity and personal struggles. These concentrated efforts resulted in them receiving an unprecedented amount of compensation in the 1830s.

A sense of frustration with the constant attacks from abolitionists and the public's disapproval and growing influence on parliamentary proceedings is evident in their chosen language. The increased use of the term "absurd" reflects this growing frustration and their desire to reassert Parliament's authority over popular opinion. For example, on May 24, 1832, during a discussion of petitions asking for relief for the West Indians, Charles Weatherell remarked, "With all due deference to the abolitionist party—to the piety or saintship of one class, the eloquence of another and the eagerness of a third—it was his opinion that the idea of the immediate emancipation of the slave-population of the West-India colonies was an absurdity."[4] On June 25, 1833, Lord Ellenborough echoed Weatherell's word choice during a debate over compensation for West Indian planters: "But the measure [for emancipation] was thrust upon his Majesty's Government by the people of England. Were his Majesty's Government afraid of the House of Commons? If so it was an absurd fear."[5] At the same time as these discussions were being held, West Indian colonists were agreeing to numerous resolutions for ameliorating conditions in the West Indies in an effort to postpone the more drastic decision to emancipate all slaves. These strategies required the adoption of a defensive and conciliatory tone. Thus their direct attacks on the abolition movement practically ceased in Parliament after the abolition of the slave trade. In contrast, their rhetoric remained heated and argumentative in print as reflected in Chapter 2.

There were certainly exceptions to the defensive, reactive tone adopted throughout these decades. Prior to abolition, the anti-abolitionists had intentionally focused on the futility of Britain alone abolishing the slave trade.[6] The foreign trade in slaves did increase following 1807, as did the profits of Britain's rival trading nations in Europe.[7] Planters could now demonstrate to both Houses of Parliament that their predictions that the slave trade of foreign competitors would continue had unfortunately come true. As the anti-slavery lobby produced petitions of greater length and in unprecedented numbers from across the country, anti-abolitionists challenged their legitimacy and the methods used to gather the tens of thousands of signatures of men and women who had never witnessed colonial slavery nor realized slave labor's continuing contribution to Britain's economy and manufacturing. As the above quotation from Lord Ellenborough demonstrates, anti-abolitionists were able to question the government's decision-making and strength by highlighting its willingness to bow before public opinion and defer to the mood of the Commons rather than follow legal precedent or logic.

One of the greatest difficulties anti-abolitionists faced in Parliament was how to prove the success of amelioration in the colonies.

Few abolitionists had witnessed nineteenth-century colonial slavery for themselves. Planters exploited this weakness by highlighting their own personal knowledge and challenging the legitimacy of the abolitionists' claims and the evidence used to support these claims.[8] The West Indian interest, in turn, was regularly charged with bias and self-interest and its testimony was classed as tainted and untrustworthy in Parliament. When several colonial assemblies refused to submit to various elements of the 1823 resolutions for amelioration and the controversial 1831 Orders in Council, colonists and anti-abolitionists in Parliament found themselves facing severe criticism and an increase in the number of calls for immediate emancipation. MPs who supported abolition were able to argue that the interests of humanity and justice would compel the British government to assert its authority if the colonists were unwilling to take practical measures to facilitate a rapid emancipation on their own initiative. The anti-abolitionists, therefore, had no choice but to react. They focused their efforts on defending the colonists' property as the institution of slavery was officially destroyed.

This chapter will focus on the arguments put forth by MPs and peers who advocated gradual emancipation and by those who argued that amelioration and emancipation should be enacted but not at the expense of the white population in the colonies or in Britain. These MPs were not publicly against abolition and thus the definition of "anti-abolitionist" has changed. For the purposes of this study, to be anti-abolitionist in the 1820s and 1830s was to be against the immediate abolition of slavery in the colonies without clear guidelines for compensation. West Indian MPs were able to promote gradual, eventual abolition and join in the calls for the amelioration of conditions on the plantations while remaining opposed to some of the demands of the abolitionists. To be anti-abolitionist in this period therefore did not necessarily mean that one was opposed to the actions, motions, and suggestions of the abolitionists, or to the idea of abolition, but to the immediate imposing of abolition upon Britain's West Indian colonies.

As this chapter turns to the detailed analysis of the arguments and rhetoric of British anti-abolition, it again becomes necessary to stress one important point. While Britain's trade in slaves was abolished in 1807 and made illegal only a few years later, and all sides of the slavery debate publically condemned the institution of slavery by the early 1820s, emancipation was not inevitable. It was an action taken by politicians and one that had received varying levels of popular and parliamentary support over the decades. This chapter will examine the many strategies undertaken in Parliament to delay, modify, and halt emancipation.

DEMONSTRATING ABOLITION'S DAMAGING CONSEQUENCES

Perhaps the strongest evidence anti-abolitionists could employ to attack the abolitionists in this period was the disappointing consequences of British abolition. Despite years of negotiations and financial incentives, European nations were slow to join Britain in enacting and enforcing an international abolition of the slave trade. Some countries even experienced an increase in both trade and profits as a result of Britain's withdrawal from the slave trade.[9] Both Houses of Parliament produced addresses to the monarch requesting that he do more to encourage other nations to abolish the trade. During these discussions plantation-owning MPs were able to reiterate their earlier objections to abolition on the grounds that Africa and Africans would not materially benefit from abolition if other nations did not take part. As Joseph Foster Barham remarked on March 12, 1810: "[he] had always been of the opinion, that unless the trade was abolished by other governments it would soon revive in our own colonies. It was only by treaty with other powers that the trade could be effectually abolished."[10] During another discussion of a similar address to be sent on May 2, 1814, Joseph Marryat the elder commented on the unchanged number of transported slaves:

> From the Report of the African Society it appeared, that up to the year 1810, the average number of slaves obtained from Africa annually amounted to 80,000; one half of which were carried away by the Spaniards, and the other half by the Portuguese. The traffic which was formerly carried on in English ships was thus kept up in Spanish and Portuguese vessels.[11]

Anti-abolitionists had predicted that the number of Africans being exported to the West Indies would not noticeably change without a universal abolition. Neither Marryat nor Foster Barham commented on Britain's lost profits, but their statements implied that its European rivals were also gaining great financial benefits that Britain had chosen to forego. They were therefore vindicated in their earlier objections and could claim to have a better understanding of the potential outcomes of any further proposed legislation for the colonies.

The other contentious outcome of abolition was Britain's continued reliance on slave labor for the production of foodstuffs and material. In the 1820s and 1830s West Indian MPs focused on the hypocritical elements of the anti-slavery argument and a British public that desired cheap sugar while objecting to the manner in which it was obtained. On March 5, 1828, during a discussion of William Joseph Denison's request for additional duties on imported sugar, Ralph Bernal argued that such a measure would encourage further slave imports:

> he [Denison] seemed to forget that, by imposing a duty on the sugar exported from our colonies, a bounty would be given on the increase of the slave-trade, by the encouragement which would thereby be given to the importation of sugar from Martinique, the Havannah, the Brazils, &c. where, the slave trade was still carried on to a horrible extent; more especially under the French flag.[12]

He stated that such a measure would only perpetuate slave labor and the atrocities of the foreign slave trade. In fact, to meet domestic demands, Britain continued to import affordable slave-grown sugar from Cuba and Brazil beyond 1833, while the price of West Indian sugar increased and production declined in some of Britain's own colonies.[13]

William Robert Keith Douglas questioned the logic, sincerity, and knowledge of the thousands of Britons who, having signed petitions calling for an end to slavery, still demanded cheap sugar. On February 21, 1831, during a discussion of Lord Althorp's motion to assist the West Indians, Douglas argued that, without financial assistance, West Indian sugar would become too expensive:

> The country was hardly consistent in its wishes to abolish slavery in our colonies while it was anxious to benefit by the low price of slave-grown sugar.... those people who had been so anxious to abolish slavery, would find that they must draw all their supplies from countries that still carried on the Slave-trade, and over which they had not the slightest control. By not assisting the English planter, then, they would perpetuate that crime which the public voice had loudly condemned, and which the country had been at great expense to put down.[14]

Douglas was careful to refer to the planters as "British" in his request for financial aid for the colonies. Richard Godson challenged the Commons to consider a similar outcome during a discussion of emancipation on May 31, 1833:

> If, after losing the West Indies, we depended for our supply of sugar upon the produce of other countries, would the object so anxiously desired be

accomplished? Where were we to obtain sugar, the produce of free labour? From Brazil? No. From Cuba? No. From the French colonies? No. Slavery existed in them all.[15]

On June 20, 1833, the duke of Wellington went further in arguing that, if the proposed emancipation resulted in the complete stoppage of production in the colonies, there would develop in its place an illegal underground slave trade and British markets would find themselves relying on this slave-produced sugar to meet consumer demand.[16] Members of the West Indian interest and their supporters were able to argue that Britain's continuing desire for sugar and other plantation produce would prevent abolitionists from achieving their goals of ending the country's dependence on slave labor. They argued that, on the contrary, the colonies would probably cease production, resume the hated trade in slaves, or leave the British Empire. Each of these potential outcomes meant that Britons would be forced to hand over their money to foreign powers, which would in turn be encouraged to use slave labor and import more slaves to meet Britain's demands as well as their own. Overall, they stressed that the abolitionists would inevitably fail to achieve their objectives and instead cause more Africans to be enslaved. Some of these predictions indeed came true. British and American legislation for abolition in 1807 appears to have had only a temporary effect on the volume of slaves being transported from Africa. Other groups took over supplying French and Spanish colonies with slaves.[17]

Warning of Rebellion

The threat of rebellion and violence in the West Indies was constantly on the minds of British politicians. Slave uprisings occurred throughout the period with Barbados, Demerara, and Jamaica all experiencing large rebellions between 1816 and 1832. Members of the West Indian interest continued to point to the devastating effects of St. Domingo's rebellion as a warning of emancipation's likely outcomes: revolt against the white colonists; mass bloodshed and uncontrollable violence; and the loss of entire colonies. Some MPs maintained that merely debating emancipation in Parliament could provoke a rebellion. Colonial newspapers imposed self-censorship into the 1820s, thereby demonstrating the colonists' concerns about arming slaves with contradictory political information.[18] Rioting at home and abroad already terrified Britain's landed classes; many believed that revolution was imminent.[19] The colonists threatened to rebel and secede in the face of government orders. These events made a dramatic impression upon the ruling classes in Britain. It was in this unsettled revolutionary landscape that the West Indian interest painted vivid images of bloodshed and violence as part of their efforts to postpone emancipation in the 1820s and early 1830s.

In the 1830s many MPs warned of the risk of violence breaking out immediately following emancipation. On May 24, 1832, during a discussion of two petitions from the West Indian interest in the midst of the reform crisis, Sir Charles Weatherell stated: "in the present state of the West Indies, a declaration of the House of Commons in favour of unqualified emancipation would be the signal for revolt."[20] That same day William Burge also advanced such a warning: "if they could that night succeed in obtaining a vote declaring slavery to be immediately abolished in Jamaica, they would desolate that colony—they would deluge it with blood."[21] Burge argued that not only would emancipation result in death and destruction in the colonies, but that it would lead to freed slaves living in a state of desperation and poverty in a lawless land cut off from international aid. Burge conjured up images of St. Domingo's downfall and its current state of despair. The threat of revolt would have seemed all the more real to a Parliament which some MPs believed had narrowly avoided revolution at home during the reform crisis of that very month.

Several MPs were also concerned that violence incited by the slavery debates or the passing of emancipation might result in the loss of the colonies altogether. On May 15, 1823, during a discussion of amelioration, Alexander Baring put forth the following warning:

> It would be absurd to suppose that a free black population, so enlightened and cultivated as to value their rights, and duly appreciate their strength; that a population so instructed and so civilized, would consent to continue to devote their labours to proprietors, the greater portion of whom are resident in England.[22]

Baring's somewhat sarcastic depiction of the consequences of granting freedom to slaves, who according to the abolitionists were fit to receive it, is quite fascinating. Britain had lost her American colonies only 50 years earlier to free men who had banded together to defend the right to govern themselves. If the slaves were as organized and learned as the abolitionists argued in their calls for immediate emancipation, why should they be content to remain under British rule?

After the loss of their American colonies, British politicians were concerned that amelioration and emancipation would reduce the colonial assemblies' powers, frustrate the colonists, and confuse the slaves. Total emancipation was a dangerous prospect; no one could be sure how the slaves or the colonists would react. A number of MPs with ties to the colonies therefore attempted to delay such legislation by urging their counterparts to work with the colonists, rather than dictating to them from above. They also stressed the importance of the colonies to the British Empire. On May 30, 1816, Lord Holland remarked that slave registration should be handled by the colonies, noting: "The utmost reluctance ought to be felt to legislate here in matters which concerned the internal regulations of the colonies; and such a mode of proceeding would have the strongest tendency to defeat the very object in view."[23] He argued that forcing the colonies to enact legislation that they opposed would result in the legislation being ignored, rejected, or thwarted. Similarly, on July 13, 1830, after Henry Brougham asserted that the colonists had not undertaken amelioration, Robert John Wilmot Horton argued that Parliament needed the colonists' help in order to implement the desired changes on the ground:

> nothing could be more unwise than to irritate the West-Indians by attempting to force laws upon them,—because he was sure that that attempt would not only be unjustifiable, but that it would fail entirely. He had heard a great deal . . . about the impropriety and injustice of our interfering with the legislative assemblies of Canada.[24]

Wilmot Horton stated that they should treat the colonists with respect if they hoped to accomplish emancipation at some point in the future. If the House had found it improper to interfere with Canada's legislative assemblies, surely it would be equally improper to interfere with those in the West Indies.

MPs also warned that, by legislating for the colonies, they might be encouraging the colonists to rebel. On March 6, 1828, during discussion on the impact of amelioration in the colonies, Ralph Bernal brought forth such a warning: "The West-Indians might be a weak body; but if driven and forced together, it might be found that they could muster both strength and courage to resist those opposed to them, and who attempted to destroy their just rights."[25] Bernal argued that the West Indians would not allow their rights to be taken away. On July 13, 1830, Robert John Wilmot Horton and Sir Robert Peel compared the present situation to that which Parliament had faced in the previous century when dealing with their American colonies. Peel asked his fellow MPs:

Could any one dwell for a moment on the horrors to be apprehended from being, in consequence of such an interference by Parliament with the internal concerns of these islands, forced to the awful emergency of waging war upon the white population of our own colonies and the colonial legislatures?[26]

On May 31, 1833, Richard Godson challenged Parliament's right to legislate for people who were not represented in Parliament:

He would begin by denying the right of the Parliament in Great Britain to legislate for the internal regulation or taxation of the colonies which had Local Legislatures. The laws of Great Britain had ever recognised . . . the right Jamaica acquired by charter to an independent legislature. The inhabitants of that island would insist that the Legislature of England had no right to pass a law to bind them; and they would not receive it.[27]

These men were concerned that the colonists and their assemblies were not being treated as their equals. Regardless of whether Parliament could legitimately legislate for those colonies with their own assemblies, such action could be dangerous.

The colonists resented the Colonial Office's interference as it infringed upon what they believed to be their right to self-regulation.[28] In late 1831, a highly controversial Order in Council was devised by the government and sent to the West Indian colonies specifying rules and regulations for the management of the colonial plantations without allowing for the colonies to adapt the policies to suit their individual circumstances. Colonies with their own legislatures would receive preferential sugar duties upon adopting them. This contentious element led to protests in the colonial legislatures, particularly in Jamaica, and growing white dissent throughout the colonies.[29] It caused tension and anger among the colonists who believed their attempts at amelioration were not being given sufficient credit or were being unreasonably rushed. It also caused divisions between crown and legislative colonies as crown colonies were forced to implement the orders immediately. Some of the stipulations contained within the orders were deemed unreasonable or unsuitable to the plantation system, the environment, and the slaves' actual needs. These stipulations then allowed planters to argue that the British government was unaware of actual plantation conditions.

On October 6, 1831, while the Order in Council was still being modified, Joseph Hume declared:

> if the Government were anxious to excite a civil war between the colonies and the mother country, they could do no better than to adopt this Order in Council. He had not seen one individual connected with the West Indies who did not protest against such an Order being sent out.[30]

Hume warned that the colonists could revolt against this level of repression. On March 9, 1832, William Burge argued that the Order contained dangerous elements that negated the rights of the colonial assemblies:

> No man who respected the rights of a legislative assembly, could by possibility approve of their conduct, when they made an Order in Council, and imperiously commanded what they were pleased to call a legislative assembly to register that Order, without the slightest alteration, as a law made, considered, and adopted by the assembly. Such a proceeding, he contended, was monstrous.[31]

The West Indian lobby strongly opposed the principles behind the Order in Council, as they implied British dominance over her West Indian colonies and proved that the government lacked an understanding of each colony's individual needs. While the Order automatically became law in the Crown colonies, those colonies with local legislatures rejected it and fought back. The Order also decreed that the colonies that implemented them would receive financial benefits and those that rejected them would not. This situation allowed the West Indian lobby to draw a further connection to the American conflict by recalling the contentious issue of taxation without representation. Throughout the slavery debates, therefore, the West Indian interest was able to warn of impending rebellion and violence by drawing on past examples of both black and white rebellions and revolutions. With unrest at home and abroad, the threat of rebellion remained a pressing issue and a convincing argument in Westminster for much of the early nineteenth century.

Attacks on Individual Abolitionists

After the abolition of the slave trade anti-abolitionists rarely attacked individual abolitionists in Parliament. They did respond to individuals over their use of unfair accusations or inflammatory language but, in doing so, commented only on their actions and language rather than their character or motives. The only abolitionist to face strong and continuous opposition during the slavery debates in Parliament throughout the post-1807 period was William Wilberforce. His central role in securing the abolition of the slave trade and pushing for international abolition made him the object of direct attacks on any element of abolition that did not unfold as planned. Even so, these attacks were neither malicious nor slanderous but instead focused on mistakes made and lessons to be learned. For example, during a discussion of Wilberforce's motion asking the Prince Regent for details on the slave population in Jamaica on June 19, 1816, Joseph Foster Barham challenged the propriety of Wilberforce's earlier bill that had been intended to end the illegal trade in slaves under foreign flags in the West Indies:

> The bill in question was brought in on the ground that there actually existed a contraband trade in slaves. Such was the plain understanding of the preamble, and such the point on which the arguments rested, by which it was supported; and yet now, when it turns out, that no such trade has existed, the author of the bill wheels round, and pretends, that this never was the foundation on which the bill was rested![32]

Anti-abolitionists had fervently argued that the bill in question was neither based on solid evidence nor on grounds of necessity because no such illegal trade existed in the British West Indies. They believed that because no proof of such illegal activity had been found, they remained justified in their continued support of the colonies. This also allowed Foster Barham to attack Wilberforce's change of position and to question his knowledge and credibility. Foster Barham's arguments remained focused on Wilberforce and his mistakes during this debate:

> But where will my hon. friend (Mr. W.) hide himself, when at some still and solitary hour, these poor slaughtered blacks seem to approach him and to say, "this time twelve-month we were innocent and contented, and but for you we should have been innocent and contented still!" If ever I have envied any man's fame; if ever I have envied any man's feelings, it had been the fame and the feeling to which my hon. friend was entitled, on his accomplishment of his great work, the abolition . . . now that, urged on by desperate counsels, he has produced calamities of which no man can foresee the conclusion, he will I fear need all the consolation, which the good he has heretofore done can afford him.[33]

Here Foster Barham expressed great admiration for Wilberforce's recent accomplishments (outwardly if not genuinely) but emphasized the unforeseen consequences that his work had produced for the slaves. Rather than providing them with security and happiness, he argued, the slaves were now in greater despair because of the efforts and "achievements" of the abolitionists. He admitted that Wilberforce's memories of his great work might console him, so long as he viewed the colonies from afar, but it was the unfortunate colonists and the slaves who had been forced to live with the consequences of his actions.

ATTACKS ON THE ABOLITIONISTS' METHODS

Anti-abolitionists attacked many of the Anti-Slavery Society's methods that appeared to have an impact on Parliament as well as the abolitionist MPs and peers' strategies in Parliament. They objected to the ways in which anti-slavery petitions originated and the means by which signatures were gathered. They wholeheartedly disagreed with the practice of requiring pledges from parliamentary candidates and forcing those standing for election to make public their views on (and any personal connections to) slavery. Abolitionists were also accused of creating spectacles and sharing dramatic, but false or outdated, stories in order to gain public support from their uneducated and ill-informed audiences and readers. Anti-abolitionists denounced these practices in Parliament throughout the years leading up to emancipation as a means of discrediting the anti-slavery activists and countering the hundreds of petitions that some abolitionist MPs maintained clearly reflected the British public's overwhelming support for their cause.

Anti-abolitionists and the West Indian lobby fought to convince Parliament that the numerous anti-slavery petitions arriving in Parliament were not truly representative of the views of the British people and, therefore, should not be allowed to influence parliamentary action. Unable or unwilling to procure thousands of signatures in support of counter petitions, anti-abolitionists were forced to discredit the appearance and legitimacy of anti-slavery petitions. On May 15, 1823, during a discussion of Thomas Fowell Buxton's bill for amelioration, Alexander Baring commented:

> I trust his majesty's ministers will not be unduly influenced by the petitions on that table, which have, in fact, been got up by a few persons in the metropolis. I know no question upon which petitions have been procured with more trick and management than on the present; or where they have come so notoriously from persons having no means whatever of exercising a judgement upon the question.[34]

He dismissed the petitions as the work of a few men in London containing signatures that were not only gained through trickery, but that also belonged to men who were not in any position to comment on the subject (and, perhaps more important, did not possess the vote). Parliament had been rejecting petitions on the basis of informal or inappropriate language since the early 1790s; anti-abolitionists could also use these precedents to challenge the origins and validity of the anti-slavery petitions without having to argue against the petitioners' sentiments.

On March 15, 1824, George Watson Taylor discussed the improper methods used to gather signatures during the presentation of several anti-slavery petitions:

> itinerant adventurers had come down with petitions ready prepared .... They addressed themselves to the passions of the people on the subject of negro slavery, rather than to reason. The poor artisan, mechanic, and peasant, were asked, whether they objected to seeing persons in perpetual slavery; and on answering, of course, in the affirmative, they were requested to sign the petitions presented to them. He could not think this a fair way of collecting the opinions of the public on this important subject.[35]

Watson Taylor objected to pre-crafted petitions being presented as though they had originated in the local communities from which the signatures were gathered. He also argued that the way in which people were approached was intentionally deceptive rather than being for the purposes of spreading and gaining information. Both Baring and Watson Taylor implied that these practices should lead their fellow MPs to ignore these petitions and instead focus on facts and evidence produced within Westminster.

Anti-abolitionists also objected to the methods anti-slavery societies used to gain financial backing for their activities. On March 16, 1824, during a discussion of the resolutions for amelioration, Baring reflected on London's Anti-Slavery Society's fund-raising practices:

> This society had raised large subscriptions, and was in the practice of sending its emissaries about to disturb every market town in the kingdom ... he had seen, on market days, men come into the town [Taunton], who related stories and exhibited pictures. The country people were asked, whether they would not vote against slavery? Some of the pamphlets of the society were placed in their hands, and they were told many dreadful stories of women who were tied down to the ground and shockingly beaten. These stories, however, were, he would say, gross exaggerations.[36]

He argued that abolitionists were systematically targeting innocent people on busy market days in towns across Britain and employing shock tactics to gain sympathy for their cause and money for their activities. Baring then elaborated on the exaggerated stories abolitionists shared with the crowds to acquire money from the market-goers by referring to them as "stock stories." He argued that these same shocking stories were used time and again because no new, relevant stories had emerged from the West Indies in support of the anti-slavery cause.[37] He suggested that abolitionists across the country were regularly and intentionally misleading a sympathetic, gullible, and uninformed British public for financial gain.

On April 15, 1831, during a debate on Thomas Fowell Buxton's motion for emancipation, Baring recalled a spectacle in Yorkshire during the election period: "there were persons led about in chains, with blackened faces, in order to rouse the feelings of the people."[38] He claimed that such visual propaganda was meant to gain sympathy for the anti-slavery cause rather than give the electors any genuine information on the subject and were thus unnecessary and "ridiculous." Sir Richard Vyvyan objected to another controversial practice of Britain's anti-slavery societies: requiring men standing for election to publicly pledge their support for emancipation or face public scorn and humiliation. On May 30, 1833, as the Commons discussed emancipation, he challenged his fellow MPs' ability to speak freely and vote freely on the subject of slavery and emancipation: "He was aware that he was addressing an assembly, many Members of which had deeply pledged themselves, though the system of pledges was ruinous to the best interests of the country. Was not a pledge a bribe, far more injurious to the Empire at large, than bribery by money?"[39] Baring and Sir Richard objected to these practices because they were directed at the unenfranchised wider public who had been continually subjected to what they regarded as false and one-sided information produced by the abolitionists. They argued that, by making pledges, MPs were then prevented from having open, honest debates and voting on the subject of slavery as their own conscience and reason dictated. This, in turn, would hurt the colonies and the empire. His decision to use the word "bribe" further emphasized his argument that this was an underhanded practice and one intended to earn votes.

Finally, as in the era of Wilberforce's almost annual motions for the abolition of the slave trade prior to 1807, West Indian MPs complained of the abolitionists' habit of continually bringing up motions to address and readdress the state of slavery in the colonies. They continued to argue that such discussions could have disastrous effects on the minds of the slaves and the stability of the colonies. On April 17, 1832, after presenting a West Indian petition to the House of Lords, Henry Lascelles, the Earl of Harewood, reflected on this worrying practice:

> Considering the situation in which the West-India interests at present stood, he would seriously ask, whether this was a proper time to irritate the slaves, and excite discontent and agitation among them by frequent motions in Parliament, having reference to their condition? Yet such motions were frequently made, and if the practice should be continued, the consequences, in all probability, would be fatal.[40]

Like many had done before him, Lascelles argued that the abolitionists' efforts to make Parliament constantly discuss colonial slavery could have dangerous or even fatal consequences. He stated that certain abolitionists willingly ignored the potential dangers of their practices in order to continue agitating for emancipation and further their personal goals. Like the anti-abolitionists' refusal to discuss emancipation without clear plans for compensation, however, this argument could also be interpreted as a desperate attempt to delay the proceedings that were threatening to emancipate hundreds of thousands of slaves.

Defending the Colonies

Much anti-abolitionist rhetoric in Parliament after 1807 possessed a distinctly defensive tone. Members of the West Indian interest emphatically defended themselves and one another when accused by abolitionists of self-interest or misconduct. These MPs were sometimes able to defend the colonists and the colonial assemblies by favorably comparing their actions to those taken in Britain. They strengthened their objections to immediate emancipation by arguing that abolitionists were being unrealistic in their depictions of a post-emancipation society in the colonies.[41] Finally, some MPs rejected the abolitionists' accusations of partisanship and interest by arguing that they were all against perpetual, inhumane slavery in the West Indies. These rhetorical strategies helped defend the colonies and the colonists' actions, prolong the emancipation debates, and extend the use of slave labor into the 1830s.

Some anti-abolitionist MPs strove to counter and deflect abolitionist charges of inhumanity by stressing the ways in which humanity was inherent in the institution of slavery in Britain's West Indian colonies.[42] They demonstrated the humanity of the colonists by comparing their laws to those enforced in Britain. On April 15, 1831, during a debate on Thomas Fowell Buxton's motion for emancipation, Horace Twiss argued: "England was hardly entitled to take a very high tone of moral indignation on this subject, when it was remembered that it was only a very few years ago, in 1822, that even in this country of humanity, civilization, and freedom, the whipping of females was finally abolished."[43] He had begun his defense by stating that he completely agreed that the whipping of female slaves was regrettable. Twiss then demonstrated the British government's own reluctance to act earlier on the issue of corporal punishment for women in an attempt to demonstrate that colonial law was not as far from Britain's laws as the abolitionists were making out. He therefore defended the colonies by highlighting the similarities between Britons and the colonists and showing that his fellow MPs were being selective in their recollection of past legislation that might appear unfavorable or inhumane in the present circumstances and yet had been enforced and condoned in Britain in recent years.

Anti-abolitionist MPs frequently challenged the abolitionists' optimistic forecasts of the outcomes of emancipation for the slaves, the colonists, and Britain's West Indian colonies. They were able to argue that the abolitionists were being unrealistic and misleading about the likely consequences of their proposed measures. On May 15, 1823, during a discussion of the bill for amelioration, Alexander Baring provided his own speculations as to the results: "If we were to arrive at a free black population, the inevitable consequence would be, that the whole of the islands would be lost to this country; there would be an end to our colonial system."[44] He argued that it was unfair to condemn the colonists for not actively pushing for emancipation when the prevailing belief was that it would inevitably lead to the destruction of property and human life. This argument had been repeatedly brought forward in Parliament prior to 1807. Baring then proceeded to challenge the abolitionists' claims that freed slaves would labor for wages.[45] He rejected the abolitionists' arguments of a slave population ready for the rights and privileges of freedom by questioning why such a massive, strong, and supposedly enlightened group of individuals would choose to continue laboring under British rule after emancipation.

The duke of Wellington employed a similar strategy in his discussion of the need for compensation for the planters. On June 20, 1833, as the lords discussed the bill for emancipation, Wellington stated:

> He wished to know why they were to give or to lend 15,000,000*l*. to the colonists, if the freed negroes were likely to work? He could easily understand the principle of compensation for the difference in the amount of labour done by the slave and the free negro; but then, what became of their boasted improvement of the negro, and of his willingness to work, when he was placed in a great degree at his own disposal? If these improvements were as they were described, why give compensation?—if no such improvement was yet to be found, then all these measures were premature.[46]

Like Baring, he challenged the abolitionists' claims that the slaves were fully ready for freedom. Wellington argued that compensation would be unnecessary if the freed slaves were truly willing to continue working as before, thus maintaining production levels in the colonies, yet here they were debating how many millions to send to the colonists as compensation for lost labor, property, and production. He contended that the abolitionists did not honestly believe that current production rates, property values, and perhaps the security of the colonies and their inhabitants would be maintained following emancipation; if they did, and could persuade the House to agree, they would all see that compensation (and a period of apprenticeship) was unnecessary. He was therefore able to argue that the act of debating compensation proved the flaws in the bill and in the entire basis for immediate emancipation.

Finally, MPs who voiced their opinions against immediate emancipation defended their positions by reflecting on the nature of the debate and the similarities of the two sides. They argued that they all wanted the same things: a better life for the West Indian slaves and a stable empire with colonists who were safe and protected by the British government. On March 6, 1828, during a discussion of the origins and nature of the 1823 resolutions for amelioration, Sir Robert John Wilmot Horton argued: "The West-Indian must be insane, who would not rather employ free labour than slaves, if the former would answer his purpose; but then, he said, very fairly, 'You are bound to shew me that there is a chance of free labour succeeding.'"[47] He attempted to convince the house that the West Indians relied on slave labor not from choice but out of necessity. They would prefer to employ free labor but were stuck in the unhappy and precarious situation that had been handed down to them. This blurred the lines between abolitionists and anti-abolitionists and made it more difficult for abolitionists to attack the West Indian position. Sir Robert also showed that the onus was on the abolitionists to prove that free labor could meet the needs of the British public, maintain production in the colonies, and be safely implemented. The editor of this speech appears to have agreed, describing Sir Robert's challenge as "fair." Shortly after, in a response to Henry Brougham's earlier speech, Sir Robert specifically questioned the meaning and usefulness of the term "abolitionist":

> He had also been accused by the same learned gentleman [Brougham], of being an opponent to the abolitionists. But when that learned gentleman told him, that he was an opponent to the abolitionists, he must beg leave to ask, who were meant by the term abolitionists? They were all pledged in one way—all agreed to the resolutions of 1823—all were bound to carry them into execution; and he challenged any honourable member to say that he had ever done any thing which did not tend to the accomplishment of these resolutions.[48]

He argued that every MP in the House was on the same side and that he was no exception. The term "abolitionist" had been used to denote a specific group of activists and their followers; now Sir Robert suggested that in fact everyone was an abolitionist in that they had all agreed on the resolutions for amelioration and therefore all wished for the improvement of the institution of colonial slavery. Sir Robert found Brougham's use of the term "abolitionist" to be unnecessary, divisive, and exclusive.

The language and rhetoric employed by anti-abolitionists in Parliament in the years following the abolition of the slave trade was defensive in nature and more often given in response to an abolitionist speech or petition than as a positive, spontaneous assertion of the anti-abolitionist position. Having lost the debate over slave trading MPs with interests in the West Indies found that they now needed to defend the colonies and their importance to the British Empire. One of the most important ways in which they achieved this aim was to stress the innate Britishness of the colonists of British descent. By emphasizing the similarities between Britons at home and abroad, the colonists' rejections of parliamentary interference in private and commercial ventures could be justified.

The rhetorical strategies discussed earlier reflect a very different strategy and mentality about the permanence of colonial slavery compared to that in existence before the abolition of the slave trade. The abolition in 1807 abruptly ended the way in which slaves had been obtained; planters and sympathetic MPs alike were now well aware of how quickly slavery could be ended by a simple act of Parliament. Their strategic shift in rhetoric, from attacking the popular abolitionists and challenging the possibility of emancipation to willingly adopting ameliorative reforms, supporting the colonies, and defending their rights to property, reflects the changed nature of the slavery debates and the damaged proslavery position in Parliament after the abolition of the slave trade.

Conclusion

In the aftermath of parliamentary reform in the early 1830s, many MPs, organized abolitionists, and the British public turned their attention once again to slavery in Britain's colonies. With their power and influence severely weakened, the West Indian interest firmly upheld its right to financial compensation in return for the state's proposed confiscation of its legally acquired property. They also convinced Parliament that the newly freed slaves could not be allowed to live freely in the colonies for a number of pressing reasons, including the danger of organization and violent revolt against the small, vulnerable white populations of the islands, the predicted total loss of plantation labor and production, and the decreased land value that would result from deserted colonial plantations. Once again, their arguments stood upon convincing legal grounds and contained enough humanitarian sentiment to sway opinion where it counted: in Westminster.

Between late February and early March of 1833, the West Indian interest demanded that, as part of an agreement regarding emancipation, slaves were to be prevented from leaving the plantations for a set period of time. They also pressed for the proposed compensation amount to be raised from £10 million to £30 million.[1] Negotiations stopped when Lord Howick, the parliamentary undersecretary and the son of Prime Minister Earl Grey, turned down their demands, but Edward Stanley searched for a compromise. The West India Committee intended to block the plan for emancipation by attacking its moral and legal basis, but after negotiating the amount and type of compensation in May 1833, it privately urged Stanley to bring forth the new plan in Parliament.[2] The West Indian interest rejected Stanley's offer of a £15 million loan as compensation and held daily meetings to draft its counterproposal. On June 7, 1833, it unanimously adopted two resolutions: the first was for a £20 million gift to colonial proprietors that would satisfy mortgagees and creditors in England; the second was for a loan of an additional £10 million to secure colonial property that would allow the planters to have continued access to credit and to obtain necessary goods.[3] West Indian MPs reiterated to the Colonial Office that the sugar colonies were vital to the empire and were worth £30 million.[4] On June 10, the government replied, promising to grant £20 million in compensation to the West Indian proprietors; this was agreed upon by a vote of 286 to 77 on June 11.[5]

The amount of compensation was initially based upon transaction records from the 1820s. Using these records and slave population totals, an average cost per slave was assessed and the owners compensated for a percentage of their worth. The compensation scheme also took into account the devaluation of the slaves' worth over the prior 12 years, the fewer hours apprentices would work after emancipation, and the financial loss of any children born to slave women who would be automatically freed. Apprenticeship would be the period between slavery and emancipation that involved shorter workdays, remuneration, and education for former slaves provided they remained with their existing employers. In the end, it was terminated in 1838 (two years earlier than originally planned) due to extra-parliamentary pressure. Robert John Buxton had moved for apprenticeship to expire in 1836 rather than 1840, but his motion was defeated by 206 votes to 89.[6] By increasing the levels of compensation for the slaveholders and halving the length of apprenticeship, Stanley was able to find a suitable compromise and achieve emancipation. Compensation allowed Stanley to secure the cooperation of the West Indian interest or at least of those members of the interest who possessed slaves.

Parliament voted to emancipate Britain's 800,000 West Indian slaves of African descent from August 1, 1834. Three out of the four main principles of the Slave Emancipation Bill could be deemed gestures and assurances to the West Indian interest.[7] These vital elements were apprenticeship, monetary payment funded by the government through taxes, and revenue raised via colonial sugar duties to ensure compensation for slaveholders. The granting of compensation showed a widespread acceptance in Parliament that slaves were property and that the planters and merchants would likely face significant financial losses as a result of emancipation. Landowners dominated the government. They would have been risking their own rights to property ownership if they had passed the act without a clause for compensation because without compensation, abolition would have been an act of Parliament that confiscated millions of pounds worth of property. It also would have set a dangerous precedent.[8] The slaves received no compensation. Sugar production declined after the end of apprenticeship in 1838.[9]

Over the years that followed, Britons chose to remember and celebrate emancipation as a great humanitarian triumph with abolitionists having overcome the wicked, self-interested West Indians in their quest to save the slaves and their own reputations. The agency of crucial other groups, including the colonists and the slaves, was all but removed from the popular story of British abolition. The West Indian interest, however, made a significant impact on the timing and nature of abolition and emancipation. They created thoughtful, convincing arguments to encourage slaveholding and Britain's participation in the slave trade. They employed rhetorical strategies to defend their position, the colonies, and undermine the abolition movement. They drew on external events, historical and legal precedent, and first-hand knowledge to further support and legitimate their positions. And they utilized a full range of sources as they attempted to share their viewpoints with a wider segment of the British public. Their efforts worked, delaying abolition and emancipation for decades despite popular and political support for abolition. In the end, the evidence shows that there were at least two sides to the story of British abolition, and they all need to be told.

Notes

Introduction

1. *Parliamentary History of England* [hereafter *PHE*] XXXIII, col. 1027.
2. For example, see Chapter 3 for an introduction to proslavery in the arts and literature of the late 1700s and early 1800s.
3. Many studies of British abolition have depicted abolition as inevitable and the planters as destined to fail. For example, see Lowell Joseph Ragatz, *The Fall of the Planter Class in the British Caribbean, 1763–1833* (1928. Reprint, New York: Octagon Books Inc., 1963), vii. See also Eric Williams, *Capitalism and Slavery* (1944. Reprint, London: Lowe and Brydon Ltd., 1964), 135.
4. Larry E. Tise, *Proslavery: A History of the Defense of Slavery in America, 1701–1840* (Athens: University of Georgia Press, 1987), xv.
5. See Chapter 5 for discussion of post-1807 anti-abolitionist rhetoric.
6. Larry E. Tise has also defined the term "anti-abolitionist" using a specific time period, which he states in the American case refers to individuals who opposed both slavery and abolition after 1831. See Tise, *Proslavery: A History of the Defense of Slavery in America, 1701–1840,* xvi. In her study of the rhetoric of the slavery debate to 1815, Srividhya Swaminathan limits her use of the term to describe the opposite of abolitionist writings. The narrower time frame of her study helps explain why the term is rarely used in her study of the slavery debate, as many of the politicians and writers she examines are clearly proslavery or anti-slavery/abolitionist in this period. See Srividhya Swaminathan, *Debating the Slave Trade: Rhetoric of British National Identity, 1759–1815* (Surrey: Ashgate Publishing Limited, 2009), 40–2. Roger Anstey employs the term to refer to MPs who voted against abolition in Parliament in the 1790s and early 1800s. His study of British abolition ends in the year 1810 before the definition of anti-abolitionist necessarily becomes more complicated and nuanced. For example, see Roger Anstey, *The Atlantic Slave Trade and British Abolition 1760–1810* (London: Macmillan Press, 1975), 309.
7. J. R. Ward, *British West Indian Slavery, 1750–1834: The Process of Amelioration* (1988. Reprint, Oxford: Clarendon Press, 2001), 2–7.

Robert E. Luster has suggested that amelioration developed out of Enlightenment philosophy and the Evangelical movement and was the principle around which many aspects of British politics revolved in the late eighteenth and early nineteenth centuries. See Robert E. Luster, *The Amelioration of the Slaves in the British Empire, 1790–1833* (New York: Peter Lang, 1995), Ch. 1.

8. Ward, *British West Indian Slavery, 1750–1834: The Process of Amelioration*, 276.
9. David Turley, *The Culture of English Antislavery, 1780–1860* (London: Routledge, 1991), 2.
10. Douglas Hamilton, "Representing Slavery in British Museums: The Challenges of 2007," in *Imagining Transatlantic Slavery*, ed. Cora Kaplan and J. R. Oldfield (Basingstoke: Palgrave Macmillan, 2010), 141–2.
11. Abolitionists started this trend. For example, see Thomas Clarkson, *The History of the Rise, Progress, and Accomplishment of the Abolition of the African Slave Trade by the British Parliament*, 2 vols. (London: Longman, Hurst, Rees, and Orme, 1808). For a more recent history of British abolition with a similar view of abolitionists, see Roger Anstey's *The Atlantic Slave Trade and British Abolition 1760–1810* (London: Macmillan Press Ltd., 1975). Following on David Brion Davis' research, Anstey's study emphasized the role of Evangelicals and Quakers in the anti-slavery movement. See David Brion Davis, *The Problem of Slavery in the Age of Revolution 1770–1823* (London: Cornell University Press, 1975). Seymour Drescher called Anstey's study a revival of the Clarksonian tradition. See Seymour Drescher, *Capitalism and Antislavery: British Mobilization in Comparitive Perspective* (Basingstoke: Macmillan Press Ltd., 1986), 1.
12. Christer Petley, "Rethinking the Fall of the Planter Class," *Atlantic Studies*, 9 (2012), 7.
13. In his "decline thesis," Eric Williams suggested that economics was the major factor in determining if and when abolition would occur in the British West Indies. He argued that slavery would have continued as long as it remained profitable. See Williams, *Capitalism and Slavery*. In the 1970s, Seymour Drescher set out to challenge the consensus on the decline thesis by demonstrating growth in colonial production and the value of the trade with the West Indies. He concluded that it was abolitionists pressuring Parliament that led to abolition. See Seymour Drescher, *Econocide: British Slavery in the Era of Abolition* (Pittsburg: University of Pittsburg Press, 1977). Recent years have witnessed a return to stressing the important role economics played in abolishing the slave trade. For example, see Joseph E. Inikori, *Africans and the Industrial Revolution in England: A Study in International Trade and Economic Development*

(Cambridge: Cambridge University Press, 2002). See also Selwyn H. H. Carrington, *The Sugar Industry and the Abolition of the Slave Trade, 1775–1810* (Gainesville: University of Florida Press, 2002). In his study of the West Indian interest in Britain, David Beck Ryden finds that the essence of Williams' decline thesis continues to hold up. See David Beck Ryden, *West Indian Slavery and British Abolition, 1783–1807* (Cambridge: Cambridge University Press, 2009), Ch. 1.

14. Eugene Genovese studied the lives, work, and ideology of slaveholders in the American south for decades. For an entry into to his body of work, see Eugene D. Genovese, *The World the Slaveholders Made: Two Essays in Interpretation* (1969. Reprint with new introduction, Hanover: University Press of New England, 1988). Larry E. Tise later firmly credited British anti-abolitionists with devising and advancing every proslavery argument later adopted in the American case. See Tise, *Proslavery: A History of the Defense of Slavery in America, 1701–1840,* 78. He also lamented that every history of proslavery written since the Civil War had treated proslavery in a moral rather than historical manner, resulting in historians making moral rather than historical judgments and misunderstanding its true nature. See Tise, *Proslavery: A History of the Defense of Slavery in America, 1701–1840,* xiii–xiv.
15. Christer Petley, "'Devoted Islands' and 'That Madman Wilberforce': British Proslavery Patriotism During the Age of Abolition," *The Journal of Imperial and Commonwealth History,* 39 (2011), 395.
16. For a detailed study of pro- and anti-slavery rhetoric in Parliament over a select number of debates, see Seymour Drescher, "People and Parliament: The Rhetoric of the British Slave Trade," *Journal of Interdisciplinary History,* 20 (1990), 561–80. Gordon K. Lewis provided a general overview of proslavery arguments in Gordon K. Lewis, "Proslavery Ideology," in *Caribbean Slavery in the Atlantic World,* ed. Verene Shepherd and Hilary Beckles (Oxford: Ian Randal, 2000), 544–79. Srividhya Swaminathan produced a detailed analysis of both sides of the slavery debates up to 1815 and argued that pro- and anti-slavery rhetoric during this period was closely connected to development and shape of a British national identity. See Swaminathan, *Debating the Slave Trade: Rhetoric of British National Identity, 1759–1815.*
17. For example, in the opening pages of his 1928 study, *The Fall of the Planter Class in the British Caribbean,* Lowell Joseph Ragatz argued that slavery would have come to an end in the islands regardless of abolition because of moral, social, and economic deterioration, the planters' loss of political influence, and the unwillingness of colonists to adapt to new progressive farming methods. See Ragatz, *The Fall of the Planter Class in the British Caribbean, 1763–1833,*

vii. Christer Petley echoed Ragatz's thesis of planter decline and expanded upon it, citing the planters' hesitance to defend their position using moral arguments as a critical missed opportunity. See Christer Petley, *Slaveholders in Jamaica: Colonial Society and Culture During the Era of Abolition* (London: Pickering and Chatto, 2009), 47. In contrast, Trevor Burnard recently asserted that, without popular abolitionism leading to the end of their participation in the slave trade, the West Indians' drive for wealth and the continuing demand for colonial produce would have allowed their power to continue on into the nineteenth century. See Trevor Burnard, "Et in Arcadia Ego: West Indian Planters in Glory, 1674–1784," *Atlantic Studies*, 9 (2012), 34–5. See also Trevor Burnard, *Mastery, Tyranny, and Desire: Thomas Thistlewood and His Slaves in the Anglo-Jamaican World* (Chapel Hill: University of North Carolina Press, 2004).

18. Ryden, *West Indian Slavery and British Abolition, 1783–1807*, 17.
19. Ibid., 18.
20. For example, see Ryden, *West Indian Slavery and British Abolition, 1783–1807*, 12. See also Srividhya Swaminathan, "Developing the West Indian Proslavery Position after the Somerset Decision," *Slavery & Abolition*, 24 (2003), 42.

CHAPTER 1

1. *The Parliamentary Debates* [hereafter *PD*] VIII, col. 980.
2. See the Introduction.
3. The Society of West India Planters and Merchants had been formed as a pressure group to lobby the government on behalf of the West Indian colonists and absentees in London. Jamaican planters and merchants dominated the society. See David Beck Ryden, *West Indian Slavery and British Abolition, 1783–1807* (Cambridge: Cambridge University Press, 2009), 194.
4. Christer Petley, "Rethinking the Fall of the Planter Class," *Atlantic Studies*, 9 (2012), 9.
5. David Lambert, *White Creole Culture, Politics and Identity During the Age of Abolition* (Cambridge: Cambridge University Press, 2005), 61.
6. For example, uprisings occurred in Barbados in 1816, in Demerara in 1823, and in Jamaica in 1831–2. The year 1830 witnessed a wave of revolutions sweeping across Europe, affecting France, Poland, Switzerland, Belgium and the Netherlands, and the surrounding territories. There was also a great deal of instability within Britain as the country experienced rapid population growth, agricultural depression, economic depression, and a cholera epidemic. Finally, the rejection of the second bill for parliamentary reform in October 1831 led to

pillaging, riots, mob violence, deaths, an attack on a jail, and threats by the political unions to begin military-style drills. See Malcolm I. Thomis and Peter Holt, *Threats of Revolution in Britain 1784–1848* (London: Macmillan Press Ltd., 1977), 87.

7. Brycchan Carey, *British Abolitionism and the Rhetoric of Sensibility: Writing, Sentiment and Slavery, 1760–1807* (Basingstoke: Macmillan Publishers Ltd., 2005), 144.
8. Seymour Drescher, "People and Parliament: The Rhetoric of the British Slave Trade," *Journal of Interdisciplinary History,* 20 (1990), 579.
9. Several historical studies of British slavery and abolition include rhetorical analysis of the parliamentary debates on slavery that relied on published speeches from the period. For example, see Seymour Drescher, "People and Parliament: The Rhetoric of the British Slave Trade," *Journal of Interdisciplinary History,* 20 (1990), 561–80. See also Carey, *British Abolitionism and the Rhetoric of Sensibility: Writing, Sentiment and Slavery, 1760–1807,* Ch. 5.
10. Overall, the argument of abolition being based upon revolutionary principles was brought up 24 times between 1783 and 1807: five times in 1793; once in 1794, 1796, and 1797; twice in 1798; three times in 1799; twice in 1804; once in 1805 and 1806; and seven times in 1807.
11. The argument of the slave trade providing a nursery for seamen was advanced 12 times during the abolition debates held between 1783 and 1807: once in 1788 and 1789; twice in 1791; once in 1796; three times in 1805 during the War of the Third Coalition; and three times in 1806 during the War of the Fourth Coalition.
12. Joseph E. Inikori, *Africans and the Industrial Revolution in England: A Study in International Trade and Economic Development* (Cambridge: Cambridge University Press, 2002), 479.
13. Srividhya Swaminathan, "Developing the West Indian Proslavery Position after the Somerset Decision," *Slavery & Abolition,* 24 (2003), 41.
14. Seymour Drescher, "Abolitionist Expectations," *Slavery & Abolition,* 21 (2000), 42.
15. Linda Colley, *Britons: Forging the Nation, 1707–1837* (New Haven: Yale University Press, 1992), 358.
16. *Parliamentary History of England* [hereafter *PHE*] XXXIV, col. 536.
17. Kenneth Morgan, "Slave Women and Reproduction in Jamaica, ca. 1776–1834," in *Women and Slavery: The Modern Atlantic,* ed. Gwyn Cambell, Suzanne Miers, and Joseph C. Miller (Athens: Ohio University Press, 2008), 27.
18. Ibid., 45.
19. Ibid., 33.

20. While statistics underwent significant development in the nineteenth century, their use in the social sciences was far less developed than in other scientific disciplines. However, statistical theory and analysis dramatically increased in Britain beginning in 1830. See Stephen M. Stigler, *The History of Statistics: The Measurement of Uncertainty before 1900* (Cambridge, MA: Harvard University Press, 1986), 4–5 and Part Two. See also Theodore M. Porter, *The Rise of Statistical Thinking, 1820–1900* (Princeton: Princeton University Press, 1986), Ch. 1.
21. *PHE* XXXIV, col. 1105.
22. *PD* II, col. 554.
23. *PD* VII, col. 33.
24. *PD* VII, col. 593.
25. David Beck Ryden, "Sugar, Spirits, and Fodder: The London West India Interest and the Glut of 1807–15," *Atlantic Studies,* 9 (2012), 46.
26. Ryden, *West Indian Slavery and British Abolition, 1783–1807,* 277.
27. Seymour Drescher, "Public Opinion and Parliament in the Abolition of the British Slave Trade," *Parliamentary History,* 26 Supplement (2007), 63.
28. Douglas, a planter, served as the major spokesman for London's West India Planters and Merchants Committee from 1829. He had served as the colonial agent for Tobago from 1823 to 1826.
29. *PD* 3rd Series XIII, col. 1243.
30. Seymour Drescher, "The Decline Thesis of British Slavery since *Econocide* (1986)," in Seymour Drescher, *From Slavery to Freedom: Comparitive Studies in the Rise and Fall of Atlantic Slavery* (New York: New York University Press, 1999), 103.
31. Lambert, *White Creole Culture, Politics and Identity During the Age of Abolition,* 182.
32. *PD* 3rd Series III, col. 1448.
33. The slave revolt began in the French colony of St. Domingo in 1791. In 1801 Toussaint Louverture outlawed slavery in the territory and in 1804 Haiti was established as an independent nation. Anti-abolitionists used Haiti as an example of the lost productivity and territory that could result from abolitionist principles.
34. *PD* New Series XVIII, col. 1037.
35. *PD* 3rd Series XVIII, col. 1886.
36. *PD* 3rd Series XIX, col. 1216.
37. Andrew J. O'Shaughnessy, *An Empire Divided: The American Revolution and the British Caribbean* (Philadelphia: University of Pennsylvania Press, 2000), 34.
38. Andrew J. O'Shaughnessy, "The Formation of a Commercial Lobby: The West Indian Interest, British Colonial Policy and the American Revolution," *The Historical Journal,* 40 (1997), 77.

39. O'Shaughnessy, *An Empire Divided: The American Revolution and the British Caribbean*, 247.
40. Adam Hochschild, *Bury the Chains: Prophets and Rebels in the Fight to Free an Empire's Slaves* (Boston and New York: Houghton Mifflin Company, 2005), 275.
41. Ibid.
42. Roger N. Buckley, *Slaves in Red Coats: The British West India Regiments, 1795–1815* (New Haven and London: Yale University Press, 1979), 78.
43. Hochschild, *Bury the Chains: Prophets and Rebels in the Fight to Free an Empire's Slaves*, 276.
44. R. G. Thorne, ed., *The House of Commons, 1790–1820*, vol. 5 (London: Secker and Warburg, 1986), 332–6.
45. *PHE* XXXII, col. 741.
46. Ibid., col. 864.
47. See *PD* III, col. 643.
48. Buckley, *Slaves in Red Coats: The British West India Regiments, 1795–1815*, 78.
49. Estimates Database, *Voyages: The Transatlantic Slave Trade Database* (Emory University, 2009) [www.slavevoyages.org/tast/assessment/estimates.faces, accessed December 14, 2012].
50. David Eltis, *Economic Growth and the Ending of the Trans-Atlantic Slave Trade* (New York: Oxford University Press, 1987), 249.
51. Richard B. Sheridan, "Slave Demography in the British West Indies and the Abolition of the Slave Trade," in *The Abolition of the Atlantic Slave Trade*, ed. David Eltis and James Walvin (Madison: University of Wisconsin Press, 1981), 269.
52. Ibid.
53. Ibid., 271.
54. Margarette Lincoln, *Representing the Royal Navy: British Sea Power, 1750–1815* (Aldershot: Ashgate, 2002), 90.
55. *PD* VI, col. 918.
56. Ibid.
57. Lincoln, *Representing the Royal Navy: British Sea Power, 1750–1815*, 78.
58. *PD* VII, col. 587.
59. Stephen Farrell, "'Contrary to the Principles of Justice, Humanity and Sound Policy': The Slave Trade, Parliamentary Politics and the Abolition Act, 1807," in *The British Slave Trade: Abolition, Parliament and People*, ed. Stephen Farrell, Melanie Unwin, and James Walvin (Edinburgh: University of Edinburgh Press, 2007), 161.
60. *PHE* XXIX, col. 1354.
61. *PD* VIII, col. 1043.
62. *PHE* XXIX, col. 281.
63. *PHE* XXXIII, cols. 279–80.

64. Ibid., cols. 280–1.
65. For further examples of MPs and peers quoting acts that abolition would violate, see James Baillie on April 2, 1792 (*PHE* XXIX, col. 1080), the duke of Clarence on July 5, 1799 (*PHE* XXXIV, cols. 1092–3), Alderman John Prinsep on April 25, 1806 (*PD* VI, col. 919), and George Hibbert on March 16, 1807 (*PD* IX, cols. 117 and 128). Anti-abolitionists also referred generally to existing legislation that condoned and encouraged participation in the slave trade, including William Manning on May 30, 1804 (*PD* II, col. 470), George Rose on June 27, 1804 (*PD* II, cols. 867–8), the duke of Clarence on July 3, 1804 (*PD* II, col. 932), and Isaac Gascoyne and Manning on June 10, 1806 (*PD* VII, cols. 593 and 601).
66. *PD* XXXVIII, col. 849.
67. For example, see Patrick Stewart's assessment of the island from May 30, 1833, in *PD* 3rd Series XVIII, col. 156.
68. *PD* 3rd Series XVIII, col. 321.
69. Swaminathan, "Developing the West Indian Proslavery Position after the Somerset Decision," 41.
70. Ibid., 41, 44–5.
71. John W. Cairns, "The Definition of Slavery in Eighteenth-Century Thinking: Not the True Roman Slavery," in *The Legal Understanding of Slavery: From the Historical to the Contemporary,* ed. Jean Allain (Oxford: Oxford University Press, 2012), 71.
72. Ibid., 83.
73. *PHE* XXXII, col. 865. Dent represented the port of Lancaster and was one of 18 MPs who voted against the bill for abolition in 1807.
74. Hibbert had been educated in Liverpool and served as director of the West India Dock Company and chairman of the West India Committee. He also acted as agent for Jamaica from 1812 to 1830. See Thorne, ed., *The House of Commons, 1790–1820,* vol. 4, 193–4.
75. *PD* IX, col. 117.
76. B. W. Higman, "The West India 'Interest' in Parliament, 1807–1833," *Historical Studies,* 13 (1967), 1.
77. Christer Petley, *Slaveholders in Jamaica: Colonial Society and Culture During the Era of Abolition* (London: Pickering and Chatto, 2009), 87.
78. Ibid., 67.
79. David Turley, *The Culture of English Antislavery, 1780–1860* (London: Routledge, 1991), 53–5.
80. William A. Green, *British Slave Emancipation: The Sugar Colonies and the Great Experiment* (1976. Reprint, New York: Oxford University Press, 1991), 105.
81. *PD* New Series X, col. 1332.

82. *PD* 3rd Series XII, col. 630.
83. *PD* New Series XVIII, col. 1029.
84. *PD* 3rd Series XIX, col. 1198.
85. *PHE* XXIX, col. 1084.
86. *PHE* XXXIII, col. 260.
87. *PHE* XXX, cols. 1141–2.
88. *PD* 3rd Series I, col. 1057.
89. *PD* 3rd Series XVIII, col. 1220.
90. *PD* II, col. 459.
91. *PD* VIII, col. 1041.
92. *PD* 3rd Series XX, cols. 63–4. James officially opposed slavery, but his grandfather had made his fortune as a West India merchant and, in 1798, James became the heir to a Jamaican estate and his family's mercantile fortune. See Fisher, ed., *The House of Commons, 1820–1832,* vol. 5, 839–44.
93. David Brion Davis, *The Problem of Slavery in the Age of Revolution 1770–1823* (London: Cornell University Press, 1975), 365–6.
94. Marcus Wood, *Slavery, Empathy, and Pornography* (New York: Oxford University Press, 2002), 151–3.
95. For example, see the anonymous pamphlet, *The Condition of the West Indian Slave Contrasted with That of the Infant Slave in Our English Factories* (London: W. Kidd, 1833). See also Gordon K. Lewis, "Proslavery Ideology," in *Caribbean Slavery in the Atlantic World,* ed. Verene Shepherd and Hilary Beckles (Oxford: Ian Randal, 2000), 558.
96. Larry E. Tise, *Proslavery: A History of the Defense of Slavery in America, 1701–1840* (Athens: University of Georgia Press, 1987), 95.
97. *PHE* XXIX, col. 1075.
98. *PD* II, col. 459.
99. *PD* New Series IX, col. 344.
100. *PD* 3rd Series XX, col. 64.
101. Boyd Hilton, *The Age of Atonement: The Influence of Evangelicalism on Social and Economic Thought 1785–1865* (Oxford: Oxford University Press, 1986), 215–7.
102. *PD* New Series X, col. 1162.
103. *PD* 3rd Series XVIII, col. 470.
104. *PHE* XXXIII, col. 257.
105. Ibid.
106. *PHE* XXIX, col. 315.
107. *PHE* XXXIV, cols. 1136–7.
108. Ibid., col. 1138.
109. *PD* II, col. 865.
110. *PD* VII, col. 592.
111. Ibid., cols. 592–3.

112. *PD* VIII, col. 982.
113. *PD* New Series IX, col. 279.
114. *PD* New Series XIV, col. 1156.
115. *PD* New Series XIV, col. 1162.
116. *PD* 3rd Series I, cols. 1048–9.
117. *PD* 3rd Series XVII, col. 1341.
118. Burge, a plantation owner, served as a colonial agent for Jamaica from 1830 and as Jamaica's attorney general. He was a member of London's West India Planters and Merchants Committee. See D. R. Fisher, ed., *The House of Commons, 1820–1832,* (Cambridge: Cambridge University Press, 2009) vol. 1, 274, and vol. 4, 450–5.
119. *PD* 3rd Series XIII, col. 85.
120. Colin Kidd, *The Forging of Races: Race and Scripture in the Protestant Atlantic World, 1600–2000* (Cambridge: Cambridge University Press, 2006), 116.
121. Ibid.
122. H. F. Augstein, "Introduction," in *Race: The Origins of An Idea, 1760–1850,* ed. H. F. Augstein (Bristol: Thoemmes Press, 1996), ix–x.
123. Mervyn C. Alleyne, *The Construction and Representation of Race and Ethnicity in the Caribbean and the World* (Kingston, Jamaica: University of the West Indies Press, 2002), 82.
124. Lewis, "Proslavery Ideology," 551.
125. *PD* II, col. 460.
126. Kidd, *The Forging of Races: Race and Scripture in the Protestant Atlantic World, 1600–2000,* 80.
127. Lewis, "Proslavery Ideology," 551.
128. *PD* II, col. 461.
129. *PHE* XXXIII, col. 1403.
130. *PD* III, col. 650.
131. *PD* III, col. 658.
132. Fully formed scientific racism and the theory of eugenics emerged later in the nineteenth century. They played an important role in defending American slavery following Britain's abolition.
133. Out of 66 recorded uses of racial arguments during the slave trade and slavery debates in Parliament, 37 (56 percent) were made in the debates leading up to abolition and 29 (44 percent) were made following abolition.
134. See Andrew Wells, "Sex and Racial Theory in Britain, 1690–1833" (Unpublished Oxford University D. Phil. thesis, 2009), 282–7.
135. *PD* New Series X, col. 1103.
136. Boyd Hilton, *A Mad, Bad, Dangerous People? England 1783–1846* (Oxford: Oxford University Press, 2006), 477.

137. For information on contemporary racial thought as utilized in the slavery debates, see Peter J. Kitson, *Romantic Literature, Race, and Colonial Encounter* (New York: Palgrave Macmillan, 2007), Ch. 3.
138. *PD* 3rd Series XVIII, col. 342.
139. Wells, "Sex and Racial Theory in Britain, 1690–1833," 299.

CHAPTER 2

1. [John Gibson Lockhart], "Art. IV–1. Journal of a West India Proprietor," *The Quarterly Review,* 50.100 (January 1834), 374.
2. See Chapter 3 for further examples of ways in which proslavery culture was depicted and shared to a wider British audience.
3. Gordon K. Lewis, "Proslavery Ideology," in *Caribbean Slavery in the Atlantic World*, ed. Verene Shepherd and Hilary Beckles (Oxford: Ian Randal, 2000), 549.
4. For a detailed discussion of the origins of the proslavery position in Britain in this period, see Srividhya Swaminathan, "Developing the West Indian Proslavery Position after the Somerset Decision," *Slavery & Abolition,* 24 (2003), 40–60.
5. Brycchan Carey, *British Abolitionism and the Rhetoric of Sensibility: Writing, Sentiment and Slavery, 1760–1807* (Basingstoke: Macmillan Publishers, 2005), 2.
6. H. T. Dickinson, *Caricatures and the Constitution, 1760–1832* (Cambridge: Chadwyk-Healey Ltd., 1986), 12.
7. Carey, *British Abolitionism and the Rhetoric of Sensibility: Writing, Sentiment and Slavery, 1760–1807,* 15 and 90.
8. John Brewer, *The Pleasures of the Imagination: English Culture in the Eighteenth Century* (London: HarperCollins Publishers, 1997), 100.
9. Anand C. Chitnis, *The Scottish Enlightenment: A Social History* (London: Croom Helm, Ltd., 1976), 6.
10. Vic Gatrell, *City of Laughter: Sex and Satire in Eighteenth Century London* (London: Atlantic Books, 2006), 16.
11. Roy Porter and Lesley Hall, *The Facts of Life: The Creation of Sexual Knowledge in Britain, 1650–1950* (New Haven: Yale University Press, 1995), 18. For further discussion on the outward display of politeness in public settings, see Helen Berry, "Polite Consumption: Shopping in Eighteenth-Century England," *Transactions of the Royal Historical Society,* Sixth Series 12 (2002), 375–94.
12. Brewer, *The Pleasures of the Imagination: English Culture in the Eighteenth Century,* 114–7.
13. Philip Babcock Grove, ed., "Utilitarianism," in *Webster's Third New International Dictionary of the English Language Unabridged* (Springfield: Merriam-Webster Inc., 1993), 2525.

14. Bart Schultz and Georgios Varouxakis, "Introduction," in *Utilitarianism and Empire,* ed. Bart Schultz and Georgios Varouxakis (Oxford: Lexington Books, 2005), 7.
15. Frederick Rosen, "Jeremy Bentham on Slavery and the Slave Trade," in *Utilitarianism and Empire,* ed. Bart Schultz and Georgios Varouxakis (Oxford: Lexington Books, 2005), 45.
16. Brewer, *The Pleasures of the Imagination: English Culture in the Eighteenth Century,* 133.
17. Olivia Smith, *The Politics of Language, 1791–1819* (Oxford: Oxford University Press, 1984), 158.
18. Brewer, *The Pleasures of the Imagination: English Culture in the Eighteenth Century,* xxvi–xxvii.
19. Ibid., 172.
20. Ibid., 167.
21. Ibid.
22. Ibid., 168.
23. Ibid., 188.
24. Ibid., 93.
25. For a detailed overview of the abolitionist works and arguments that influenced the British public in the 1780s and 1790s, see Srividhya Swaminathan's *Debating the Slave Trade* (London: Ashgate, 2009), Ch. 3.
26. Christer Petley, "Slavery, Emancipation and the Creole World View of Jamaican Colonists, 1800–1834," *Slavery & Abolition,* 26 (2005), 100.
27. Ibid.
28. Srividhya Swaminathan, *Debating the Slave Trade: Rhetoric of British National Identity, 1759–1815* (Surrey: Ashgate Publishing Limited, 2009), 142–3.
29. For example, see the introductory pages of Jesse Foot's *A Defence of the Planters in the West Indies; Comprised in Four Arguments,* 2nd edn. (London: J. Debrett, 1792), discussed in this chapter.
30. For a detailed look at the rhetorical strategies and intended readership of early pro- and anti-slavery pamphlets, see Brycchan Carey's *British Abolitionism and the Rhetoric of Sensibility* (New York: Palgrave Macmillan, 2005), Ch. 4.
31. Brewer, *The Pleasures of the Imagination: English Culture in the Eighteenth Century,* 172.
32. Thomas Maxwell Adams, *A Cool Address to the People of England, on the Slave Trade* (London: R. Faulder and J. Stockdale, 1788), 18–9.
33. Carey, *British Abolitionism and the Rhetoric of Sensibility: Writing, Sentiment and Slavery, 1760–1807,* 128.
34. Adams, *A Cool Address,* 36–7.
35. See Chapter 1 for examples of this strategy being employed in the parliamentary debates.

36. Adams, *A Cool Address,* 34.
37. Swaminathan, *Debating the Slave Trade: Rhetoric of British National Identity, 1759–1815,* 192.
38. Foot remarks that he will leave the "modern pioneers of humanity" to inform the others. See Foot, *A Defence of the Planters in the West Indies; Comprised in Four Arguments,* iii.
39. See Srividhya Swaminathan's discussion of women becoming involved in the abolition movement in Swaminathan, *Debating the Slave Trade: Rhetoric of British National Identity, 1759–1815,* 190.
40. Foot, *A Defence of the Planters in the West Indies; Comprised in Four Arguments,* 93.
41. Ibid., 95.
42. Ibid., 8.
43. Ibid., 7.
44. See Chapter 1 for examples of this argument being employed in Parliament.
45. See Alexander McDonnell, *The West India Legislatures Vindicated from the Charge of Having Resisted the Call of the Mother Country for the Amelioration of Slavery* (London: John Murray, 1826), 89–102.
46. Ibid., 7–8.
47. James Walvin, *England, Slaves and Freedom 1776–1838* (Basingstoke: Macmillan, 1986), 19.
48. A Resident, *Sketches and Recollections of the West Indies* (London: Smith, Elder, & Co., 1828), ix.
49. F. W. N. Bayley, *Four Years' Residence in the West Indies* (London: William Kidd, 1830), vi–vii.
50. Ibid.
51. The popular *Domestic Manners of the Americans* by Frances Trollope had been published one year earlier. The author or publisher would have been trying to capitalize on the earlier travel journal's success.
52. Mrs. Carmichael, *Domestic Manners and Social Condition of the White, Coloured, and Negro Population of the West Indies,* 2 vols. (London: Whittaker, Treacher, and Co., 1833), vol. 1, 32.
53. A Resident, *Sketches and Recollections,* vii; xii–xiii.
54. Ibid., 269.
55. Ibid., 292–3.
56. Ibid., 316.
57. These works are discussed later in this chapter.
58. Bayley, *Four Years' Residence,* 372.
59. Ibid., 373.
60. Carmichael, *Domestic Manners and Social Condition of the White, Coloured, and Negro Population of the West Indies,* vol. 1, 324.
61. Allan Gallay, "'The Origins of Slaveholders' Paternalism: George Whitefield, the Bryan Family, and the Great Awakening in the South," *Journal of Southern History,* 53 (1987), 393–4.

62. Carmichael, *Domestic Manners and Social Condition of the White, Coloured, and Negro Population of the West Indies*, vol. 1, 244–5.
63. Andrew Lewis, "'An Incendiary Press': British West Indian Newspapers during the Struggle for Abolition," *Slavery & Abolition*, 16 (1995), 348–51.
64. Rev. George Wilson Bridges, *A Voice from Jamaica in Reply to William Wilberforce, Esq. M.P.* (London: Longman, Hurst, Rees, Orme, Brown, and Green, 1823), 19.
65. Ibid., 8.
66. Ibid., 46.
67. Robert Hibbert Jun., *Facts, Verified Upon Oath, in Contradiction of the Report of Rev. Thomas Cooper, Concerning the General Condition of the Slaves in Jamaica; and More Especially Relative to the Management and Treatment of the Slaves Upon Georgia Estate, in the Parish of Hanover, in That Island* (London: John Murray, 1824) ix.
68. James MacQueen, *The West India Colonies; The Calumnies and Misrepresentations Circulated Against Them by The Edinburgh Review, Mr. Clarkson, Mr. Cropper, etc. etc.* (London: Baldwin, Cradock, and Joy, 1824), 1–2.
69. David Lambert, *White Creole Culture, Politics and Identity During the Age of Abolition* (Cambridge: Cambridge University Press, 2005), 145.
70. James MacQueen, *The Colonial Controversy, Containing a Refutation of the Anticolonists; the State of Hayti, Sierra Leone, India, China, Cochin China, Java, &c. &c.; the Production of Sugar, &c. and the State of the Free and Slave Labourers in those Countries; Fully Considered, in a Series of Letters, Addressed to the Earl of Liverpool; With a Supplementary Letter to Mr. Macaulay* (Glasgow: Khull, Blackie, & Co., 1825), 5.
71. Ibid., 9.
72. Alexander Barclay, *A Practical View of the Present State of Slavery in the West Indies; or, An Examination of Mr. Stephen's "Slavery of the British West India Colonies"* (London: Smith, Elder & Co., 1826), i–ii.
73. Ibid., ii.
74. Alexander McDonnell, *Compulsory Manumission; Or an Examination of the Actual State of the West India Question* (London: John Murray, 1827), 6–7.
75. Ibid., 62.
76. Brewer, *The Pleasures of the Imagination: English Culture in the Eighteenth Century*, 172.
77. Richard Watson, *The Religious Instruction of Slaves in the West India Colonies Advocated and Defended. A Sermon Preached before the Wesleyan Methodist Missionary Society, in the New Chapel, City-Road, London, April 28, 1824*, 4th edn. (London: Butterworth and Son, n.d.), 6.

78. Ibid., 8–9; Rev. B. Bailey, *The House of Bondage. A Dissertation upon the Nature of Service or Slavery under Levitical Law, among the Hebrews in the Earliest Ages, and in the Gentile World, Until the Coming of Christ*... (London: C. & J. Rivington, 1824), 15–7. Vincent Carretta and Philip Gould have noted that by interpreting Genesis Chapter Nine to mean that Africans were Ham's descendants, writers could argue that Africans were meant to be slaves. See Vincent Carretta and Philip Gould, "Introduction," in *Genius in Bondage: Literature of the Early Black Atlantic*, ed. Vincent Carretta and Philip Gould (Lexington: The University Press of Kentucky, 2001), 5.
79. Bailey, *The House of Bondage. A Dissertation upon the Nature of Service or Slavery under Levitical Law, among the Hebrews in the Earliest Ages, and in the Gentile World, Until the Coming of Christ*..., 22.
80. Ibid., 23.
81. Ibid., 24; Watson, *The Religious Instruction of Slaves in the West India Colonies Advocated and Defended. A Sermon Preached before the Wesleyan Methodist Missionary Society, in the New Chapel, City-Road, London, April 28, 1824*, 15.
82. Joanne Shattock, *Politics and Reviewers: The Edinburgh and the Quarterly in the Early Victorian Age* (London: Leicester University Press, 1989), 10–11.
83. Biancamaria Fontana, *Rethinking the Politics of Commercial Society: The Edinburgh Review 1802–1832* (Cambridge: Cambridge University Press, 1985), 6.
84. John Clive, *Scotch Reviewers: The Edinburgh Review, 1802–1815* (London: Faber and Faber Ltd., 1956), 84–5.
85. Fontana, *Rethinking the Politics of Commercial Society: The Edinburgh Review 1802–1832.*
86. Jonathan Cutmore, "Introduction," in *Conservativism and the Quarterly Review: A Critical Analysis*, ed. Jonathan Cutmore (London: Pickering & Chatto, 2007), 10.
87. Shattock, *Politics and Reviewers: The Edinburgh and the Quarterly in the Early Victorian Age*, 11–12.
88. Ibid., 12–13.
89. Ibid., 13–14.
90. John O. Hayden, *The Romantic Reviewers, 1802–1824* (London: Routledge and Kegan Paul, 1969), 11.
91. "Art. VIII. Substance of the Debate in the House of Commons on 15th May, 1823 ...," *The Quarterly Review* 29.58 (1823), 477.
92. William Christie, *The Edinburgh Review in the Literary Culture of Romantic Britain: Mammoth and Megalonyx* (London: Pickering and Chatto, 2009), 20–3.
93. Cutmore, "Introduction," 14.
94. Christie, *The Edinburgh Review in the Literary Culture of Romantic Britain: Mammoth and Megalonyx*, 51.

95. Anne H. Stevens, *British Historical Fiction before Scott* (London: Palgrave Macmillan, 2010), 124.
96. Ibid., 125.
97. Hayden, *The Romantic Reviewers, 1802–1824,* 244.
98. [George Ellis], "Art. II. The History of Barbadoes, from the first Discovery of the Island in the Year 1605, till the Accession of Lord Seaforth, 1801," *The Quarterly Review* 1.2 (1809), 267.
99. The contributor was likely Joseph Lowe who had published an *Inquiry into the State of the British West Indies* in 1807. See Jonathan Cutmore, *Contributors to the Quarterly Review: A History, 1809–1825* (London: Pickering & Chatto, 2008), 176.
100. "Art. VIII. Substance of the Debate in the House of Commons on 15 May, 1823 . . . ," 477.
101. Ibid.
102. Ibid., 478.
103. See Chapter 1 for information on how these arguments were presented in Parliament.
104. "Art. VIII. Substance of the Debate in the House of Commons on 15 May, 1823 . . . ," 496–7 and 507.
105. Ibid., 507.
106. Ibid., 508.
107. [Charles Rose Ellis and Robert John Wilmot Horton], "Art. XIII–1. Speech of the Right Honourable George Canning . . . ," *The Quarterly Review* 30.60 (January 1824), 566–7.
108. Ibid., 572.
109. Ibid., 570–1.
110. Brycchan Carey and Sara Salih, "Introduction," in *Discourses of Slavery and Abolition: Britain and its Colonies, 1760–1838,* ed. Brycchan Carey, Markman Ellis, and Sara Salih (Basingstoke: Palgrave Macmillan, 2004), 2–3.
111. Steven Fuller, *The Representation of Steven Fuller, Esq; Agent for Jamaica, to His Majesty's Ministers* (London: n.p., 1785), 1.
112. Lambert, *White Creole Culture, Politics and Identity During the Age of Abolition*, 61.
113. Brewer, *The Pleasures of the Imagination: English Culture in the Eighteenth Century,* 181.
114. Ibid., 193.
115. Lewis, "Proslavery Ideology," 546–7.
116. Marcus Wood, *Slavery, Empathy, and Pornography* (New York: Oxford University Press, 2002), 142–3.
117. Edward Long, *The History of Jamaica. Or, General Survey of the Antient and Modern State of That Island: with Reflections on its Situation, Settlements, Inhabitants, Climate, Products, Commerce, Laws, and Government,* 3 vols. (London: T. Lowndes, 1774), vol. 1, 2.

118. Ibid., vol. 2, 370. Note that orangutans are native to Indonesia and Malaysia, not Africa.
119. Lewis, "Proslavery Ideology," 551.
120. Bryan Edwards, *The History, Civil and Commercial, of the British Colonies in the West Indies*, 2 vols. (London: John Stockdale, 1793), vol. 1, xvii.
121. Ibid., vol. 1, xviii.
122. Ibid., vol. 1, xx–xxi.
123. Bryan Edwards, *An Historical Survey of the French Colony in the Island of St. Domingo: Comprehending a Short Account of its Ancient Government, Political State, Population, Productions, and Exports; A Narrative of the Calamities which have Desolated the Country ever since the year 1789, with some Reflections on their Causes and Probable Consequences, and a Detail of the Military Transactions of the British Army in that Island to the End of 1794* (London: John Stockdale, 1797), xxii.
124. Ibid., 83–5.
125. Ibid., 86.
126. Ibid., 7.
127. Lambert, *White Creole Culture, Politics and Identity During the Age of Abolition*, 77–8.
128. John Poyer, *The History of Barbados, from the First Discovery of the Island, in the Year 1605, Till the Accession of Lord Seaforth in 1801* (London: J. Mawman, 1808), xiv.
129. Ibid., xiv–xv.
130. Ibid., xxi.
131. Lambert, *White Creole Culture, Politics and Identity During the Age of Abolition*, 77–8.
132. J. Stewart, *A View of the Past and Present State of the Island of Jamaica; With Remarks on the Moral and Physical Condition of the Slaves, and on the Abolition of Slavery in the Colonies* (Edinburgh: Oliver & Boyd, 1823), v-vi.
133. Ibid., vi–vii.
134. Ibid., 242.
135. Ibid., 243–4.
136. Ibid., 244.
137. Lambert, *White Creole Culture, Politics and Identity During the Age of Abolition*, 69.
138. George Boulukos, *The Grateful Slave: The Emergence of Race in Eighteenth-Century British and American Culture* (Cambridge: Cambridge University Press, 2008), 6–7.
139. Lambert, *White Creole Culture, Politics and Identity During the Age of Abolition*, 66.
140. James Grainger, *An Essay on the More Common West-India Diseases; and the Remedies which that Country Itself Produces: To Which are*

Added, Some Hints on the Management, etc. of Negroes, 2nd edn. (Edinburgh: Mundell & Son, and London: Longman & Rees, 1802), vi–viii.

141. Ibid., v–vi.
142. Ibid., i.
143. Ibid., v–vi.
144. Ibid., 8.
145. Ibid.
146. Ibid., 89.
147. Ibid., 88.
148. The manual was advertised as "a Work necessary to the West India Planters at all times, but more especially adapted to the circumstance of a cessation of the Slave Trade." In "Multiple Classified Ads," *Morning Post* (August 31, 1804), 2.
149. "The Following Address to the People of Great Britain and Ireland has been of Late Most Extensively Circulated throughout the United Kingdom by the West India Body in this Country," *The Anti-Slavery Reporter* 82 (June 25, 1831), 296.
150. A Professional Planter, *Practical Rules for the Management and Medical Treatment of Negro Slaves, in the Sugar Colonies* (London: J. Barfield, 1803), 9–10.
151. Ibid., 25.
152. Ibid., 28.
153. Ibid., 35.
154. Ibid., 47–8.
155. Ibid, 85.
156. Peter Kitson, "'Candid Reflections': The Idea of Race in the Debate over the Slave Trade and Slavery in the Late Eighteenth and Early Nineteenth Century," in *Discourses of Slavery and Abolition: Britain and its Colonies, 1760–1838,* ed. Brycchan Carey, Markman Ellis, and Sara Salih (Basingstoke: Palgrave Macmillan, 2004), 22.
157. Boulukos, *The Grateful Slave: The Emergence of Race in Eighteenth-Century British and American Culture,* 202.
158. Peter J. Kitson, *Romantic Literature, Race, and Colonial Encounter* (New York: Palgrave Macmillan, 2007), 103.
159. H. F. Augstein, "Introduction," in *Race: The Origins of An Idea, 1760–1850,* ed. H. F. Augstein (Bristol: Thoemmes Press, 1996), ix–x.
160. Kitson, *Romantic Literature, Race, and Colonial Encounter,* 19, 93.
161. Carretta and Gould, "Introduction," 5.
162. Kitson, "'Candid Reflections': The Idea of Race in the Debate over the Slave Trade and Slavery in the Late Eighteenth and Early Nineteenth Century," 20.

163. Walvin, *England, Slaves and Freedom 1776–1838*, 24.
164. Charles White, *An Account of the Regular Gradation in Man, and in Different Animals and Vegetables; and from the Former to the Latter* (London: C. Dilly, 1799), iii.
165. Ibid., 43.
166. Andrew Wells, "Sex and Racial Theory in Britain, 1690–1833" (Unpublished Oxford University DPhil thesis, 2009), 285.
167. A name given to pastoral people of Southwestern Africa now deemed derogatory.
168. White, *Account of the Regular Gradation in Man*, 134.
169. Ibid., 137.
170. James Cowles Prichard, *Researches into the Physical History of Mankind*, 2nd edn., 2 vols. (London: John and Arthur Arch, 1826), vol. 1, 2.
171. Ibid., vol. 1, 240.
172. Ibid., vol. 2, 533.
173. Augstein, "Introduction," xiii.
174. Ibid., xxiv.
175. Prichard, *Researches into the Physical History of Mankind*, vol. 1, 337.
176. John Bigland, *An Historical Display of the Effects of Physical and Moral Causes on the Character and Circumstances of Nations: Including a Comparison of the Ancients and Moderns in Regard to their Intellectual and Social State* (London: Longman, Hurst, Rees, Orme, and Brown, 1816), 4.
177. Ibid., 13.
178. Ibid., 61.
179. Ibid., 28.
180. Ibid.

CHAPTER 3

1. [Sir Phillip Gibbes], *Instructions for the Treatment of Negroes &c. &c. &c.*, 3rd edn. (London: Shepperson and Reynolds, 1797), 107.
2. Kay Dian Kriz, *Slavery, Sugar, and the Culture of Refinement: Picturing the British West Indies, 1700–1840* (New Haven: Yale University Press, 2008), 2.
3. John Brewer, *The Pleasures of the Imagination: English Culture in the Eighteenth Century* (London: HarperCollins Publishers, 1997), 450–1.
4. Ibid., 453.
5. Ibid., xxvi.
6. Ibid., 228.
7. Ibid., 206.
8. Ibid., 276.

9. Ibid., 208.
10. See Albert Boime, *The Art of Exclusion: Representing Blacks in the Nineteenth Century* (London: Thames and Hudson, 1990), 1–2.
11. David Dabydeen, *Hogarth's Blacks: Images of Blacks in Eighteenth Century English Art* (Kingston-Upon-Thames, Surrey: Dangaroo Press, 1985), 21–7.
12. Marcus Wood, *Blind Memory: Visual Representation of Slavery in England and America 1780–1865* (New York: Routledge, 2000), 153.
13. Marcia Pointon, *Hanging the Head: Portraiture and Social Formation in Eighteenth-Century England* (New Haven and London: Yale University Press, 1993), 141.
14. Ibid., 9.
15. It is interesting to note that the exhibition was held the same month that the abolition campaign was launched. See Jan Marsh, "The Black Presence in British Art 1800–1900: Introduction and Overview," in *Black Victorians: Black People in British Art 1800–1900*, ed. Jan Marsh (Aldershot: Lund Humphries, 2005), 17.
16. Pointon, *Hanging the Head: Portraiture and Social Formation in Eighteenth-Century England*, 38.
17. David Bindman, "Subjectivity and Slavery in Portraiture," in *Slave Portraiture in the Atlantic World*, ed. Agnes Lugo-Ortiz and Angela Rosenthal (New York: Cambridge University Press, 2013), 85.
18. Pointon, *Hanging the Head: Portraiture and Social Formation in Eighteenth-Century England*, 146.
19. Bindman, "Subjectivity and Slavery in Portraiture," 73.
20. Dabydeen, *Hogarth's Blacks: Images of Blacks in Eighteenth Century English Art*, 30.
21. Pointon, *Hanging the Head: Portraiture and Social Formation in Eighteenth-Century England*, 146.
22. Kriz, *Slavery, Sugar, and the Culture of Refinement: Picturing the British West Indies, 1700–1840*, 79.
23. Pointon, *Hanging the Head: Portraiture and Social Formation in Eighteenth-Century England*, 81.
24. Ibid., 61.
25. Diana Donald, *The Age of Caricature: Satirical Prints in the Reign of George III* (New Haven and London: Yale University Press, 1996), 15.
26. Pascal Dupuy, "Informations et désinformations: Les tentatives d'abolition de l'esclavage en Angleterre à traverse la caricature anglaise, 1760–1810," *Actes de Colloque de 1999*, 25 (2001), 182.
27. Donald, *The Age of Caricature: Satirical Prints in the Reign of George III*, 19–20.
28. Vic Gatrell, *City of Laughter: Sex and Satire in Eighteenth Century London* (London: Atlantic Books, 2006), 7.

29. Eirwen E. C. Nicholson, "Consumers and Spectators: The Public of the Political Print in Eighteenth-Century England," *History*, 81 (1996), 19.
30. Ibid., 17.
31. H. T. Dickinson, *Caricatures and the Constitution, 1760–1832* (Cambridge: Chadwyk-Healey Ltd., 1986), 15.
32. Nicholson, "Consumers and Spectators: The Public of the Political Print in Eighteenth-Century England," 18.
33. Dickinson, *Caricatures and the Constitution, 1760–1832*, 13.
34. Gatrell, *City of Laughter: Sex and Satire in Eighteenth Century London*, 14.
35. Dickinson, *Caricatures and the Constitution, 1760–1832*, 19.
36. Ibid., 20.
37. Ibid., 17–18.
38. Ibid., 20.
39. Gatrell, *City of Laughter: Sex and Satire in Eighteenth Century London*, 11.
40. Dickinson, *Caricatures and the Constitution, 1760–1832*, 13.
41. Ibid., 21.
42. Gatrell, *City of Laughter: Sex and Satire in Eighteenth Century London*, 9.
43. Ibid., 10.
44. Dickinson, *Caricatures and the Constitution, 1760–1832*, 13.
45. Nicholson, "Consumers and Spectators: The Public of the Political Print in Eighteenth-Century England," 10.
46. Ibid., 10–11.
47. Ibid.
48. Dickinson, *Caricatures and the Constitution, 1760–1832*, 13.
49. Brewer, *The Pleasures of the Imagination: English Culture in the Eighteenth Century*, 457–9.
50. Dickinson, *Caricatures and the Constitution, 1760–1832*, 14.
51. Ibid.
52. Wood, *Blind Memory: Visual Representation of Slavery in England and America 1780–1865*, 152. See also Donald, *The Age of Caricature: Satirical Prints in the Reign of George III*, 2.
53. Kriz, *Slavery, Sugar, and the Culture of Refinement: Picturing the British West Indies, 1700–1840*, 99–100.
54. Ibid., 99.
55. Henrice Altink, "Deviant and Dangerous: Pro-Slavery Representations of Jamaican Slave Women's Sexuality, c. 1780–1834," *Slavery & Abolition*, 26 (2005), 272–5.
56. Kriz, *Slavery, Sugar, and the Culture of Refinement: Picturing the British West Indies, 1700–1840*, 100.
57. Wood, *Blind Memory: Visual Representation of Slavery in England and America 1780–1865*, 154.

58. Ibid., 156.
59. Donald, *The Age of Caricature: Satirical Prints in the Reign of George III*, 15.
60. Kriz, *Slavery, Sugar, and the Culture of Refinement: Picturing the British West Indies, 1700–1840*, 99–100.
61. Ibid., 106.
62. Charmaine Nelson, "Venus Africaine: Race, Beauty and African-ness," in *Black Victorians: Black People in British Art 1800–1900*, ed. Jan Marsh (Aldershot: Lund Humphries, 2005), 47.
63. Miles Taylor, "John Bull and the Iconography of Public Opinion in England c. 1712–1929," *Past & Present*, 134 (1992), 106.
64. Kriz, *Slavery, Sugar, and the Culture of Refinement: Picturing the British West Indies, 1700–1840*, 1.
65. Donald, *The Age of Caricature: Satirical Prints in the Reign of George III*, 44.
66. Roy Porter, "Review: Seeing the Past," *Past & Present*, 118 (1988), 200.
67. Kriz, *Slavery, Sugar, and the Culture of Refinement: Picturing the British West Indies, 1700–1840*, 2.
68. Ibid.
69. Anon., *Cruelty & Oppression Abroad* (London: W. Holland, 1792).
70. Brewer, *The Pleasures of the Imagination: English Culture in the Eighteenth Century*, 352.
71. Ibid., 354.
72. Ibid., 352.
73. Ibid., 327–31.
74. Ibid., 438.
75. Ibid., 61.
76. Ibid., 330.
77. Ibid., 94.
78. Ibid., 76.
79. Ibid., 351.
80. "Theatre Royal, Hay Market," *Times* [London] (August 3, 1789), 1.
81. See *The New Vocal Enchantress Containing An Elegant Selection of All The Newest Songs Lately Sung at the Theatres Royal Drury Lane, Covent Garden, Haymarket, Royalty Theatre, Vaux Hall, &c. &c. &c.* (London: C. Stalker, 1791), 29–30. See also *The Muse in Good Humour; or Momus's Banquet: A Collection of Choice Songs, Including the Modern* (London: William Lane, n.d.), 123.
82. John Whitaker and Gilbert Stuart, "Monthly Catalogue," *The English Review, or An Abstract of English and Foreign Literature* 14 (1789), 387.
83. John Gilmore, "Introduction," in *Creoleana and The Fair Barbadian and Faithful Black*, ed. John Gilmore (Oxford: Macmillan Education, 2002), 15.

84. Thomas Bellamy, *The Benevolent Planters* (London: J. Debrett, 1789), 3.
85. Ibid., 3–4.
86. George Boulukos, *The Grateful Slave: The Emergence of Race in Eighteenth-Century British and American Culture* (Cambridge: Cambridge University Press, 2008), 9–13.
87. Bellamy, *The Benevolent Planters,* 13.
88. J. W. Orderson, *The Fair Barbadian and Faithful Black; or, A Cure for the Gout. A Comedy in Three Acts* (Liverpool: Ross and Nightingale, 1835), in *Creoleana and The Fair Barbadian and Faithful Black,* ed. John Gilmore (Oxford: Macmillan Education, 2002), 158.
89. Olivia Smith, *The Politics of Language, 1791–1819* (Oxford: Oxford University Press, 1984), 3.
90. David Lambert, *White Creole Culture, Politics and Identity During the Age of Abolition* (Cambridge: Cambridge University Press, 2005), 202.
91. Heather S. Nathans, *Slavery and Sentiment on the American Stage, 1787–1861: Lifting the Veil of Black* (New York: Cambridge University Press, 2009), 6.
92. Brewer, *The Pleasures of the Imagination: English Culture in the Eighteenth Century,* 352.
93. George E. Boulukos, "Maria Edgeworth's 'Grateful Negro' and the Sentimental Argument for Slavery," *Eighteenth-Century Life,* 23 (1999), 23.
94. Orderson, *The Fair Barbadian and Faithful Black,* 181.
95. Ibid.
96. Brewer, *The Pleasures of the Imagination: English Culture in the Eighteenth Century,* 172.
97. James G. Basker, ed., *Amazing Grace: An Anthology of Poems about Slavery* (New Haven: Yale University Press, 2002), xxxiii.
98. Ibid., xlvii.
99. Brycchan Carey, *British Abolitionism and the Rhetoric of Sensibility: Writing, Sentiment and Slavery, 1760–1807* (Basingstoke: Macmillan Publishers, 2005), 92.
100. Karen O'Brien, "Imperial Georgic, 1660–1789," in *The Country and the City Revisited: England and the Politics of Culture, 1550–1850,* ed. Gerald Maclean, Donna Landry, and Joseph P. Ward (Cambridge: Cambridge University Press, 1999), 174–5.
101. Anon., "The Field Negro, or the Effect of Civilization," in *Poems, on Subjects arising in England, and the West Indies* (London: R. Faulder, 1783), 15–16.
102. Basker, ed., *Amazing Grace: An Anthology of Poems about Slavery,* 237.
103. James Boswell, *No Abolition of Slavery; or the Universal Empire of Love* (London: R. Faulder, 1791), 8.

104. Ibid., 17.
105. Ibid., 21–2.
106. Rev. H. E. Holder, *Fragments of a Poem, Intended to have been Written in Consequence of Reading Major Majoribanks's Slavery* (Bath: R. Cruttwell, 1792), 19.
107. Ibid., 18.
108. [Gibbes], *Instructions for the Treatment of Negroes,* 107.
109. Ibid., 108.
110. [Sir Phillip Gibbes], "A Negro's Address to his Fellows," in *Instructions for the Treatment of Negroes &c. &c. &c.,* 3rd edn. (London: Shepperson and Reynolds, 1797), 133.
111. Ibid.
112. C. F. D., "Bonja Song," in *Contrary Voices: Representations of West Indian Slavery, 1657–1834,* ed. Karina Williamson (Kingston, Jamaica: University of the West Indies Press, 2008), 491.
113. Ibid., 492.
114. For example, see the discussion of F. W. N. Bayley's *Four Years Residence in the West Indies* (1830) in Chapter 2.
115. M. J. Chapman, *Barbadoes, and Other Poems* (London: James Fraser, 1833), vii–viii.
116. Ibid., 41–2.
117. See Chapters 4 and 5 for further discussion of these stories.
118. See Chapter 1 for similar discussions of the term "slave" in the parliamentary debates.
119. Chapman, *Barbadoes, and Other Poems,* 80.
120. See Chapter 1 for examples of similar paternalist arguments put forth in the parliamentary debates.
121. Markman Ellis, *The Politics of Sensibility: Race, Gender and Commerce in the Sentimental Novel* (Cambridge: Cambridge University Press, 1996), 8–9.
122. Anne H. Stevens, *British Historical Fiction before Scott* (London: Palgrave Macmillan, 2010), 53–4.
123. Ibid., 55.
124. Brewer, *The Pleasures of the Imagination: English Culture in the Eighteenth Century,* xviii.
125. Janina Nordius, "Racism and Radicalism in Jamaican Gothic: Cynric R. Williams's *Hamel, The Obeah Man,*" *ELH,* 73 (2006), 674–5.
126. Karina Williamson, "Introduction," in *Marly; or, A Planter's Life in Jamaica,* Karina Williamson, ed. (Oxford: Macmillan, 2005), xxxiii.
127. Colonists viewed Obeah as alarming and dangerous. Slaves throughout Britain's West Indian colonies were banned from practicing it. See Randy M. Browne, "The 'Bad Business' of Obeah: Power, Authority,

and the Politics of Slave Culture in the British Caribbean," *William and Mary Quarterly*, 3rd ser. 68 (2011), 455.

128. John Gilmore, "Series Editor's Preface," in *Marly; or, A Planter's Life in Jamaica*, Karina Williamson, ed. (Oxford: Macmillan, 2005), viii.
129. Nordius, "Racism and Radicalism in Jamaican Gothic: Cynric R. Williams's *Hamel, The Obeah Man*," 673.
130. [Cynric R. Williams], *Hamel, The Obeah Man*, 2 vols. (London: Hunt and Clark, 1827), vol. 2, 313.
131. Anon., *Marly; or, A Planter's Life in Jamaica* (Glasgow: Richard Griffin and Co., 1828); Reprint: Karina Williamson, ed. (Oxford: Macmillan, 2005), 2.
132. Nordius, "Racism and Radicalism in Jamaican Gothic: Cynric R. Williams's *Hamel, The Obeah Man*," 679.
133. Williamson, "Introduction," in *Marly; or, A Planter's Life*, xxiv.

CHAPTER 4

1. *Parliamentary History of England* [hereafter *PHE*] XXVII, col. 638.
2. Ibid., col. 639.
3. Ibid., 645.
4. Ibid., 641.
5. Srividhya Swaminathan, *Debating the Slave Trade: Rhetoric of British National Identity, 1759–1815* (Surrey: Ashgate Publishing Limited, 2009), Ch. 5.
6. Brycchan Carey, *British Abolitionism and the Rhetoric of Sensibility: Writing, Sentiment and Slavery, 1760–1807* (Basingstoke: Macmillan Publishers Ltd., 2005), 90–2.
7. Stephen Farrell, "'Contrary to the Principles of Justice, Humanity and Sound Policy': The Slave Trade, Parliamentary Politics and the Abolition Act, 1807", in *The British Slave Trade: Abolition, Parliament and People*, ed. Stephen Farrell, Melanie Unwin, and James Walvin (Edinburgh: University of Edinburgh Press, 2007), 145.
8. *PHE* XXIX, col. 281.
9. Ibid., col. 1225.
10. Sheffield was the author of *Observations on the Project for Abolishing the Slave Trade* (London: J. Debrett, 1790) that was published in at least two editions.
11. Seymour Drescher, "Whose Abolition? Popular Pressure and the Ending of the British Slave Trade," *Past & Present*, 143 (1994), 165.
12. *PHE* XXX, col. 659.
13. Ibid., col. 1440.
14. James A. Epstein, *Radical Expression: Political Language, Ritual, and Symbol in England, 1790–1850* (New York: Oxford University Press, 1994), 27.

15. H. T. Dickinson, *Liberty and Property: Political Ideology in Eighteenth-Century Britain* (London: Methuen & Co., 1977), 289.
16. William C. Lowe, "Bertie, Willoughby, fourth earl of Abingdon (1740–1799)," *Oxford Dictionary of National Biography* (Oxford: Oxford University Press, 2004) [www.oxforddnb.com/view/article/2280, accessed December 3, 2012].
17. *PHE* XXXI, col. 468.
18. Thomas L. Haskell, "Capitalism and the Origins of the Human Sensibility," *American Historical Review*, 90 (1985), 345–50.
19. *PHE* XXXIII, col. 1387.
20. *The Parliamentary Debates* [hereafter *PD*] IX, cols. 142–6.
21. Ibid., col. 143.
22. *PHE* XXXIII, col. 1387.
23. Ibid., col. 1388.
24. *PD* II, col. 651.
25. *PD* III, col. 642.
26. Ibid., col. 657.
27. *PHE* XXVII, col. 644.
28. *PHE* XXIX, cols. 331–2.
29. *PHE* XXX, col. 1441.
30. *PHE* XXXII, col. 869.
31. *PHE* XXXIII, col. 573.
32. Linda Colley, *Britons: Forging the Nation, 1707–1837* (New Haven: Yale University Press, 1992), 373.
33. *PD* IX, col. 115.
34. Seymour Drescher, "People and Parliament: The Rhetoric of the British Slave Trade," *Journal of Interdisciplinary History*, 20 (1990), 567.
35. Frank O'Gorman, *Voters, Patrons, and Parties: The Unreformed Electoral System of Hanoverian England, 1734–1832* (Oxford: Oxford University Press, 1989), 291.
36. *PHE* XXIX, col. 1229.
37. Ibid., col. 1241.
38. Olivia Smith, *The Politics of Language, 1791–1819* (Oxford: Oxford University Press, 1984), vii.
39. Janet Sorensen, "Vulgar Tongues: Canting Dictionaries and the Language of the People in Eighteenth-Century Britain," *Eighteenth-Century Studies*, 37 (2004), 436.
40. Smith, *The Politics of Language, 1791–1819*, 30–4.
41. *PHE* XXX, col. 657.
42. *PHE* XXIX, cols. 1281–2.
43. *PHE* XXXI, col. 1330. East was a member of the Society of West Indian Planters and Merchants in London and the great-grandson of an early Jamaican colonist. See Thorne, ed., *The House of Commons, 1790–1820*, vol. 3, 659–60.

44. Smith, *The Politics of Language, 1791–1819*, 162.
45. Dror Warhman, "Virtual Representation: Parliamentary Reporting and Languages of Class in the 1790s," *Past and Present*, 136 (1992), 85.
46. *PHE* XXXIV, col. 1110.
47. *PHE* XXX, col. 513.
48. *PD* II, col. 873.
49. Ibid., col. 931.
50. *PD* XVI, col. 919.
51. *PHE* XXXII, col. 742.
52. *PD* VIII, col. 719.
53. Drescher, "People and Parliament: The Rhetoric of the British Slave Trade," 575.
54. *PHE* XXVII, col. 578.
55. This paternalist argument is explored in greater detail in Chapter 1.
56. *PHE* XXIX, col. 316.
57. O'Gorman, *Voters, Patrons, and Parties: The Unreformed Electoral System of Hanoverian England, 1734–1832*, 227–32.
58. *PHE* XXXII, cols. 863–4.
59. David Roberts, *Paternalism in Early Victorian England* (London: Croom Helm Ltd., 1979), 4–6 and 22.
60. Kim Lawes, *Paternalism & Politics: The Revival of Paternalism in Nineteeth-Century Britain* (London: Macmillan, 2000), 25.
61. *PHE* XXIX, cols. 315–6.
62. Ibid., col. 1082.
63. *PHE* XXXII, col. 869.
64. *PHE* XXXIV, col. 537.
65. *PD* II, col. 469.
66. See Chapter 1 for a detailed overview of legal arguments advanced during the slavery debates.
67. *PHE* XXVIII, col. 78.
68. *PHE* XXXI, col. 468.
69. Dickinson, *Liberty and Property: Political Ideology in Eighteenth-Century Britain*, 280 and 310.
70. Jeff D. Bass, "An Efficient Humanitarianism: The British Slave Trade Debates, 1791–1792," *Quarterly Journal of Speech*, 75 (1989), 153.
71. *PHE* XXXII, col. 890. Rose was an agent for Dominica where his wife held property.
72. *PD* II, cols. 868–9.
73. *PD* III, col. 650.
74. Clive Emsley, *British Society and the French Wars* (London: Macmillan, 1979), 2–3.
75. Ibid., 13.
76. *PHE* XXVIII, col. 1208.

77. *PD* II, col. 932.
78. Clive Emsley, "Revolution, War and the Nation State: the British and French Experiences 1789–1801," in *The French Revolution and British Popular Politics,* ed. Mark Philp (Cambridge: Cambridge University Press, 1991), 111.
79. Michael Duffy, "War, Revolution, and the Crisis of the British Empire," in *The French Revolution and British Popular Politics,* ed. Mark Philp (Cambridge: Cambridge University Press, 1991), 125.
80. *PHE* XXX, col. 653.
81. Ibid., col. 654.
82. Ibid.
83. Ibid., col. 655.
84. On February 27, 1807, Thomas Hughan depicted the destruction of St. Domingo as a result of intentionally disseminated revolutionary doctrines. See *PD* VIII, cols. 1041–2. On March 16, 1807, George Hibbert argued that the French believed revolution in St. Domingo was related to abolition. See *PD* IX, col. 126. This argument was explored in Chapter 1.
85. *PHE* XXXII, col. 868. Anthony Browne also challenged the wisdom of dismantling long-established institutions during a debate on abolition on February 27, 1807. See *PD* VIII, col. 1048.
86. The French Revolution threatened this belief. See Epstein, *Radical Expression: Political Language, Ritual, and Symbol in England, 1790–1850,* 31.
87. *PHE* XXXII, cols. 873–4.
88. Ibid., col. 878.
89. Ibid., col. 890.
90. James T. Boulton, *The Language of Politics in the Age of Wilkes and Burke,* ed. Michael Hurst, Studies in Political History (Westport: Greenwood Press, 1975), 75–6.
91. Epstein, *Radical Expression: Political Language, Ritual, and Symbol in England, 1790–1850,* 5.
92. H. T. Dickinson, "Popular Conservatism and Militant Loyalism, 1789–1815," in *Britain and the French Revolution,* ed. H. T. Dickinson (Basingstoke: Macmillan, 1989), 106.
93. Dickinson, *Liberty and Property: Political Ideology in Eighteenth-Century Britain,* 237.
94. Clive Emsley, "The Social Impact of the French Wars," in *Britain and the French Revolution,* ed. H. T. Dickinson (Basingstoke: Macmillan Education, 1989), 212.
95. Mark Philp, "Introduction," in *The French Revolution and British Popular Politics,* ed. Mark Philp (Cambridge: Cambridge University Press, 1991), 13.
96. Emsley, *British Society and the French Wars,* 67–70 and 94.
97. *PD* III, col. 655.

98. David Owen, *English Philanthropy, 1660–1960* (London: Oxford University Press, 1965), 98.
99. *PD* VIII, col. 667.
100. Ibid., col. 992.
101. David Eastwood, "Patriotism and the English State in the 1790s," in *The French Revolution and British Popular Politics,* ed. Mark Philp (Cambridge: Cambridge University Press, 1991), 168.
102. *PD* IX, col. 136. Windham was Secretary of State for War and Colonies and the son-in-law of a former plantation-owning commander-in-chief of Jamaica.

CHAPTER 5

1. *The Parliamentary Debates* [hereafter *PD*] New Series IX, col. 296.
2. *PD* New Series XVIII, col. 1048.
3. See *PD* XVII, cols. 679–81.
4. *PD* 3rd Series XIII, cols. 68–9.
5. *PD* 3rd Series XVIII, col. 1215.
6. Seymour Drescher, "People and Parliament: The Rhetoric of the British Slave Trade," *Journal of Interdisciplinary History,* 20 (1990), 575.
7. Howard Temperley, "Capitalism, Slavery and Ideology," *Past & Present,* 75 (1977), 104.
8. Srividhya Swaminathan, *Debating the Slave Trade: Rhetoric of British National Identity, 1759–1815* (Surrey: Ashgate Publishing Limited, 2009), 142.
9. Temperley, "Capitalism, Slavery and Ideology," 104.
10. *PD* XVI, col. 14******b.
11. *Parliamentary History of England* [hereafter *PHE*] XXVII, col. 645.
12. *PD* New Series XVIII, col. 976.
13. Temperley, "Capitalism, Slavery and Ideology," 103–10.
14. *PD* New Series II, cols. 787–8.
15. *PD* 3rd Series XVIII, col. 221.
16. Ibid., cols. 1189–90.
17. David Eltis, "Was Abolition of the U.S. and British Slave Trade Significant in the Broader Atlantic Context?," *William and Mary Quarterly,* 3rd ser. 66 (2009), 222.
18. Andrew Lewis, "'An Incendiary Press': British West Indian Newspapers during the Struggle for Abolition," *Slavery & Abolition,* 16 (1995), 347–9.
19. Boyd Hilton, *A Mad, Bad, Dangerous People? England 1783–1846* (Oxford: Oxford University Press, 2006), 417. See also James J. Sack, *From Jacobite to Conservative: Reaction and Orthodoxy in Britain, c. 1760–1832* (Cambridge: Cambridge University Press, 1993), 103.
20. *PD* 3rd Series XIII, col. 67.

21. Ibid., col. 85.
22. *PD* New Series IX, col. 347.
23. *PD* XXXIV, col. 909.
24. *PD* New Series XXV, col. 1198.
25. *PD* New Series XVIII, col. 1045.
26. *PD* New Series XXV, col. 1209.
27. *PD* 3rd Series XVIII, col. 205.
28. Christer Petley, *Slaveholders in Jamaica: Colonial Society and Culture During the Era of Abolition* (London: Pickering and Chatto, 2009), 95.
29. Ibid., 98–100.
30. *PD* 3rd Series VIII, cols. 180–1.
31. *PD* 3rd Series XI, col. 40.
32. *PHE* XXXIV, col. 1193.
33. Ibid., col. 1194.
34. *PD* New Series IX, col. 348.
35. *PD* New Series X, col. 1012.
36. Ibid., col. 1159.
37. Ibid., col. 1161.
38. *PD* 3rd Series III, col. 1464.
39. *PD* 3rd Series XVIII, col. 131.
40. *PD* 3rd Series XII, col. 599.
41. Swaminathan, *Debating the Slave Trade: Rhetoric of British National Identity, 1759–1815*, 145.
42. Ibid., 142.
43. *PD* 3rd Series III, col. 1453.
44. *PD* New Series IX, col. 347.
45. Ibid.
46. *PD* 3rd Series XVIII, col. 1187.
47. *PD* New Series XVIII, cols. 1029–30.
48. Ibid., col. 1030.

CONCLUSION

1. Izhak Gross, "The Abolition of Negro Slavery and British Parliamentary Politics 1832–3," *The Historical Journal*, 23 (1980), 69.
2. Ibid., 73–4.
3. Richard B. Sheridan, "The West India Sugar Crisis and British Slave Emancipation, 1830–1833," *The Journal of Economic History*, 21 (1961), 547.
4. Gross, "The Abolition of Negro Slavery and British Parliamentary Politics 1832–3," 74.
5. Sheridan, "The West India Sugar Crisis and British Slave Emancipation, 1830–1833," 547.

6. Gross, "The Abolition of Negro Slavery and British Parliamentary Politics 1832–3," 78.
7. Seymour Drescher, *The Mighty Experiment: Free Labor versus Slavery in British Emancipation* (New York: Oxford University Press, 2002), 128. For a detailed examination of the compensation scheme, see Nicholas Draper, *The Price of Emancipation: Slave-Ownership, Compensation and British Society at the End of Slavery* (Cambridge: Cambridge University Press, 2010), Ch. 2.
8. William A. Green, *British Slave Emancipation: The Sugar Colonies and the Great Experiment* (1976. Reprint, New York: Oxford University Press, 1991), 121.
9. Howard Temperley, "Capitalism, Slavery and Ideology," *Past & Present,* 75 (1977), 103.

Bibliography

Printed Primary Sources

Parliamentary Records

Cobbett, William, ed. *Cobbett's Parliamentary Debates.*

———. *The Parliamentary History of England.*

Hansard, T. C., ed. *The Parliamentary Debates.*

Newspapers and Periodicals

The Anti-Slavery Reporter

La Belle Assemblée, or Bell's Court and Fashionable Magazine Addressed Particularly to the Ladies

Blackwood's Edinburgh Magazine (formerly *The Edinburgh Monthly Magazine*)

Bury and Norwich Post

The Christian Observer

Derby Mercury

Edinburgh Evening Post

Edinburgh Journal of Natural and Geographical Science

Edinburgh Review

The English Review, or An Abstract of English and Foreign Literature

Essex Standard

Examiner [London]

The Gentleman's Magazine, and Historical Chronicle

Hull Packet

John Bull

The Ladies Monthly Museum

Leeds Times

The Literary Panorama and National Register

Liverpool Mercury

London Chronicle

London Evening Post

London Review

The Monthly Repository of Theology and General Literature

Morning Chronicle [London]

Morning Herald [London]

Morning Post [London]
The Quarterly Review
The Scots Magazine and Edinburgh Literary Miscellany
Scottish Missionary Register
The Standard [London]
The Times [London]
True Briton
Western Times [Exeter]
Westminster Review
Whitehall Evening Post

Books, Pamphlets, and Other Printed Material

Anon. "The Condition of the West Indian Slave Contrasted with That of the Infant Slave in Our English Factories." London: W. Kidd, 1833.

Anon. "The Field Negro, or the Effect of Civilization." In *Poems, on Subjects Arising in England, and the West Indies*. London: R. Faulder, 1783.

Anon. *Marly; or, A Planter's Life in Jamaica*. Glasgow: Richard Griffin and Co., 1828. Reprint with introductions by John Gilmore and Karina Williamson. Oxford: Macmillan Education, 2005.

Anon. *The Muse in Good Humour; or Momus's Banquet: A Collection of Choice Songs, Including the Modern*. London: William Lane, n.d.

Anon. *The New Vocal Enchantress Containing an Elegant Selection of All the Newest Songs Lately Sung at the Theatres Royal Drury Lane, Covent Garden, Haymarket, Royalty Theatre, Vaux Hall, &c. &c. &c.* London: C. Stalker, 1791.

Bailey, Rev. B. *The House of Bondage. A Dissertation upon the Nature of Service or Slavery under Levitical Law, among the Hebrews in the Earliest Ages, and in the Gentile World, Until the Coming of Christ*.... London: C. & J. Rivington, 1824.

Barclay, Alexander. *A Practical View of the Present State of Slavery in the West Indies; or, An Examination of Mr. Stephen's "Slavery of the British West India Colonies."* London: Smith, Elder & Co., 1826.

Bayley, F. W. N. *Four Years' Residence in the West Indies*. London: William Kidd, 1830.

Beck, Theodric Romeyn and John B. Beck. *Elements of Medical Jurisprudence*. 11th edn. Philadelphia: J.B. Lippincott & Co., 1860.

Bellamy, Thomas. *The Benevolent Planters*. London: J. Debrett, 1789.

Bigland, John. *An Historical Display of the Effects of Physical and Moral Causes on the Character and Circumstances of Nations: Including a Comparison of the Ancients and Moderns in Regard to Their Intellectual and Social State*. London: Longman, Hurst, Rees, Orme, and Brown, 1816.

Boswell, James. *No Abolition of Slavery; or the Universal Empire of Love*. London: R. Faulder, 1791.

Boulard, A. M. H. *Catalogue des Livres Anglais.* Paris: Chez M. Commendeur, 1828.

Bridges, Rev. George Wilson. *A Voice from Jamaica in Reply to William Wilberforce, Esq. M.P.* London: Longman, Hurst, Rees, Orme, Brown, and Green, 1823.

Burke, Edmund. *Reflections on the Revolution in France (1790)*, ed. Connor Cruise O'Brien. London: Penguin Books, 1986.

Carmichael, Mrs. *Domestic Manners and Social Condition of the White, Coloured, and Negro Population of the West Indies.* 2 vols. London: Whittaker, Treacher, and Co., 1833.

Chapman, M. J. *Barbadoes, and Other Poems.* London: James Fraser, 1833.

Clarkson, Thomas. *The History of the Rise, Progress, and Accomplishment of the Abolition of the African Slave-Trade by the British Parliament.* 2 vols. London: Paternoster-Row, 1808.

Cobb, Thomas Read Rootes. *An Inquiry into the Law of Negro Slavery in the United States of America: to which Is Prefixed an Historical Sketch of Slavery.* 2 vols. Philadelphia: T. & J.W. Johnson & Co., 1858.

Cruikshank, Isaac Robert. *John Bull Taking a Clear View of the Negro Slavery Question.* 1826.

D., C. F. "Bonja Song." In *Contrary Voices: Representations of West Indian Slavery, 1657–1834*, ed. Karina Williamson. Kingston, Jamaica: University of the West Indies Press, 2008.

Edwards, Bryan. *An Historical Survey of the French Colony in the Island of St. Domingo: Comprehending a Short Account of Its Ancient Government, Political State, Population, Productions, and Exports; A Narrative of the Calamities Which have Desolated the Country Ever since the Year 1789, with Some Reflections on their Causes and Probable Consequences, and a Detail of the Military Transactions of the British Army in that Island to the End of 1794.* London: John Stockdale, 1797.

———. *The History, Civil and Commercial, of the British Colonies in the West Indies.* 2 vols. London: John Stockdale, 1793.

[Gibbes, Sir Phillip.] *Instructions for the Treatment of Negroes &c. &c. &c.* 3rd edn. London: Shepperson and Reynolds, 1797.

Gillray, James. *Philanthropic Consolations on the Loss of the Slave Bill.* 1796.

Grainger, James. *An Essay on the More Common West-India Diseases; and the Remedies which That Country Itself Produces: To which Are Added, Some Hints on the Management, etc. of Negroes.* 2nd edn. Edinburgh: Mundell & Son, and London: Longman & Rees, 1802.

Hibbert Jun., Robert. *Facts, Verified Upon Oath, in Contradiction of the Report of Rev. Thomas Cooper, Concerning the General Condition of the Slaves in Jamaica; and More Especially Relative to the Management and Treatment of the Slaves Upon Georgia Estate, in the Parish of Hanover, in That Island.* London: John Murray, 1824.

Holder, Rev. H. E. *Fragments of a Poem, Intended to Have Been Written in Consequence of Reading Major Majoribanks's Slavery.* Bath: R. Cruttwell, 1792.

Holland, William, publisher. *The Blind Enthusiast.* 1792a.

———. *Cruelty and Oppression Abroad.* 1792b.

Long, Edward. *The History of Jamaica. Or, General Survey of the Antient and Modern State of That Island: With Reflections on Its Situation, Settlements, Inhabitants, Climate, Products, Commerce, Laws, and Government.* 3 vols. London: T. Lowndes, 1774.

McDonnell, Alexander. *Compulsory Manumission; or an Examination of the Actual State of the West India Question.* London: John Murray, 1827.

———. *The West India Legislatures Vindicated from the Charge of Having Resisted the Call of the Mother Country for the Amelioration of Slavery.* London: John Murray, 1826.

McQueen, James. *The Colonial Controversy, Containing a Refutation of the Anticolonists; the State of Hayti, Sierra Leone, India, China, Cochin China, Java, &c. &c.; the Production of Sugar, &c. and the State of the Free and Slave Labourers in Those Countries; Fully Considered, in a Series of Letters, Addressed to the Earl of Liverpool; with a Supplementary Letter to Mr. Macaulay.* Glasgow: Khull, Blackie, & Co., 1825.

———. *The West India Colonies; The Calumnies and Misrepresentations Circulated Against Them by The Edinburgh Review, Mr. Clarkson, Mr. Cropper, etc. etc.* London: Baldwin, Cradock, and Joy, 1824.

Orderson, J. W. *The Fair Barbadian and Faithful Black; or, A Cure for the Gout. A Comedy in Three Acts.* Liverpool: Ross and Nightingale, 1835. Reprint, in *Creoleana and The Fair Barbadian and Faithful Black*, ed. John Gilmore. Oxford: Macmillan Education, 2002.

Poyer, John. *The History of Barbados, from the First Discovery of the Island, in the Year 1605, Till the Accession of Lord Seaforth in 1801.* London: J. Mawman, 1808.

Prichard, James Cowles. *Researches into the Physical History of Mankind.* 2nd edn. 2 vols. London: John and Arthur Arch, 1826.

A Professional Planter. *Practical Rules for the Management and Medical Treatment of Negro Slaves, in the Sugar Colonies.* London: J. Barfield, 1803.

A Resident. *Sketches and Recollections of the West Indies.* London: Smith, Elder, & Co., 1828.

Reynolds, Sir Joshua. Portrait of George IV When Prince of Wales with a Negro Page. c. 1787.

Stewart, J. *A View of the Past and Present State of the Island of Jamaica; with Remarks on the Moral and Physical Condition of the Slaves, and on the Abolition of Slavery in the Colonies.* Edinburgh: Oliver & Boyd, 1823.

Taylor, Robert Eveleigh. *Inauguralis, de Hominum Varietatibus.* Edinburgh: Excudebant Adamus Neill et Socii, 1800.

Watson, Richard. *The Religious Instruction of Slaves in the West India Colonies Advocated and Defended. A Sermon Preached before the Wesleyan Methodist Missionary Society, in the New Chapel, City-Road, London, April 28, 1824.* 4th edn. London: Butterworth and Son, n.d.

White, Charles. *An Account of the Regular Gradation in Man, and in Different Animals and Vegetables; and from the Former to the Latter*. London: C. Dilly, 1799.

[Williams, Cynric R.]. *Hamel, The Obeah Man*. 2 vols. London: Hunt and Clark, 1827.

SECONDARY SOURCES

Monographs

Alleyne, Mervyn C. *The Construction and Representation of Race and Ethnicity in the Caribbean and the World*. Kingston, Jamaica: University of the West Indies Press, 2002.

Anstey, Roger. *The Atlantic Slave Trade and British Abolition 1760–1810*. London: Macmillan Press Ltd., 1975.

Basker, James G., ed. *Amazing Grace: An Anthology of Poems about Slavery*. New Haven: Yale University Press, 2002.

Bebbington, D. W. *Evangelicalism in Modern Britain: A History from the 1730s to the 1980s*. London: Routledge, 1989.

Boime, Albert. *The Art of Exclusion: Representing Blacks in the Nineteenth Century*. London: Thames and Hudson, 1990.

Boulton, James T. *The Language of Politics in the Age of Wilkes and Burke*, ed. Michael Hurst. Westport: Greenwood Press, 1975.

Boulukos, George. *The Grateful Slave: The Emergence of Race in Eighteenth-Century British and American Culture*. Cambridge: Cambridge University Press, 2008.

Brewer, John. *The Pleasures of the Imagination: English Culture in the Eighteenth Century*. London: HarperCollins Publishers, 1997.

Briggs, Asa. *The Age of Improvement, 1783–1867*. London: Longmans, 1962.

Brown, Christopher Leslie. *Moral Capital: Foundations of British Abolitionism*. Chapel Hill: The University of North Carolina Press, 2006.

Buckley, Roger N. *Slaves in Red Coats: The British West India Regiments, 1795–1815*. New Haven and London: Yale University Press, 1979.

Burlingame, Michael. *Abraham Lincoln: A Life*. 2 vols. Baltimore: Johns Hopkins University Press, 2008.

Burnard, Trevor. *Mastery, Tyranny, and Desire: Thomas Thistlewood and His Slaves in the Anglo-Jamaican World*. Chapel Hill: University of North Carolina Press, 2004.

Carey, Brycchan. *British Abolitionism and the Rhetoric of Sensibility: Writing, Sentiment and Slavery, 1760–1807*. Basingstoke: Macmillan Publishers Ltd., 2005.

Carrington, Selwyn H. H. *The Sugar Industry and the Abolition of the Slave Trade, 1775–1810*. Gainesville: University Press of Florida, 2002.

Chitnis, Anand C. *The Scottish Enlightenment: A Social History*. London: Croon Helm, Ltd., 1976.

Christie, William. *The Edinburgh Review in the Literary Culture of Romantic Britain: Mammoth and Megalonyx*. London: Pickering and Chatto, 2009.

Clive, John. *Scotch Reviewers: The Edinburgh Review, 1802–1815*. London: Faber and Faber Ltd., 1956.

Colley, Linda. *Britons: Forging the Nation, 1707–1837*. New Haven: Yale University Press, 1992.

Coupland, Sir Richard. *The British Antislavery Movement*. 1933. Reprint with preface by J. D. Fage. London: Frank Cass and Co., 1964.

Cutmore, Jonathan. *Contributors to the Quarterly Review*. London: Pickering & Chatto, 2008.

Dabydeen, David. *Hogarth's Blacks: Images of Blacks in Eighteenth Century English Art*. Kingston-Upon-Thames: Dangaroo Press, 1985.

Davis, David Brion. *The Problem of Slavery in the Age of Revolution 1770–1823*. London: Cornell University Press, 1975.

Dickinson, H. T. *Caricatures and the Constitution, 1760–1832*. Cambridge: Chadwyk-Healey Ltd., 1986.

———. *Liberty and Property: Political Ideology in Eighteenth-Century Britain*. London: Methuen & Co., 1977.

Donald, Diana. *The Age of Caricature: Satirical Prints in the Reign of George III*. New Haven and London: Yale University Press, 1996.

Draper, Nicholas. *The Price of Emancipation: Slave-ownership, Compensation and British Society at the End of Slavery*. Cambridge: Cambridge University Press, 2010.

Drescher, Seymour. *Capitalism and Antislavery: British Mobilization in Comparative Perspective*. Basingstoke: Macmillan Press, 1986.

———. *Econocide: British Slavery in the Era of Abolition*. Pittsburgh: University of Pittsburgh Press, 1977.

———. *From Slavery to Freedom: Comparative Studies in the Rise and Fall of Atlantic Slavery*. New York: New York University Press, 1999.

———. *The Mighty Experiment: Free Labor versus Slavery in British Emancipation*. New York: Oxford University Press, 2002.

Ellis, Markman. *The Politics of Sensibility: Race, Gender and Commerce in the Sentimental Novel*. Cambridge: Cambridge University Press, 1996.

Eltis, David. *Economic Growth and the Ending of the Transatlantic Slave Trade*. New York: Oxford University Press, 1987.

Emsley, Clive. *British Society and the French Wars*. London: Macmillan Press, 1979.

Epstein, James A. *Radical Expression: Political Language, Ritual, and Symbol in England*, 1790–1850. New York: Oxford University Press, 1994.

Fisher, D. R., ed. *The House of Commons, 1820–1832*. 7 vols. Cambridge: Cambridge University Press, 2009.

Fontana, Biancamaria. *Rethinking the Politics of Commercial Society: The Edinburgh Review 1802–1832*. Cambridge: Cambridge University Press, 1985.

Gatrell, Vic. *City of Laughter: Sex and Satire in Eighteenth Century London.* London: Atlantic Books, 2006.

Genovese, Eugene. *The World the Slaveholders Made: Two Essays in Interpretation.* New York: Pantheon Books, 1969.

Green, William A. *British Slave Emancipation: The Sugar Colonies and the Great Experiment, 1830–1865.* 1976. Reprint, New York: Oxford University Press, 1991.

Hamburger, Joseph. *James Mill and the Art of Revolution.* New Haven and London: Yale University Press, 1963.

Hayden, John. O. *The Romantic Reviewers, 1802–1824.* London: Routledge and Kegan Paul, 1969.

Hilton, Boyd. *The Age of Atonement: The Influence of Evangelicalism on Social and Economic Thought 1785–1865.* Oxford: Oxford University Press, 1986.

———. *A Mad, Bad, Dangerous People? England 1783–1846.* Oxford: Oxford University Press, 2006.

Hochschild, Adam. *Bury the Chains: Prophets and Rebels in the Fight to Free an Empire's Slaves.* Boston and New York: Houghton Mifflin Company, 2005.

Inikori, Joseph E. *Africans and the Industrial Revolution in England: A Study in International Trade and Economic Development.* Cambridge: Cambridge University Press, 2002.

James, C. L. R. *The Black Jacobins: Toussaint L'Ouverture and the San Domingo Revolution.* 1938. New Edition, London: Allison and Busby, 1980.

Jennings, Judith. *The Business of Abolishing the British Slave Trade 1783–1807.* London: Frank Cass and Co., 1997.

Kidd, Colin. *The Forging of Races: Race and Scripture in the Protestant Atlantic World, 1600–2000.* Cambridge: Cambridge University Press, 2006.

Kielstra, Paul Michael. *The Politics of British Slave Trade Suppression in Britain and France, 1814–48: Diplomacy, Morality, and Economics.* Basingstoke: Macmillan Press Ltd., 2000.

Kitson, Peter. *Romantic Literature, Race, and Colonial Encounter.* New York: Palgrave Macmillan, 2007.

Kitson, Peter J. and Debbie Lee, eds. *Slavery, Abolition and Emancipation: Writings in the British Romantic Period.* 8 vols. London: Pickering & Chatto, 1999.

Klingberg, Frank J. *The Anti-Slavery Movement in England: A Study in English Humanitarianism.* 1926. Reprint, Hamden: Archon Books, 1968.

Kriz, Kay Dian. *Slavery, Sugar, and the Culture of Refinement: Picturing the British West Indies, 1700–1840.* New Haven: Yale University Press, 2008.

Lambert, David. *White Creole Culture, Politics and Identity During the Age of Abolition.* Cambridge: Cambridge University Press, 2005.

Lawes, Kim. *Paternalism & Politics: The Revival of Paternalism in Nineteenth-Century Britain*. London: Macmillan, 2000.

LoPatin, Nancy D. *Political Unions, Popular Politics, and the Great Reform Act of 1832*. Basingstoke: Macmillan Press Ltd., 1999.

Lincoln, Margarette. *Representing the Royal Navy: British Sea Power, 1750–1815*. Aldershot: Ashgate, 2002.

Luster, Robert E. *The Amelioration of the Slaves in the British Empire, 1790–1883*. New York: Peter Lang, 1995.

Mathieson, William Law. *British Slavery and its Abolition 1823–1838*. London: Longman, Green and Co. Ltd., 1926.

Morgan, Kenneth, ed. *The British Transatlantic Slave Trade*. 4 vols. London: Pickering & Chatto, 2003.

Namier, Lewis and John Brooke, eds. *The House of Commons 1754–1790*. 3 vols. London: Her Majesty's Stationary Office, 1964.

Nathans, Heather S. *Slavery and Sentiment on the American Stage, 1787–1861: Lifting the Veil of Black*. New York: Cambridge University Press, 2009.

O'Gorman, Frank. *Voters, Patrons, and Parties: The Unreformed Electoral System of Hanoverian England, 1734–1832*. Oxford: Oxford University Press, 1989.

O'Shaughnessy, Andrew Jackson. *An Empire Divided: The American Revolution and the British Caribbean*. Philadelphia: University of Pennsylvania Press, 2000.

Oldfield, J. R. *"Chords of Freedom": Commemoration, Ritual, and British Transatlantic Slavery*. Manchester: Manchester University Press, 2007.

———. *Popular Politics and British Anti-Slavery: The Mobilisation of Public Opinion Against the Slave Trade 1787–1807*. Manchester: Manchester University Press, 1995.

Owen, David. *English Philanthropy, 1660–1960*. London: Oxford University Press, 1965.

Pearce, Edward. *Reform! The Fight for the 1832 Reform Act*. London: Jonathan Cape, 2003.

Petley, Christer. *Slaveholders in Jamaica: Colonial Society and Culture During the Era of Abolition*. London: Pickering and Chatto, 2009.

Pointon, Marcia. *Hanging the Head: Portraiture and Social Formation in Eighteenth-Century England*. New Haven and London: Yale University Press, 1993.

Porter, Theodore M. *The Rise of Statistical Thinking, 1820–1900*. Princeton: Princeton University Press, 1986.

Porter, Roy and Lesley Hall. *The Facts of Life: The Creation of Sexual Knowledge in Britain, 1650–1950*. New Haven: Yale University Press, 1995.

Ragatz, Lowell Joseph. *The Fall of the Planter Class in the British Caribbean, 1763–1833: A Study in Social and Economic History*. 1928. Reprint, New York: Octagon Books Inc., 1963.

Roberts, David. *Paternalism in Early Victorian England.* London: Croom Helm Ltd., 1979.

Royle, Edward. *Revolutionary Britannia: Reflections on the Threat of Revolution in Britain, 1789–1848.* Manchester: Manchester University Press, 2000.

Rushton, J. Phillipe. *Race, Evolution, and Behaviour: A Life History Perspective.* 1995. 2nd abridged edn., Port Huron: Charles Darwin Research Institute, 2000.

Ryden, David, ed. *The British Transatlantic Slave Trade, Vol. 4, The Abolitionist Struggle: Promoters of the Slave Trade.* London: Pickering and Chatto, 2003.

———. *West Indian Slavery and British Abolition, 1783–1807.* Cambridge: Cambridge University Press, 2009.

Sack, James J. *From Jacobite to Conservative: Reaction and Orthodoxy in Britain, c. 1760–1832.* Cambridge: Cambridge University Press, 1993.

Shattock, Joanne. *Politics and Reviewers: The Edinburgh and the Quarterly in the Victorian Age.* London: Leicester University Press, 1989.

Smith, Olivia. *The Politics of Language, 1791–1819.* Oxford: Oxford University Press, 1984.

Stevens, Anne H. *British Historical Fiction before Scott.* Houndsmills, Basingtoke: Palgrave Macmillan, 2010.

Stigler, Stephen M. *The History of Statistics: The Measurement of Uncertainty before 1900.* Cambridge, MA: Harvard University Press, 1986.

Swaminathan, Srividhya. *Debating the Slave Trade: Rhetoric of British National Identity, 1759–1815.* Farnham: Ashgate, 2009.

Thomas, Helen. *Romanticism and Slave Narratives: Transatlantic Testimonies.* Cambridge: Cambridge University Press, 2000.

Thomas, Malcolm I. and Peter Holt. *Threats of Revolution in Britain 1789–1848.* London: Macmillan Press Ltd., 1977.

Thorne, R. G., ed. *The House of Commons, 1790–1820.* 5 vols. London: Secker and Warburg, 1986.

Tise, Larry E. *Proslavery: A History of the Defense of Slavery in America, 1701–1840.* Athens: University of Georgia Press, 1987.

Turley, David. *The Culture of English Antislavery, 1780–1860.* London: Routledge, 1991.

Turner, Michael J. *The Age of Unease: Government and Reform in Britain, 1782–1832.* Midsomer Norton, Somerset: Sutton Publishing Ltd., 2000.

Walvin, James. *England, Slaves and Freedom 1776–1838.* Basingstoke: Macmillan Press, 1986.

Ward, J. R. *British West Indian Slavery, 1750–1834: The Process of Amelioration.* Oxford: Clarendon Press, 2001.

Whyte, Iain. *Scotland and the Abolition of Black Slavery, 1756–1838.* Edinburgh: Edinburgh University Press, 2006.

Wilbur, Samuel Howell. *Eighteenth-Century British Logic and Rhetoric.* Princeton: Princeton University Press, 1971.

Williams, Eric. *Capitalism and Slavery.* London: Lowe and Brydon Ltd., 1964.

Williamson, Karina, ed. *Contrary Voices: Representations of West Indian Slavery, 1657–1834.* Kingston, Jamaica: University of the West Indies Press, 2008.

Wood, Marcus. *Blind Memory: Visual Representation of Slavery in England and America 1780–1865.* New York: Routledge, 2000.

———. *The Horrible Gift of Freedom: Atlantic Slavery and the Representation of Emancipation.* Athens: University of Georgia Press, 2010.

———. *Radical Satire and Print Culture 1790–1822.* Oxford: Clarendon Press, 1994.

———. *Slavery, Empathy, and Pornography.* New York: Oxford University Press, 2002.

Articles

Altink, Henrice. "Deviant and Dangerous: Pro-Slavery Representations of Jamaican Slave Women's Sexuality, c. 1780–1834." *Slavery & Abolition*, 26 (2005): 271–88.

Bacchus, M. K. "Education and Society among the Non-Whites in the West Indies Prior to Emancipation." *History of Education*, 19 (1990): 85–104.

Bass, Jeff D. "An Efficient Humanitarianism: The British Slave Trade Debates, 1791–1792." *Quarterly Journal of Speech*, 75 (1989): 152–65.

Berry, Helen. "Polite Consumption: Shopping in Eighteenth Century England." *Transactions of the Royal Historical Society*, Sixth Series, 12 (2002): 375–94.

Boulukos, George. "Maria Edgeworth's 'Grateful Negro' and the Sentimental Argument for Slavery." *Eighteenth-Century Life*, 23 (1999): 12–29.

Browne, Randy M. "The 'Bad Business' of Obeah: Power, Authority, and the Politics of Slave Culture in the British Caribbean." *The William and Mary Quarterly*, 3rd ser. 68 (2011): 451–80.

Burnard, Trevor. "Et in Arcadia Ego: West Indian Planters in Glory, 1674–1784." *Atlantic Studies*, 9 (2012): 19–40.

———. "Passengers Only: The Extent and Significance of Absenteeism in Eighteenth-Century Jamaica." *Atlantic Studies*, 1 (2004): 178–95.

———. "Powerless Masters: The Curious Decline of Jamaican Sugar Planters in the Foundational Period of British Abolitionism." *Slavery & Abolition*, 32 (2011): 185–98.

Cain, P. J. and A. G. Hopkins. "Gentlemanly Capitalism and British Expansion Overseas I. The Old Colonial System, 1688–1850." *Economic History Review*, 2nd ser. 39 (1986): 510–25.

———. "The Political Economy of British Expansion Overseas, 1750–1914." *Economic History Review*, 2nd ser. 33 (1980): 463–90.

Chaplin, Joyce E. "Slavery and the Principle of Humanity: A Modern Idea in the Early Lower South." *Journal of Southern History*, 24 (1990): 299–315.

Cooke, Anthony. "An Elite Revisited: Glasgow West India Merchants, 1783–1877." *Journal of Scottish Historical Studies*, 32 (2012): 127–65.

Cotter, William R. "The Somerset Case and the Abolition of Slavery in England." *History*, 79 (1994): 31–56.

Draper, Nicholas. "The City of London and Slavery: Evidence from the First Dock Companies, 1795–1800." *Economic History Review*, 61 (2008): 432–66.

———. "The Rise of a New Planter Class? Some Countercurrents from British Guiana and Trinidad, 1807–33." *Atlantic Studies*, 9 (2012): 65–83.

Drescher, Seymour. "Abolitionist Expectations." *Slavery & Abolition*, 21 (2000): 41–66.

———. "People and Parliament: The Rhetoric of the British Slave Trade." *Journal of Interdisciplinary History*, 20 (1990): 561–80.

———. "Public Opinion and Parliament in the Abolition of the British Slave Trade." *Parliamentary History*, 26 Supplement (2007): 42–65.

———. "The Slaving Capital of the World: Liverpool and National Opinion in the Age of Abolition." *Slavery & Abolition*, 9 (1988): 128–43.

———. "Whose Abolition? Popular Pressure and the Ending of the British Slave Trade." *Past & Present*, 143 (1994): 136–66.

Dupuy, Pascal. "Informations et Désinformations: Les Tentatives d'Abolition de l'Esclavage en Angleterre à Traverse la Caricature Anglaise, 1760–1810." *Actes de Colloque de 1999*, 25 (2001): 175–93.

Eltis, David. "Was Abolition of the U.S. and British Slave Trade Significant in the Broader Atlantic Context?" *The William and Mary Quarterly*, 3rd ser. 66 (2009): 715–36.

Epstein, James A. "The Constitutional Idiom: Radical Reasoning, Rhetoric and Action in Early Nineteenth-Century England." *Journal of Social History*, 23 (1990): 553–74.

Furstenberg, François. "Atlantic Slavery, Atlantic Freedom: George Washington, Slavery, and Transatlantic Abolitionist Networks." *The William and Mary Quarterly*, 68 (2011): 247–86.

Gallay, Allan. "The Origins of Slaveholders' Paternalism: George Whitefield, the Bryan Family, and the Great Awakening in the South." *Journal of Southern History*, 53 (1987): 369–94.

Greene, Jack P. "Liberty, Slavery, and the Transformation of British Identity in the Eighteenth-Century West Indies." *Slavery & Abolition*, 21 (2000): 1–31.

Gross, Izhak. "The Abolition of Negro Slavery and British Parliamentary Politics 1832–3." *The Historical Journal*, 23 (1980): 63–85.

Haskell, Thomas L. "Capitalism and the Origins of the Human Sensibility." *American Historical Review*, 90 (1985): 339–61 and 547–66.

Higman, B. W. "The West India 'Interest' in Parliament, 1807–1833." *Historical Studies*, 13 (1967): 1–19.

Hoppit, Julian. "Political Arithmetic in Eighteenth-Century England." *Economic History Review*, 49 (1996): 516–40.

Jenks, Timothy. "Language and Politics at the Westminster Election of 1796." *The Historical Journal*, 44 (2001): 419–39.

Lambert, David. "The 'Glasgow King of Billingsgate': James MacQueen and an Atlantic Proslavery Network." *Slavery & Abolition*, 29 (2008): 389–414.

Lewis, Andrew. "'An Incendiary Press': British West Indian Newspapers during the Struggle for Abolition." *Slavery & Abolition*, 16 (1995): 346–62.

Littlefield, Daniel C. "Plantations, Paternalism, and Profitability: Factors Affecting African Demography in the Old British Empire." *Journal of Southern History*, 47 (1981): 167–82.

Mason, Matthew. "Keeping Up Appearances: The International Politics of Slave Trade Abolition in the Nineteenth-Century Atlantic World." *The William and Mary Quarterly*, 3rd ser. 66 (2009): 809–32.

Morgan, Kenneth. "Bristol West India Merchants in the Eighteenth Century." *Transactions of the Royal Historical Society*, 6th Series 3 (1993): 185–208.

Nicholson, Eirwen E. C. "Consumers and Spectators: The Public and the Political Print in Eighteenth-Century England." *History*, 81 (1996): 5–21.

Nordius, Janina. "Racism and Radicalism in Jamaican Gothic: Cynric R. Williams's *Hamel, The Obeah Man*." *English Literary History*, 73 (2006): 673–93.

O'Shaughnessy, Andrew Jackson. "The Formation of a Commercial Lobby: The West Indian Interest, British Colonial Policy and the American Revolution." *The Historical Journal*, 40 (1997): 71–95.

Oldfield, J. R. "Abolition: A History of Slavery and Anti-Slavery." *Slavery & Abolition*, 32 (2011): 309–10.

Otele, Olivette. "British Slavers Against Abolition." *Revue Français de Civilisation Britannique*, 15 (2008): 61–76.

Petley, Christer. "'Devoted Islands' and 'That Madman Wilberforce': British Proslavery Patriotism During the Age of Abolition." *The Journal of Imperial and Commonwealth History*, 39 (2011): 393–415.

———. "Gluttony, Excess, and the Fall of the Planter Class in the British Caribbean." *Atlantic Studies*, 9 (2012): 85–106.

———. "Rethinking the Fall of the Planter Class." *Atlantic Studies*, 9 (2012): 1–17.

———. "Slavery, Emancipation and the Creole World View of Jamaican Colonists, 1800–1834." *Slavery & Abolition*, 26 (2005): 93–115.

Porter, Roy. "Review: Seeing the Past." *Past & Present*, 118 (1988): 186–205.

Quinault, Roland. "The French Revolution of 1830 and Parliamentary Reform." *History* 79 (1994): 377–93.

———. "Gladstone and Slavery." *The Historical Journal*, 52 (2009): 363–83.

Rawley, James A. "London's Defense of the Slave Trade, 1787–1807." *Slavery & Abolition*, 14 (1993): 48–69.

Reckford, Mary. "IV. The Colonial Office and the Abolition of Slavery." *The Historical Journal*, 14 (1971): 723–34.

Ryden, David Beck. "Sugar, Spirits, and Fodder: The London West India Interest and the Glut of 1807–15." *Atlantic Studies*, 9 (2012): 41–64.

Sheridan, Richard B. "The West India Sugar Crisis and British Slave Emancipation, 1830–1833." *The Journal of Economic History*, 21 (1961): 539–51.

Sorensen, Janet. "Vulgar Tongues: Canting Dictionaries and the Language of the People in Eighteenth-Century Britain." *Eighteenth-Century Studies*, 37 (2004): 435–54.

Swaminathan, Srividhya. "Developing the West Indian Proslavery Position after the Somerset Decision." *Slavery & Abolition*, 24 (2003): 40–60.

Taylor, Miles. "John Bull and the Iconography of Public Opinion in England c. 1712–1929." *Past & Present*, 134 (1992): 93–128.

Temperley, Howard. "Capitalism, Slavery and Ideology." *Past & Present*, 75 (1977): 94–118.

Thompson, E. P. "The Moral Economy of the English Crowd in the Eighteenth Century." *Past & Present*, 50 (1971): 76–136.

Walvin, James. "Freedom and Slavery and the Shaping of Victorian Britain." *Slavery & Abolition*, 15 (1994): 246–59.

———. "Why Did the British Abolish the Slave Trade? *Econocide* Revisited." *Slavery & Abolition*, 32 (2011): 583–8.

Ward, J. R. "The Profitability of Sugar Planting in the British West Indies, 1650–1834." *The Economic History Review*, New Series 31 (1978): 197–213.

Warhman, Dror. "Virtual Representation: Parliamentary Reporting and Languages of Class in the 1790s." *Past & Present*, 136 (1992): 83–113.

Winch, Donald. "Adam Smith: Scottish Moral Philosopher as Political Economist." *The Historical Journal*, 35 (1992): 91–113.

Wood, Marcus. "Debating the Slave Trade: Rhetoric of British National Identity, 1759–1815." *Slavery & Abolition*, 32 (2011): 594–6.

Essays

Augstein, H. F. "Introduction." In *Race: The Origins of An Idea, 1760–1850*, ed. H. F. Augstein (Bristol: Thoemmes Press, 1996): ix–xxxiii.

Bindman, David. "Subjectivity and Slavery in Portraiture." In Slave Portraiture in the Atlantic World, ed. Agnes Lugo-Ortiz and Angela Rosenthal (New York: Cambridge University Press, 2013): 71–88.

Bohls, Elizabeth A. "The Gentleman Planter and the Metropole: Long's *History of Jamaica* (1774)." In *The Country and the City Revisited: England and the Politics of Culture, 1550–1850*, ed. Gerald Maclean, Donna Landry, and Joseph P. Ward (Cambridge: Cambridge University Press, 1999): 180–96.

Cairns, John W. "The Definition of Slavery in Eighteenth-Century Thinking: Not the True Roman Slavery." In *The Legal Understanding of Slavery: From the Historical to the Contemporary*, ed. Jean Allain (Oxford: Oxford University Press, 2012): 61–84.

Carey, Brycchan, and Sara Salih. "Introduction." In *Discourses of Slavery and Abolition: Britain and its Colonies, 1760–1838*, ed. Brycchan Carey, Markman Ellis, and Sara Salih (Basingstoke: Palgrave Macmillan, 2004): 1–8.

Carretta, Vincent, and Philip Gould. "Introduction." In *Genius in Bondage: Literature of the Early Black Atlantic*, ed. Vincent Carretta, and Philip Gould (Lexington: The University Press of Kentucky, 2001): 1–13.

Christie, Ian R. "Conservatism and Stability in British Society." In *The French Revolution and British Popular Politics*, ed. Mark Philp (Cambridge: Cambridge University Press, 1991): 169–87.

Cutmore, Jonathan. "Introduction." In *Conservatism and the Quarterly Review: A Critical Analysis*, ed. Jonathan Cutmore (London: Pickering & Chatto, 2007): 1–18.

Derry, John. "The Opposition Whigs and the French Revolution, 1789–1815." In *Britain and the French Revolution*, ed. H. T. Dickinson (Basingstoke: Macmillan, 1989) 39–60.

Dickinson, H. T. "Introduction: The Impact of the French Revolution and the French Wars, 1789–1815." In *Britain and the French Revolution*, ed. H. T. Dickinson (Basingstoke: Macmillan, 1989): 1–19.

———. "Popular Conservatism and Militant Loyalism, 1789–1815." In *Britain and the French Revolution*, ed. H. T. Dickinson (Basingstoke: Macmillan, 1989): 103–25.

Dinwiddy, John. "Interpretations of Anti-Jacobinism." In *The French Revolution and British Popular Politics*, ed. Mark Philp (Cambridge: Cambridge University Press, 1991): 38–49.

Duffy, Michael. "War, Revolution, and the Crisis of the British Empire." In *The French Revolution and British Popular Politics*, ed. Mark Philp (Cambridge: Cambridge University Press, 1991): 118–45.

Eastwood, David. "Patriotism and the English State in the 1790s." In *The French Revolution and British Popular Politics*, ed. Mark Philp (Cambridge: Cambridge University Press, 1991): 146–68.

Emsley, Clive. "Revolution, War and the Nation State: The British and French Experiences 1789- 1801." In *The French Revolution and British Popular Politics*, ed. Mark Philp (Cambridge: Cambridge University Press, 1991): 99–117.

———. "The Social Impact of the French Wars." In *Britain and the French Revolution*, ed. H. T. Dickinson (Basingstoke: Macmillan, 1989): 211–28.

Farrell, Stephen. "'Contrary to the Principles of Justice, Humanity and Social Policy': The Slave Trade, Parliamentary Politics, and the Abolition Act,

1807." In *The British Slave Trade: Abolition, Parliament, and People*, ed. Stephen Farrell, Melanie Unwin, and James Walvin (Edinburgh: Edinburgh University Press, 2007): 141–71.

Hall, Catherine. "Afterword: Britain 2007, Problematising Histories." In *Imagining Transatlantic Slavery*, ed. Cora Kaplan and John Oldfield (Basingstoke: Palgrave Macmillan, 2010): 191–201.

Hamilton, Douglas. "Representing Slavery in British Museums: The Challenges of 2007." In *Imagining Transatlantic Slavery*, ed. Cora Kaplan and John Oldfield (Basingstoke: Palgrave Macmillan, 2010): 127–44.

Kaye, Mike. "The Development of the Anti-Slavery Movement after 1807." In *The British Slave Trade: Abolition, Parliament, and People*, ed. Stephen Farrell, Melanie Unwin, and James Walvin (Edinburgh: Edinburgh University Press, 2007): 238–58.

Kitson, Peter. "'Candid Reflections': The Idea of Race in the Debate over the Slave Trade and Slavery in the Late Eighteen and Early Nineteenth Century." In *Discourses of Slavery and Abolition: Britain and its Colonies, 1760–1838*, ed. Brycchan Carey, Markman Ellis, and Sara Salih (Basingstoke: Palgrave Macmillan, 2004): 11–25.

Lewis, Gordon K. "Proslavery Ideology." In *Caribbean Slavery in the Atlantic World*, ed. Verene Shepherd and Hilary Beckles (Oxford: Ian Randal, 2000): 544–79.

Marsh, Jan. "The Black Presence in British Art 1800–1900: Introduction and Overview." In *Black Victorians: Black People in British Art 1800–1900*, ed. Jan Marsh (Aldershot: Lund Humphries, 2005): 12–22.

Morgan, Kenneth. "Slave Women and Reproduction in Jamaica, ca. 1776–1834." In *Women and Slavery: The Modern Atlantic*, ed. Gwyn Cambell *et. al.* (Athens: Ohio University Press, 2008): 27–53.

Nelson, Charmaine. "Venus Africaine: Race, Beauty and African-ness." In *Black Victorians: Black People in British Art 1800–1900*, ed. Jan Marsh (Aldershot: Lund Humphries, 2005): 46–56.

O'Brien, Karen. "Imperial Georgic, 1660–1789." In *The Country and the City Revisited: England and the Politics of Culture, 1550–1850*, ed. Gerald Maclean, Donna Landry, and Joseph P. Ward (Cambridge: Cambridge University Press, 1999): 160–79.

O'Gorman, Frank. "Pitt and the 'Tory' Reaction to the French Revolution, 1787–1815." In *Britain and the French Revolution*, ed. H. T. Dickinson (Basingstoke: Macmillan, 1989): 21–37.

Otele, Olivette. "Religion and Slavery: A Powerful Weapon for Pro-Slavery and Abolitionist Campaigners." In *Le débat sur l'abolition de l'esclavage en Grande-Bretagne (1787–1840)*, ed. Françoise Le Jeune and Michel Prum (Paris: Ellipses, 2008).

Philp, Mark. "Introduction." In *The French Revolution and British Popular Politics*, ed. Mark Philp (Cambridge: Cambridge University Press, 1991): 1–17.

———. "The Fragmented Ideology of Reform." In *The French Revolution and British Popular Politics*, ed. Mark Philp (Cambridge: Cambridge University Press, 1991): 50–77.

Quinault, Roland. "Anglo-American Attitudes to Democracy from Lincoln to Churchill." In *Anglo-American Attitudes: From Revolution to Partnership*, ed. Fred M. Leventhal and Roland Quinault (Aldershot: Ashgate, 2000): 124–41.

Rosen, Frederick. "Jeremy Bentham on Slavery and the Slave Trade." In *Utilitarianism and Empire*, ed. Bart Schultz and Georgios Varouxakis (Oxford: Lexington Books, 2005): 33–56.

Schultz, Bart and Georgios Varouxakis. "Introduction." In *Utilitarianism and Empire*, ed. Bart Schultz and Georgios Varouxakis (Oxford: Lexington Books, 2005): 1–32.

Sheridan, Richard B. "Slave Demography in the British West Indies and the Abolition of the Slave Trade." In *The Abolition of the Atlantic Slave Trade*, ed. David Eltis and James Walvin (Madison: University of Wisconsin Press, 1981): 259–86.

Stevenson, John. "Popular Radicalism and Popular Protest, 1789–1815." In *Britain and the French Revolution*, ed. H. T. Dickinson (Basingstoke: Macmillan, 1989): 61–82.

Walvin, James. "Introduction." In *The British Slave Trade: Abolition, Parliament, and People*, ed. Stephen Farrell, Melanie Unwin, and James Walvin (Edinburgh: Edinburgh University Press, 2007): 1–11.

———. "The Public Campaign in England against Slavery, 1787–1834." In *The Abolition of the Atlantic Slave Trade*, ed. David Eltis and James Walvin (Madison: The University of Wisconsin Press, 1981): 63–79.

Ward, Candice. "Sensibility, Tropical Disease, and the Eighteenth-Century Sentimental Novel." In *Discourses of Slavery and Abolition: Britain and its Colonies, 1760–1838*, ed. Brycchan Carey, Markman Ellis, and Sara Salih (Basingstoke: Palgrave Macmillan, 2004): 63–77.

Wood, Marcus. "Significant Silence: Where was Slave Agency in the Popular Imagery of 2007?" In *Imagining Transatlantic Slavery*, ed. Cora Kaplan and John Oldfield (Basingstoke: Palgrave Macmillan, 2010): 162–90.

Unpublished Theses

Barrett, Ian John. "Cultures of Pro-Slavery: The Political Defence of the Slave Trade in Britain c. 1787–1807." Unpublished PhD thesis (King's College London, 2009).

Ledford, Megan. "Enlightenment Politeness and the Female Reader: The Role of Didactic Literature in Teaching Politeness to Women in Virginia and Scotland, 1750–1850." Unpublished PhD thesis (University of Edinburgh, 2012).

Wells, Andrew. "Sex and Racial Theory in Britain, 1690–1833." Unpublished D. Phil. thesis (Oxford University, 2009).

Reference Works/Electronic Resources

Gove, Philip Babcock, et al., eds. *Webster's Third New International Dictionary of the English Language Unabridged.* Springfield: Merriam-Webster Inc., 1993.

Oxford Dictionary of National Biography (electronic resource)

Voyages: The Transatlantic Slave Trade Database (electronic resource)

The Wellesley Index to Victorian Periodicals, 1824–1900 (electronic resource)

Index

CPSIA information can be obtained
at www.ICGtesting.com
Printed in the USA
LVOW01*1612250216
476699LV00019B/343/P

9 781137 578204